CONTRACT ADMINISTRATION

This material was prepared pursuant to Contract #99-8-1383-42-20 from the U.S. Department of Labor by the author, who was commissioned by the George Meany Center for Labor Studies, AFL-CIO, in partial fulfillment of its Tripartite Program for Apprenticeship and Associate Degree in Labor Studies. The opinions contained in this material do not necessarily reflect those of the George Meany Center for Labor Studies, the American Federation of Labor-Congress of Industrial Organizations, or the U.S. Department of Labor.

CONTRACT ADMINISTRATION

A Guide for Stewards and Local Officers

Bob Repas

Professor, School of Labor and
Industrial Relations
Michigan State University

The Bureau of National Affairs, Inc., Washington, D.C.

Library of Congress Cataloging in Publication Data

Repas, Bob, 1921–
Contract administration.

Bibliography: p.
Includes index.
1. Grievance procedures—United States. 2. Grievance
arbitration—United States. 3. Collective labor agree-
ments—United States. I. Title.
KF3544.R47 1984 344.73′018896 84-9857
ISBN 0-87179-433-0 347.30418896
ISBN 0-87179-434-9 (pbk.)

Printed in the United States of America
International Standard Book Number: 0-87179-433-0 (hardbound)
0-87179-434-9 (paperback)

to my wife,

for the patience and understanding she displayed
during the numerous nights and weekends I
spent away from home teaching extension
classes for union members.

Contents

List of Tables

List of Exhibits

Preface

This is primarily a how-to-do-it book, aimed at union representatives who are involved at the first step of the grievance procedure. The book's purpose is to enable them to more effectively defend the rights of those they represent. This book also attempts to supply some background information that will enable stewards to understand better the institution of unionism in which they play an important role.

The book is based in large part on my 35 years of experience in teaching grievance handling to union members as disparate as auto workers and siderographers.

I had my first experience with unions in Milwaukee, Wisconsin, in 1941 when I joined an AFSCME local, composed primarily of foreign-born workers, many of whom were German socialists. Although we had a formal organization, we had neither a contract nor a grievance procedure. We discussed setting up a steward system a number of times, but were not sure how to do it or exactly how it would work. Meanwhile, our representatives, petitioning for a wage increase, appeared cap in hand before the city council at its 1943 annual budget meeting. The council locked its doors and refused to allow our representatives to testify. The next day we struck in protest—a strike that was to last 31 days. The city's action had a profound effect in changing my views. I came into the labor movement a member of the Norman Thomas Socialist Party and believed in the class struggle based on the private ownership of property. As a result of the city's action, I decided then, and still believe, that we have a class society based not on property ownership, but on a power relationship in both private and public employment where one person gives orders and another person takes orders. In this kind of society a union is necessary to protect the worker at the place of employment in capitalist and communist countries alike.

Having been employed for some years at a large state university, I am convinced that professionals (in this case, faculty), as well as blue-collar workers, need protection against arbitrary treatment.

Therefore, the problems associated with grievance handling at the faculty level are discussed.

I regret that the longest chapter in this book deals with arbitration, because philosophically I believe labor and management should solve their problems without the use of a third party. Furthermore, younger arbitrators do not seem to have the same feel for people, as do the old-timers who learned their trade under the War Labor Board of World War II. As a result the younger abitrators depend increasingly on legalisms in their awards. Practically, however, I see no alternative to arbitration as the last step in the grievance procedure if the parties are unable to agree.

I have been fortunate in being able to observe, learn, and steal ideas from some of the great labor educators. Larry Rogin and Russ Allen are unsurpassed as discussion leaders. Frank Marquart was able to draw out the shyest student in the class through the use of imaginative techniques. In the process, instructors learned about shop problems from the worker's viewpoint. Today, unfortunately, there seems to be a tendency for labor educators to look down on teaching grievance handling because "it's the same old stuff." I have never found that to be so. The general principles for processing grievances may remain the same, but different content arising under a variety of contracts makes the teaching of grievance handling a challenging subject. One class may concentrate on the duty of fair representation; another, on problems arising out of new technology; and a third, on the relationship of seniority to the promotion clause. Hardly dull, routine subjects.

The formalization of a grievance procedure has introduced the beginning of industrial democracy into the workplace. The fact, however, that only the Steelworkers union has negotiated a justice and dignity clause, which presumes that a worker is innocent until proven guilty, indicates that most employees still lack basic rights on the job that are taken for granted elsewhere in civilian life.

At a time when the labor movement lacks political clout, it is imperative that unions have well-trained, aggressive stewards to protect the gains unions have made over the years. It is to this purpose that this book is dedicated, because it seeks to examine grievance handling from the union's point of view.

Chapter 1, "Development of Contract Administration," examines the origins of the collective bargaining process, the development of the written contract, and the need to enforce and interpret this document. Chapter 2, "The Duties of Union Officers and Stewards," describes the responsibility of the steward for activities other than handling grievances, such as acting as a communicator or educating those persons he or she represents. Chapter 3, "Definition of a Grievance," explains that the definition of a grievance may be broader than a violation of the contract and may include complaints charging the violation of a law or a past practice. Chapter 4, "Purpose of the Grievance Procedure," discusses the value of the grievance procedure not only to the worker and the union, but to the employer as well. Chapter 5, "Processing Grievances," explains the mechanics of grievance handling, emphasizing the role of the steward and of the shop committee in processing grievances. Chapter 6, "Grievance Procedures in Public Employment," evaluates the similarities and differences in processing grievances in the public and private sector. Chapter 7, "The Duty of Fair Representation," explains the union's obligation to handle grievances free of discriminatory treatment. Chapter 8, "The Arbitration Process," discusses the development of arbitration, how the process works, the guidelines that have evolved, and the problems associated with arbitration. Chapter 9, "Problems in Contract Administration," discusses the concept of "work now and grieve later," the encroachment of law on the arbitration process, special problems in contract administration facing public and professional employees, the time and cost considerations in arbitration, and the conflict between collective and individual rights.

The use of "he" and "his" in general discussions in this book should be understood to be a shortened form of "he or she" and "his or her." Obviously individuals of both sexes are involved in all aspects of the subject dealt with here.

I wish to thank Jacqueline Brophy of the George Meany Center for Labor Studies, Inc., for her patience in editing, reediting, and once again, editing the manuscript for this book.

BOB REPAS
June 1984

1

Development of Contract Administration

Union activities do not end with bargaining over wages, hours, and working conditions. Administration of the collective bargaining agreement is also of vital importance. One author has defined "contract administration" in these words:

> Contract administration involves the settlement of grievances, the establishment of rules and regulations to implement the contract, and ... has three basic parts: 1) the introduction of the contract after its approval by the negotiating parties; 2) contract alteration and revision during its term, including possible reopening on specified issues; and 3) the actual operation of the contract, including grievance handling and pressure tactics.[1]

There can be no contract administration, however, without collective bargaining, since without the written document resulting from the bargaining process, there would be nothing to administer.

The development of the collective bargaining process in this country did not come easily. Throughout the 19th century, and in fact until passage of the Wagner Act in 1935 and the subsequent legal protection afforded collective bargaining by the federal government, unions faced serious legal obstacles.

Union Activities in a Period of Employer and Government Opposition

At first the courts harassed union activists under the common law doctrine of conspiracy. Later, under the Sherman Anti-Trust

---

[1]Randle Wortman, *Collective Bargaining, Principles and Practices*, 2nd ed. (Boston: Houghton Mifflin Co., 1966), p. 209.

1

Act of 1890 and the Clayton Act of 1914, union activities such as strikes, picketing, and boycotts were held by the courts to be "in restraint of trade" and therefore violations of antitrust law. As a result unions were subject to both injunctions and fines, and sometimes their leaders were jailed. In an effort to keep out unions, employers utilized blacklisting, violence, expulsion from company-owned housing, and the yellow dog contract.

The hostility shown by both employers and the government required unions to resort to a form of guerrilla warfare in order to exist. Because workers who joined together to improve conditions were liable to prosecution as participants in a conspiracy, no formal bargaining existed between representatives of labor and management as we know it today. Instead, unions presented their demands on a take-it-or-leave-it basis. The first offer was the last offer. Typically, a wage demand was placed secretly on the employer's desk at night. The workers were prepared to strike if the employer did not raise wages immediately. Often, in secret meetings to which entrance could be obtained only by giving a password, the workers took elaborate oaths not to work for less than the proposed scale.

At the same time employers formed associations that were committed to a common wage policy. Sometimes unions struck when employer associations rejected their wage demands. Employers tried to starve striking workers back to work either by delaying settlement, hiring strikebreakers (persons not previously employed at the workplace hired to replace strikers), or urging their workers to act as scabs (workers who had not joined the strike or returned to work before the strike was over). At other times employers took the offensive and locked out their workers until the financial resources of the striking workers were exhausted and their wage demands were withdrawn.

Those individual employers who sought to settle separately with unions could be penalized by the association. Penalties might include ostracizing the employer, underselling him, preventing access to raw materials, or stripping him of a previously agreed-upon part of the market.

Wage disputes were pure tests of economic strength, and the booms and busts of the business cycle often determined the winner. If the workers were successful in stopping production in a period of prosperity, the employers were reluctant to take a long strike because of the loss of profits. If economic conditions were bad, however, the employers had little incentive to settle. Thus workers made wage demands when economic conditions were good and employers cut wages when conditions were bad. Each party adopted its policies without consulting with the other, since the concept of joint determination of conditions of employment did not exist. The core of contract administration—a union seeking to enforce a written agreement through a grievance procedure—was unknown.

In this hostile environment only a few workers were able to organize successfully. They were primarily skilled workers: printers, construction workers (particularly bricklayers and shipyard carpenters), shoemakers (or cordwainers as they were originally called), silversmiths, tailors, and bakers. Such craftsmen were able to organize because they possessed a scarce item: the skill, acquired through training and work experience, required to perform the job. The ability to read and write, required for printing and construction work, represented a skill possessed by few workers because no free public school system existed in the early years of this country. (Although in 1828 the Workingmen's Party of Philadelphia, labor's first political organization, proposed free public schools as part of its platform, that goal was not generally attained until the 1850s.) Workers who performed skilled work were much harder to replace when they struck because they were in short supply. Therefore they had greater bargaining power with the employer than did the unskilled workers. Even today, in countries where workers are free to join unions of their own choosing, skilled workers are usually the first to organize.

Development of Collective Bargaining and Contract Administration

Collective bargaining, or the joint determinations made by labor and management representatives regarding wages and other conditions of employment, developed when employer associations and unions became stabilized and relatively equal in strength. Without some equality of bargaining power, the stronger party dictated the terms of settlement rather than determining them jointly. The joint determination of wages and working conditions took place only when both parties realized it was in their own self-interest to end the unilateral setting of employment conditions. The local union's objective of maintaining or raising the living standards of its members could not be easily achieved when the union relied on an ultimatum, with no procedure for modifying its original demands. Employers began to realize that they too had a stake in ending cutthroat wage competition generated by the substandard producer, competition that often pitted one employer against the other just as unorganized workers were pitted against each other.

The desire for joint determination of wages by the unions and the employers resulted in the negotiated agreement. Once the terms of the agreement were reached, the next logical step was the administration of the agreement.

By 1900 a distinction had been made between negotiating the terms of the original agreement and negotiating the settlement of grievances involving the application of those terms. In 1902 President Theodore Roosevelt appointed a U.S. Strike Commission to settle a strike in the anthracite coalfields. That settlement incorporated the first permanent grievance procedure to cover industrywide grievances. In 1912 this grievance procedure was expanded to apply to grievances occurring in individual mines covered by the contract. Soon thereafter the printing and clothing industries also adopted formalized grievance procedures. The craft unions in construction, because of the short duration and the seasonal nature of construction work, enforced conditions of employment in a geographic area rather than at a single workplace.

Although the concept of contract administration first occurred at the turn of the century, the handling of worker grievances by workshop representatives, usually called stewards, came later.

Industrial Steward System. The industrial steward system arose first in coal mines and printing plants. One of the earliest demands of miners, who were paid according to the amount of coal each had dug, was the right to select their own weighman who could make sure they were not shortchanged on their production. Later, they established pit committees which concerned themselves with grievances.

During World War I workers demanded workplace representation in Germany, Russia, France, Britain, Norway, and Italy. The reasons were the same everywhere. Workers, suffering from wartime inflation, requested wage increases. The speedup in war production was equally important in increasing worker militancy. In Britain the development of the shop steward movement was opposed by employers, unions, and government. Employers did not want day-to-day negotiations with representatives of their own employees; the union officers feared that the shop stewards would compete with them for workers' loyalty; and the government feared that radical elements would seize control. In spite of these fears, first the employer, then the government, and eventually the unions in Europe recognized the steward as the workers' representative with the responsibility for dealing with day-to-day problems in the workplace.

Shop Committees. In the United States a somewhat similar process took place during World War I. The National War Labor Board, created to deal with labor-management disputes, authorized the establishment of shop committees, many of which were elected by workers who were not union members. Originally, unions favored these elections (even though they took place in nonunion plants) on the grounds that some representation was better than none. They hoped that these committees would stimulate interest in bona fide unions. They soon had reason to change their minds because employers refused to grant union recognition. Instead, employers became the most enthusiastic organizers and supporters of shop committees, particularly when a legitimate union appeared on the scene. Employers controlled the committees through such devices as handpicking the officers, prohibiting meetings of the shop committee off the company premises, and supplying the meeting place and funds for the organizations. The committees were further hampered because they had no access to experienced trade unionists, lacked contact with other unions, and had no funds with which to conduct strikes. As a result the American Federation of Labor (AFL) at its 1919 convention officially condemned the shop committees as company unions.

Unions adopted a new strategy in the 1930s. Instead of denouncing shop committes, the unions infiltrated them. Their main targets were those committees that had gradually become more independent of management and were beginning to make demands for the autonomy of their organizations and for higher wages and better working conditions. Employers, hoping to keep out bona fide unions, made some concessions that succeeded only in further raising the level of expectations of the shop committees. As a result more and more union supporters were elected officers of the shop committees, and the employers' hold on them was broken.

The Congress of Industrial Organizations' (CIO) Steelworkers Organizing Committee (SWOC) was so successful in capturing control of shop committees in the 1930s that it was able to obtain union recognition in the country's largest steel company, the United States Steel Corporation, without a strike.

Although many shop committees were nothing more than company unions, they laid the basis for industrial unionism and the steward system as we know it today. These committees functioned on a plantwide basis and handled grievances arising on the shop floor. On important issues the company invariably won, but the experience proved invaluable to shop committee members who became the backbone of the new unions.

Arbitration. The widespread development of collective bargaining in the auto, steel, electrical manufacturing, rubber, and packinghouse industries during the 1930s greatly enlarged the scope of contract administration. The passage of the National Labor Relations Act, or Wagner Act, in 1935 aided this development by setting up the National Labor Relations Board (NLRB) and affording federal government recognition and protection to union organizing and collective bargaining activities.

Early in World War II the federal government created the War Labor Board (WLB) to regulate labor-management relations during a period of wage stabilization. The WLB had a major impact on contract administration because it often ordered the incorporation of arbitration into the grievance procedure when the employer was unwilling to agree to it in negotiations. After World War II, the WLB continued to exercise its influence on contract administration when many of its former staff became arbitrators.

The U.S. Supreme Court has also affected contract administration. In 1960 three decisions involving the United Steelworkers union, known as the *Trilogy* cases, established the arbitrator as the final judge on grievances arising out of the workplace. The Court stated that:

(1) Arbitrator decisions in private employment were enforceable through the federal courts;
(2) The arbitrator has the sole authority to determine whether a grievance is arbitrable except when the court finds that the contract specifically limits the arbitrator from doing so;
(3) The federal courts may not review an arbitrator's decision on its merits, which means that the courts will not substitute their judgment for that of the arbitrator; and
(4) The courts will enforce a broad award "so long as it draws its essence from the collective bargaining agreement."[2]

In its 1971 *Collyer* decision the NLRB ruled that, when the subject matter of an unfair labor practice charge was also eligible for a grievance procedure, it would defer the matter to arbitration proce-

---

[2]*Steelworkers v. Enterprise Wheel & Car Corp.*, 363 US 593, 34 LA 569 (1960).

dures as established by the collective bargaining agreement.[3] The NLRB held that the grievance procedure negotiated by the parties should be used before a government agency became involved. Unions have argued that the *Collyer* doctrine deprives workers of some of their statutory rights, because the Taft-Hartley Act does not specifically provide for deferral to arbitration. As a matter of policy, international unions have urged each of their local unions to file an unfair labor practice charge at the same time an issue is submitted to arbitration. This action ensures that the NLRB will review the arbitrator's decision to see that the settlement meets the requirements of the Taft-Hartley Act.

Pressure Tactics in Contract Administration

Pressure tactics exerted by unions play an important part in contract administration. Such tactics are actions often prohibited by the contract but hard to prevent or stop because of the difficulty of determining the responsible parties. Pressure tactics are more common in the initial stages of collective bargaining when the union feels that the employer understands only economic power. In this period each party tends to be highly suspicious of the motives and actions of the other.

Threat to Strike. Unions have used different kinds of pressure tactics over the years. Sometimes a simple threat to strike over a grievance will obtain the desired concessions from the employer. A parts supplier to one of the "Big Three" auto companies may agree to union demands if it fears a strike may cause it to miss its delivery date, which in turn might result in the loss of future orders. The same threat may be effective in the construction industry where contractors are subject to financial penalties if projects are not completed on time.

Wildcat Strikes. These strikes occur without advance notice to management, usually on the spur of the moment. While wildcat strikes are unauthorized by union officers, they sometimes have their unofficial support. This type of strike is the major tactic used by workers to place pressure on management. If a union steward is fired, the entire work force may respond by walking out, or a steward in a key department may lead a work stoppage protesting an unsafe working condition. Either action may force an entire plant to shut down, thereby placing great pressure on management.

---

[3]*Collyer Insulated Wire*, 192 NLRB 837, 77 LRRM 1931 (1971).

Work Slowdowns. Work slowdowns are another form of pressure frequently used, particularly in disputes involving production standards. Slowdowns occur when workers limit their production as part of a concerted action. A union may respond to increased workloads by systematically slowing production until the union can reach an agreement with management. Slowdowns may also be used to protest layoffs, plant closings, or harsh disciplinary actions. Even unorganized workers frequently resort to this tactic because of the difficulty of discovering the ringleaders, particularly when the workers increase production from time to time.

Flooding the Grievance Procedure. Flooding the grievance procedure with unimportant, minor, and imaginary complaints is another technique. Sometimes workers in a department use this method to call to the attention of management their unhappiness with the actions of a particular supervisor. If management is convinced that the supervisor is incapable of handling those under him, he may be transferred or let go, although the company will not publicly acknowledge its reasons for doing so. The union may also resort to this tactic during negotiations in order to place additional pressure on management. This tactic can backfire on the union, however. If hostilities are such that flooding the grievance procedure on a plantwide basis results, management may respond by pushing every grievance to arbitration in the hopes that the cost will force the union to its knees.

Tactics of Union Members. Union leaders may also be subject to pressure tactics from a membership that feels its problems are not being handled properly. Petitions may be circulated and resolutions passed taking the leadership to task. Union officers may be criticized at department meetings. They may also be harassed by irate phone calls late at night, by being picketed, or by letters to the press denouncing them for not meeting the needs of the membership.

Unions resort to pressure tactics because of frustrations arising from a wide variety of causes, ranging from management actions to international union politics. For example, on the local level there may be a revolt against what the union considers harsh measures taken by management. Or a militant union may feel that the grievance procedure has built-in delays either because of excessive time limits or because of management's constant requests for postponements at each step in the procedure.

At the international level, the grievance procedure has been viewed by some unions as a form of class collaboration. For example, prior to World War I the Industrial Workers of the World (IWW) opposed any signed contract, and with it any written grievance procedure. The IWW sought to abolish the employer rather than coexist with him. Other unions, like Region 7 of the Allied Industrial Workers (AIW), accepted the concept of a negotiated agreement, but for many years opposed arbitration on the grounds that it represented class collaboration. The union preferred to settle disputes directly with the employer without the intervention of an outside third party in the form of an arbitrator.[4]

Sometimes internal union politics are responsible for the use of pressure tactics in contract administration. For example, an opposition group may charge the incumbents with being ineffective in handling grievances because grievances have not been speedily processed. Prior to a local union election, the incumbents may resort to various forms of pressure on management to convince the membership that they are both militant and effective.

Personality clashes between labor and management may be responsible for the pressure tactics. The union representative may find that every time he meets with his counterpart in management a shouting match takes place with no rational discussion. He may conclude that talk is useless and action needed.

Use of pressure tactics by unions has declined for several reasons. A negotiated grievance procedure ending in arbitration usually includes an agreement not to strike for the duration of the contract. The no-strike clause marks a clear distinction between legal and illegal strikes and opens the union to possible damage suits if a strike takes place while the contract is in effect.

With the growth of arbitration, the union's use of pressure tactics has declined but has not disappeared. On the other hand, pressure tactics used by the membership against its officers may be on the increase. In part this may be due to the increased number of younger, more educated union activists who do not respect union leadership as their elders may have and who are more likely to challenge authority. The turbulence in much of American society in the 1960s and 1970s also reached the labor movement. As we shall see later, these factors pose a number of tough problems in contract administration.

---

[4]Bob Repas, "Grievances Procedures Without Arbitration," *Industrial and Labor Relations Review* 30 (July 1967), p. 382.

Summary

Although unions date back to the founding of this country, they did not become a permanent part of the American scene until after the Civil War. Prior to that time unions organized and then disappeared under the weight of economic pressures or legal obstacles. As the country industrialized, more workers organized and eventually built permanent organizations that utilized the collective bargaining process to raise living standards and defend the rights of its members. Out of the collective bargaining process came the written contract listing the conditions of employment. The concept of contract administration flowed naturally from the need to interpret and enforce this written document.

Key Words and Phrases

collective bargaining	skilled workers
Collyer decision	steward
contract administration	strikebreaker
flooding the grievance procedure	threat to strike
National Labor Relations Board	*Trilogy* cases
pit committees	Wagner Act
pressure tactics	War Labor Board
scab	wildcat strikes
shop committees	work slowdowns

Review and Discussion Questions

1. What were some legal obstacles making it difficult for unions to organize before the passing of the Wagner Act in 1935?

2. Which workers organized first in the United States? Why?

3. How were wage rates set before employers recognized unions?

4. How are pressure tactics used to settle grievances?

5. Has the bargaining strength of unions increased or decreased during war periods in the past? Why?

6. What factors were responsible for the development of early collective bargaining?

2

The Duties of Union Officers
and Stewards

The main responsibility of local union officers and stewards in contract administration is the handling of grievances. A grievance usually develops out of actions taken by a representative of management. In most cases, this person is the immediate supervisor or foreman. The union seeks to have its own representative in any area where an immediate supervisor has jurisdiction. The two persons meet to discuss a complaint in the first step of the grievance procedure. The union representatives responsible for processing a worker's complaint at this level are usually called stewards. Some unions refer to them as committeemen, chairladies, chairmen, delegates, association representatives, building representatives, chapel chairmen, patrolmen, or professional rights and responsibility representatives. Regardless of the title, they perform similar duties. In this chapter, the term union representative is used when stewards and other local union officers are referred to collectively. Throughout the remainder of the book, only the term steward will be used to designate this firstline union official.

Most of this book concentrates on handling grievances. This chapter, however, will describe other responsibilities expected of union officers and stewards. These include:

(1) Knowing basic labor legislation, both state and federal;
(2) Serving as a "transmission belt" between the officers and membership;
(3) Supporting such activities as the AFL-CIO Community Services Program;
(4) Supporting union activity carried out through the Committee on Political Education (COPE) in the AFL-CIO;

11

(5) Organizing and unionizing the workers in the bargaining unit; and

(6) Getting members to attend meetings.

Independent unions, those not affiliated with the AFL-CIO, often have their own community services and political action committees, and their stewards are expected to perform these same duties.

Basic Federal Labor Legislation

Local union representatives cannot know details of every piece of legislation of concern to workers. They should, however, know where to obtain specific information so that members can be told where to go for aid and assistance. Representatives should be familiar with the following federal laws:

- Davis-Bacon Act
- Social Security Act
- Occupational Safety and Health Act
- Employee Retirement Income Security Act
- Fair Labor Standards Act
- Freedom of Information Act
- Consumer Credit Protection Act
- Equal Employment Opportunity Legislation

Davis-Bacon Act. The Davis-Bacon Act, first passed in 1931 and amended several times later, is an important law affecting construction workers. The law empowers the U.S. Secretary of Labor to establish minimum wages for each craft of workers employed on construction projects costing more than $2,000 and financed wholly or in part by the federal government.[1] The minimum wage is set after surveying the average prevailing wage in a geographic area for workers in a craft employed on a similar project.

The Davis-Bacon Act was passed because of cutthroat wage competition in the construction industry. In 1932, construction workers employed on federal flood control projects who were not yet covered by Davis-Bacon were paid as low as 12.5 cents per hour, while wages in construction elsewhere averaged 87 cents per hour. Sometimes these workers received no take-home pay after wages were withheld for groceries, cooking services, tent rent, and tobacco.[2]

---

[1]Building and Construction Trades Department, AFL-CIO, *The Davis-Bacon Act: It Works for America* (Washington, D.C.: AFL-CIO, 1979).

[2]*Ibid.*

Today about 500,000 construction contractors employ 4½ million workers. Employment is highly seasonal and temporary in nature. Most of the basic construction costs are set by commercial contract; that is, the contractor must adhere to both the construction design and material specifications embodied in the contract. Since material costs are relatively equal, the major variables are managerial skills and the price of labor. As a result, contractors have considerable incentive to cut wages, and it was such action that the Davis-Bacon Act was designed to stop.

In large cities or in other areas where unions have organized substantial portions of the construction industry, the minimum rate, or "prevailing rate" as it is called under Davis-Bacon, was set at the union scale for the craft.

In 1979 a major effort to destroy the Davis-Bacon Act was launched by two groups of construction employers, the Associated General Contractors (AGC) and the Associated Builders and Contractors (ABC). In the past the AGC had negotiated master agreements with construction unions covering all of its affiliates in a geographic area. Today many members of the AGC have gone "double-breasted," which means that they operate both a union and a nonunion company, each under a different name. Typically, the nonunion company bids on smaller jobs or on residential and commercial work. As it grows larger and is able to assemble skilled workers, it often completely replaces the company's union operation. The ABC, on the other hand, has never dealt with unions, although it states it has no objections to hiring union members. It will not negotiate a union contract and says that it favors a policy of "merit employment" which, when translated, means it favors open shop employment (construction jobs operated on a nonunion basis). Both groups attack the Davis-Bacon Act principally on the grounds of its inflationary impact.

Little evidence supports the ABC's charge that the Davis-Bacon Act causes inflation. Recent studies indicate that the productivity of union construction workers is higher than nonunion workers,[3] and thus the higher wages paid to union workers are more than

---

[3]Steven G. Allen, *Unionized Construction Workers Are More Productive* (Washington, D.C.: Center to Protect Workers' Rights, 1979); and Clinton C. Bourdin and Raymond E. Levitt, *A Comparison of Wages and Labor Management Practices in Union and Non-Union Construction* (Cambridge: Massachusetts Institute of Technology, 1978). The first study was funded by the AFL-CIO Building and Construction Trades Department while the second was funded by the U.S. Department of Housing and Urban Development. They come to similar conclusions regarding the productivity of union construction workers.

compensated for by higher productivity. In part, the comprehensive training received by journeymen during their union apprenticeships is responsible. In addition, the broad range of skills acquired by union journeymen means less supervision is required, thus lowering costs. On a union job typically one foreman is employed to supervise ten journeymen, while on a nonunion job the ratio of supervisors to journeymen is one to three.[4]

Stewards and officers should vigorously police the Davis-Bacon Act, since 30 percent of all construction in the country falls under its provisions. The law requires that the prevailing minimum wage rate be posted at the construction site. This provision applies whether the contract has been awarded to a union contractor or to an open shop contractor. In addition, union officers should check to see if the state in which the construction takes place has a law similar to Davis-Bacon and if the state act applies the prevailing minimum rate to projects, such as municipal buildings and school construction, which are funded by units of local government. (See Table 1.)

Social Security Act. The Social Security Act was one of the major pieces of legislation passed in 1935 during the first term of President Franklin Roosevelt. Originally covering only retirement benefits, the law has been expanded to cover survivors, total disability, and Medicare benefits. Excellent publications in each of these areas are available, either free or at a minimum cost from the nearest Social Security office. These publications enable union representatives to answer many questions of direct concern to union members. It is important that the union representative urge those workers contemplating retirement within the near future to contact the Social Security office for an estimate of their benefits.

Occupational Safety and Health Act. The passage of the Occupational Safety and Health Act by the U.S. Congress in 1970 opened another area with which the steward should be familiar. The legislation was enacted to eliminate on-the-job health and safety hazards. To achieve this end the Occupational Safety and Health Administration (OSHA) has issued a number of "standards," administrative regulations governing health and safety at the workplace. Examples of general industry standards dealing with occupational *safety* include procedures governing the operation of hydraulic power presses; specifications for guards for power transmission; face and eye protection; and other personal protective

---

[4]Bourdin and Levitt, *A Comparison of Wages*, p. 70.

Table 1. States With Prevailing Wage Laws*

State†

Alaska	Missouri
(Arkansas)	Montana
California	(Nevada)
Colorado	New Hampshire
Connecticut	New Jersey
Delaware	New Mexico
District of Columbia	New York
Hawaii	Ohio
Idaho	Oklahoma
Illinois	Oregon
Indiana	Pennsylvania
(Kansas)	Rhode Island
Kentucky	(Tennessee)
(Louisiana)	(Texas)
Maine	(Virginia)
Maryland	Washington
Massachusetts	West Virginia
Michigan	Wisconsin
Minnesota	Wyoming

*Some laws cover only certain types of construction. The threshold figure on which the prevailing wage is based varies greatly from state to state.

†"Right to Work" states are in parentheses.

Source: [4-4A State Labor Laws] Lab. Rel. Rep. (BNA). References are to the page of BNA's *State Labor Laws* (SLL) where text of the law or section thereof begins, as of the date of this publication: Alaska SLL 11:333; Arkansas SLL 13:333; California SLL 14:375; Colorado SLL 15:341; Connecticut SLL 16:335; Delaware SLL 17:334; District of Columbia SLL 18:334; Hawaii SLL 21:336a; Idaho SLL 22:334; Illinois SLL 25:338; Indiana SLL 24:335; Kansas SLL 26:334; Kentucky SLL 27:335; Louisiana SLL 28:334; Maine SLL 29:334; Maryland SLL 30:333; Massachusetts SLL 31:347; Michigan SLL 32:337; Minnesota SLL 33:343; Missouri SLL 35:334; Montana SLL 36:334; Nevada SLL 38:334; New Hampshire SLL 39:335; New Jersey SLL 40:345; New Mexico SLL 41:333; New York SLL 42:385; Ohio SLL 45:334; Oklahoma SLL 46:333; Oregon SLL 47:336; Pennsylvania SLL 48:337; Rhode Island SLL 50:334; Tennessee SLL 53:333; Texas SLL 54:335; Virginia SLL 57:333; Washington SLL 58:341; West Virginia SLL 59:332e; Wisconsin SLL 60:343; Wyoming SLL 61:333.

equipment; while construction standards cover trenching and shoring when excavating, as well as methods for dealing with electrical hazards. Examples of standards dealing with occupational *health* are those concerning airborne contaminants and ventilation systems, noise, laser beams, microwaves, radiation, and toxic materials. Employers violating these standards may receive citations and fines. Stewards should be familiar with the specific standards governing the type of work where they are employed.

Of equal importance are those provisions of the act relating to the rights of workers: workers cannot be penalized for requesting a health or safety inspection or for testifying on any provisions of the act; the union has the right to have a walk-around representative present when the OSHA inspector makes a tour of the workplace; and the walk-around representative has the right to call the attention of the inspector to health and safety problems, as does any other worker while the tour is being conducted.

OSHA permits state plans to substitute for the federal act. Stewards should be familiar with the requirements of a state act in effect, as well as any contract clauses dealing with the union's rights: to have health and safety representatives; to have periodic health and safety inspections; to bring sampling equipment into the plant; to bring a union hygienist into the plant; and to receive information automatically about accident and health survey records and about the toxicity of new chemicals. Above all, stewards should know whether workers have a contract right to stop work on an unsafe job. Laws, to be effective, require on-the-job enforcement. The steward has an important role in this area.

Employee Retirement Income Security Act. The Employee Retirement Income Security Act (ERISA) was passed in 1974 to protect workers and their beneficiaries in employee pension and welfare plans. A 1972 statement by Ralph Nader explains the need for this law:

> At least one-half of all persons participating in private pension plans will not receive pension benefits when they retire. More than one-half of all persons who receive private pension benefits receive less than $1,000 a year. The majority of pension plans do not provide for benefits for dependent widows or widowers, or provide only limited benefits.[5]

Reasons for failure to pay pension benefits range from corruption and mismanagement to disqualifying technicalities in the plans. ERISA mandates standards of conduct for those who administer or manage these plans and requires that certain information be reported. For example, both pension and welfare plans must file an annual report with the U.S. Secretary of Labor. In addition, workers and their beneficiaries must automatically receive a summary description of the plan in easily understood language, a summary of any changes in the plan, and if a claim is denied, an explanation in writing.

ERISA does not require an employer to have a pension or welfare plan, but only to maintain certain standards if one is estab-

---

[5]Ralph Nader and Kate Blackwell, *You and Your Pension* (New York: Grossman Publishers, 1973), p. 158.

lished. ERISA also does not establish a minimum pension benefit or provide for an automatic transfer of pension benefits if the worker changes jobs.[6]

Union representatives should refer difficult questions to their organization's pension specialist or to the senior fund administrator for accurate information on eligibility and benefit levels. For example, one person contemplating a change of employment may need information about its effect on vesting rights, while other persons considering early retirement may want to know the benefits to which they are entitled.

Fair Labor Standards Act. The Fair Labor Standards Act (FLSA) which now covers most workers, deals with three major areas of concern to unions: (1) the minimum wage; (2) overtime pay; and (3) restrictions on the use of child labor.

When first passed in 1938, FLSA provided for a minimum wage of 25 cents per hour. By 1982 the minimum wage had risen to $3.35 an hour. The act requires overtime payment at the rate of one and one-half times the worker's regular pay rate for all hours worked in excess of 40 per week. Any other provision for overtime pay, such as for hours worked in excess of eight per day or for double time for Sunday work, are not required by the law but are the result of negotiations between management and the union. The act also prohibits children under the age of 16 from working in most industries.

Many states have minimum wage laws covering workers in public employment and workers in private employment who are exempted from FLSA coverage. The minimum rate set in most states' laws is lower than the FLSA rate. Some state laws do not provide for any overtime pay; others may require an overtime rate only after 44 or 48 hours. To determine whether federal or state coverage applies, the nearest office of the Wage and Hour Division of the U.S. Department of Labor should be contacted.

The wage rates of organized workers, usually set forth in the collective bargaining agreement, are nearly always higher than the minimum wage. The steward, therefore, need not be concerned

---

[6]U.S. Department of Labor, Labor-Management Services Administration, *Often Asked Questions About the Employee Retirement Income Security Act of 1974* (Washington, D.C.: Government Printing Office, 1975). Various branches of the federal government administer and enforce sections of ERISA. This pamphlet lists the offices of the Labor-Management Services Administration, which has the major responsibility for administration and enforcement. In addition, these offices can provide the names of other government offices involved with ERISA.

with this aspect of the law. However, overtime pay provisions, also set forth in the contract, may need the steward's vigilance. When the work force rotates shifts or workdays, for example, disputes arising over the definition of a workweek could effect the payment of overtime.

Freedom of Information Act. The federal Freedom of Information Act entitles an individual or organization to most information accumulated by agencies of the federal government. A number of agencies, such as the Federal Bureau of Investigation, the Central Intelligence Agency, and the Office of Personnel Management, have accumulated files relating to the peaceful political activities of union members. This information has sometimes been illegally distributed to private employers who have used it against union activists. Organizations such as the American Civil Liberties Union have pamphlets available explaining how union members can obtain their own files.

Many states have also passed their own freedom of information acts that permit individuals or organizations to obtain records from a state or local unit of government. A public employer may refuse to supply records essential for negotiations or processing grievances in states where both freedom of information and collective bargaining laws exist. If so, public employee unions may be able to get faster results by seeking information through a freedom of information request rather than filing an unfair labor practice charge. Michigan's law, typical of freedom of information acts, requires the public agency to supply the requested information, usually within five days.[7]

In comparison, filing an unfair labor practice may take six months or longer to produce the same information. Furthermore, the union may be able to obtain information unavailable under the public employment bargaining law. For example, a teachers' union interested in knowing the amount spent on administrators' salaries can usually obtain this information through a state freedom of information act, while appropriate labor boards may refuse to supply such information if the administrators are not included in the bargaining unit.

Consumer Credit Protection Act. A *garnishment* is a court order requiring an employer to deduct a specified amount from a worker's paycheck and to turn it over to a creditor. Wages may be garnisheed without the worker's consent, but not without advance notice and a court judgment. If the employee receives a summons to

---

[7]1976 Mich. Pub. Acts 442.

appear in court and fails to do so, or if the employee loses the case, the judgment and notice of garnishment is sent to the employer. A garnishment applies to only one pay period. If one garnishment does not satisfy the debt, additional garnishments may be obtained.

In the Consumer Credit Protection Act of 1969, Congress prohibits discharge of a worker garnisheed more than one time for the nonpayment of the same debt. This act also specifies the amount of pay that can be garnisheed, an amount related to the worker's total take-home pay. Take-home pay is defined as earnings after legally required deductions, such as social security and income taxes, have been subtracted. If part of a court order, alimony, separate maintenance, and child support payments are also subtracted to determine take-home pay. Under current law no garnishment can be made if take-home pay is less than $100.50 per week. Earnings between $100.50 and $134.00 can be garnisheed at a maximum rate of 25 percent. The formula used to determine the garnishment exemption is based on three-fourths the minimum wage multiplied by 40 hours ($.75 \times \$3.35 \times 40 = \$100.50$). As the minimum wage increases, so will the amount of take-home pay exempt from the garnishment process.

An employee who buys a car and who is unable to make the payments because of sudden heavy medical bills may not be discharged even though more than one garnishment is required to pay that debt. On the other hand, a worker garnisheed more than once for separate debts may be subject to discharge. Some states, however, provide greater restrictions on garnishments and some prohibit them entirely. In any case, a steward should be sure that any restrictions on garnishments are observed. Many union members do not oppose disciplinary action by management against workers who are garnisheed because they feel that "deadbeats deserve what they get." Evidence shows, however, that most workers are garnisheed because they have been laid off, have heavy medical bills, have been victims of shady or illegal practices, or have difficulty managing money matters after having moved from an agricultural society into an urban one. Garnishments are the major reason for workers filing for bankruptcy. The union representative can play an important role in educating workers as to the reasons for garnishment. In most medium and large cities, either private or government consumer-oriented agencies exist that can supply material or speakers alerting workers to fraudulent business practices.[8]

---

[8]"Congress Imposes Restrictions on Wage Garnishment," *Congressional Quarterly Weekly Report* 21 (May 24, 1968), p. 1201.

Regardless of the reasons for garnishments, it hardly makes sense to discharge workers for nonpayment of debts, since they cannot meet any financial obligations without income.

Equal Employment Opportunity Legislation. Title VII of the Civil Rights Act of 1964 and subsequent federal legislation forbid job discrimination based on race, color, religion, national origin, sex, or age. In addition, some states have enacted legislation prohibiting discrimination based on marital status, and 12 states have enacted laws prohibiting discrimination based on physical and mental handicaps unrelated to ability to perform the job. Some states also prohibit the denial of employment because of arrest records or the failure to meet height and weight requirements.

Many union contracts now contain clauses prohibiting employment discrimination. Whether or not the contract contains such a clause, the steward who feels a worker has a justified complaint should encourage the worker to file a grievance. It is important that all complaints involving the workplace be processed through the grievance procedure so that the union protects its right to exclusive representation. Equal employment opportunity complaints represent an area in which an arbitrator's decision may not be final. The U.S. Supreme Court has ruled that a discrimination charge that has gone through the grievance procedure, including arbitration, may be reheard by the federal courts on its merits.

Basic State Labor Legislation

In addition to the preceding legislation, there also exist a number of functions which are primarily under the jurisdiction of the individual states. Some of these areas with which union representatives should be familiar are:

- Unemployment insurance
- Workers' compensation
- Lie detector test restrictions
- Wage payment laws
- Access to personnel files

Unemployment Insurance. In the frequent downswings of the American economy, many workers are laid off and thus draw unemployment insurance. Union representatives, therefore, are frequently asked questions about unemployment compensation laws. Unemployment insurance is a combined federal and state program.

Under the Social Security Act, passed in 1935, the federal government pays the costs of administering the law, while state governments are responsible for raising the money to pay benefits to laid-off workers. Within broad federal guidelines, each state is free to establish its own eligibility requirements and benefit levels. The major union criticisms of the program are the inadequacy of payments and the variation in benefits between the states.

Some workers are not aware that they must file a claim with the nearest office of the state agency administering the act in order to obtain unemployment insurance benefits. Therefore, stewards should tell workers who have been laid off about this requirement. A worker denied benefits should be instructed to contact the union for assistance in filing an appeal. Appeals may take a long time to process if complicated questions are involved, such as the right of a worker to receive benefits when laid off as a result of a strike in another workplace. Stewards should keep the people they represent informed of appeal decisions and legal developments.

Unemployment insurance is created by legislative action. In addition the union contract may entitle a worker to benefits such as severance pay, retraining, relocation, early retirement, and supplemental unemployment benefits. *Severance pay* is usually a lump sum payment based on the years of service for a worker permanently laid off. *Relocation allowances* may pay the moving expenses for workers transferred to other areas.

Workers' Compensation. Workers' compensation laws are designed to help the victims of job-related accidents by paying for medical care and part of the wages lost. These laws were originally designed to provide two-thirds of lost pay, but that goal is rarely achieved, and inflation continues to erode the living standard of disabled workers.

In contrast to unemployment insurance, the federal government neither pays the administrative cost of workers' compensation programs nor sets standards for the states. State governments therefore have less incentive to pass legislation in this field. Thus Wisconsin passed the first law in 1912, but Mississippi did so only in 1948.

Workers' compensation is a form of "no fault" insurance under which the injured person is entitled to benefits regardless of personal negligence as long as the injury was not intentionally inflicted. Prior to its passage, the common law doctrine of contributory negligence applied, which meant that a victim of a work accident was forced to sue the employer to recover medical expenses and wages lost and could collect only on proof that his negligence did not contribute to the accident.

The steward should inform union members to report all accidents immediately to avoid a dispute over whether the injury is work related. If medical treatment is required, the steward should know whether the company doctor must be used or if and when the worker's doctor may be called. Likewise, the steward should be familiar with the waiting period, if any, before benefits are paid. The steward should also be aware that sometimes serious illnesses occurring off the job, such as heart attacks, may be compensable if it can be shown they are job related. The union should compile a list of competent attorneys qualified to handle workers' compensation cases which the steward could make available if the employer contests a worker's claim.

Lie Detector Test Restrictions. In recent years, lie detector, or polygraph, tests have been widely used by employers, particularly in retail trade and other service industries. Workers are often required to take them as a condition of hire as well as a condition for continued employment. Some states have passed laws prohibiting their use in either or both situations. Unions have strongly opposed their use because:

(1) Studies indicate that in many instances those persons giving the tests are not qualified to interpret them.

(2) The tests are highly unreliable, so much so that the courts refuse to allow the results of lie detector tests to be introduced as evidence.[9] A chronic liar may show no reaction on the polygraph; an innocent person, upset by the assumption of guilt that requires the test or by the types of questions asked, may react in a way interpreted as guilt.

(3) Many of the questions asked involve an invasion of privacy. For example, questions may be asked that have no bearing on workplace conduct, such as those relating to sexual activity, politics, or attitudes toward unions.

If there is a law restricting the use of lie detectors, the union representative should make sure that it is not ignored at the workplace.

---

[9]Edgar A. Jones, Jr., "'Truth' When the Polygraph Operator Sits as Operator (or Judge): The Deception of 'Detection' in the Diagnosis of Truth and Deception," *Truth, Lie Detectors, and Other Problems in Labor Arbitration,* Proceedings of the Thirty-First Annual Meeting of the National Academy of Arbitrators (Washington, D.C.: Bureau of National Affairs, Inc., 1978), pp. 75–152.

Where state laws prohibit the discharge of workers for refusal to submit to lie detector tests, the employer sometimes applies lesser penalties such as suspensions. Stewards should fight these penalties since the objections applied to lie detector tests are the same regardless of the penalty. Any effort by management aimed at getting workers to waive their right to refuse to submit to these tests should also be vigorously opposed by the steward.

Wage Payment Laws. Many state laws specify a time period within which a worker must receive payment for all work performed when the worker is laid off, quits, or is discharged from the job. Since most union members do not have large savings, the union representative should make sure that these timetables are met. State laws usually prevent deductions from the worker's paycheck without written authorization.

Access to Personnel Files. Nine states now have laws permitting workers to examine their personnel files.[10] These laws include some or all of the following rights:

(1) Workers may request and obtain a copy of any material in their files.

(2) Workers may append their own statements to any material in the files with which they disagree.

(3) Workers must be informed if any material is forwarded to another employer.

(4) Material unrelated to the workplace performance may not be placed in workers' files.[11]

Union representatives should urge those they represent to periodically examine their files. By doing so, they will know precisely what records are being kept by management and will be able to refute any material with which they disagree. In addition, in case of disciplinary action, workers will be able to challenge any evidence used that does not appear in their personnel files, because these laws require that all written personnel records be kept there.

The state labor body, the appropriate state agency, or a university labor program may have published pamphlets dealing with one or more of these laws. Stewards should obtain relevant copies since they may answer most of the questions they will be asked. In addi-

---

[10]Alaska, California, Connecticut, Maine, Michigan, Oregon, Pennsylvania, Utah, and Wisconsin.

[11]1978 Mich. Pub. Acts 397.

tion, the pamphlets usually state where more specific information can be obtained.

"Transmission Belt" of Union Communications

The steward serves as a communicator to three different groups: the membership, the officers of the union, and management. On average, less than 5 percent of the membership regularly attend local union business meetings, though exceptions occur when an important issue is scheduled such as a strike vote, election of officers, or contract ratification. If the membership is to be informed of the policies and programs of the organization, the steward must assume a major responsibility as communicator to them.

Some stewards argue that there is no reason to inform the members if they are not sufficiently interested in the affairs of the organization to attend meetings or to read the union publications. This attitude can only create problems for the union, because all evidence indicates that the union member who is informed about the organization tends to be a better member. Furthermore, the most effective communication takes place by word of mouth, which is why the steward should report to members in the department during rest periods, lunch hour, or after work.

Stewards have responsibility for communication to union officers as well. Stewards should periodically seek the views of those they represent in respect to the policy questions faced by the organization. For example, stewards ought to ask for opinions on major demands the union should make during negotiations for the next contract and those views should be conveyed to the officers and the executive board. Stewards serve in a dual capacity, both as representatives of the officers of the union and of the workers in their departments.

The importance of the steward's function as a communicator is illustrated in studies showing that the member's opinion of the steward is indicative of how the member views the labor movement as a whole. If the steward is regarded as conscientious, effective, and interested in the member's welfare, this same attitude is projected toward the local union, the international union, and the labor movement.

The larger the local union, the more important the steward's role of communicator becomes. Union members may never see the international union president and may have spoken only briefly to the local union president, but they do know the steward and have formed opinions about the steward both as an individual and as a union representative.

Successful handling of grievances requires that the steward also be able to communicate with management. Usually this is done orally but sometimes sharp personality conflicts between the steward and the immediate supervisor make oral communication impossible, and consequently few settlements may take place at this level. Written communication is also important because the initial form of the written grievance may affect its final outcome. For example, some arbitrators will award no more as a final settlement than was requested when the grievance was first put into writing.

Community Service Programs

Local unions set up community service committees to perform several valuable functions:

(1) Acquaint union members with the health and welfare services available in their own communities;
(2) Train union counselors to refer union members to the appropriate agency for help;
(3) Assist in developing coordinated fund raising for United Way agencies;
(4) Provide volunteers for the various agencies;
(5) Develop labor representatives qualified to serve on agency boards of directors; and
(6) Assist union members with strike-related problems.

In many communities, union members provide the largest share of contributions to the United Way. Yet they do not utilize these agencies to the same degree as do other segments of American society. This appears to be true for several reasons. Many local unions have no community services committee and those that do may have frequent turnover in personnel, hindering efforts to make union members aware of the agencies in the field. Also, workers are more likely to seek help when they are unemployed, and then the type of assistance they are looking for involves food, shelter, and clothing, necessities provided primarily by tax-supported agencies rather than voluntary ones. In addition, the service agencies funded by the United Way, such as the Girl Scouts, Boy Scouts, and Family Service, traditionally derive more participation from middle class than working class families.

This lack of utilization may change with the recent effort of some unions to establish, jointly with management, employee assistance committees. These joint in-plant committees seek to refer troubled employees to the appropriate agency, many of which are United Way affiliates. Referrals are based solely upon declining job performance. These committees originally concentrated on referring workers whose job performance suffered from an excessive use of alcohol. Then the objective expanded to provide the same service to workers with a poor work record resulting from the use of other drugs. The latest trend indicates that these committees will refer troubled workers who are exhibiting a decline in job performance, whether the reason is marital difficulties, mental or physical breakdowns, or other emotional problems, to professionals.

The growth of employee assistance committees poses a potential jurisdictional dispute with community services committees because it is unclear at this time where the duties of one end and the duties of the other begin.

The role of community services committees is clear, however, in respect to strikes. They may be involved in tasks ranging from supplying coffee to pickets and handling the distribution of strike relief to obtaining food stamps or welfare.

Depending on the structure of the union, the steward's relationship to the community services committee will vary. But the steward will be expected to assist workers when they have difficult problems. For example, if the steward is aware of a worker whose spouse requires catered meals because of a severe heart condition, the steward should refer that person to the union's community service committee. If none exists in that union, the full-time United Way labor representative employed in many cities should be contacted. If neither of these sources of help are available, representatives of the various agencies should be invited to the steward council meeting so that the steward will become familiar with the services existing in the community.

Political Education

Almost from the time they were first organized, unions were active politically, sometimes engaging in independent political action and at other times resorting to "rewarding friends and punishing enemies," the policy promoted by Samuel Gompers, first president of the AFL. These early political efforts were sporadic, with activity starting shortly before an election, ceasing when the polling booths closed, and not beginning again until the next election year.

Labor's first effort in politics on a year-round basis began in 1936 when John L. Lewis, president of the CIO, established Labor's Non-Partisan League for the purpose of reelecting President Franklin Roosevelt to a second term.[12] The League was to serve as a bridge between the two warring national federations, the AFL and the CIO, with the objective of getting them to cooperate politically. The Mine Workers union, through this mechanism, contributed $500,000 to Roosevelt's campaign for a second term. By the time of the 1940 election, four years later, Lewis had broken with Roosevelt and supported Wendell Wilkie, the Republican candidate for President, while the other CIO unions enthusiastically supported Roosevelt's bid for a third term. As a result of Lewis's dissatisfaction, Labor's Non-Partisan League played a limited role in this campaign.

In 1943, the CIO established its Political Action Committee (PAC) to work for the reelection of Franklin Roosevelt to a fourth term and to replace Labor's Non-Partisan League, which John L. Lewis took with him when he left the CIO in 1942. In 1947, following the passage of the Taft-Hartley Act, the AFL created its first political arm, Labor's League for Political Education (LLPE), signifying that the AFL also intended to participate in politics year-round. When the AFL-CIO was created in 1955, the PAC and the LLPE merged to form the Committee on Political Education (COPE).

The purpose of COPE is to elect, on a nonpartisan basis, candidates at federal, state, and local levels who favor legislation endorsed by organized labor. Democrats have been more frequently supported because their voting records have been more pro-labor than those of their opponents. From time to time, however, some Republicans, as well as a few socialists and independents, have been endorsed. Just as workers seek to pool their economic strength for bargaining purposes, workers also seek to pool their political strength because what is won at the bargaining table can be lost at the legislative level.

COPE engages in a wide variety of activities that involve thousands of union members at the local union level. Some of these activities are:

(1) Distributing the voting records of elected officials;
(2) Conducting voter registration campaigns;

---

[12]Irving Bernstein, *The Turbulent Years* (Boston: Houghton Mifflin Co., 1971), p. 449.

(3) Getting out the vote;
(4) Endorsing candidates; and
(5) Making political contributions.

Voting records of legislators at the federal and state levels are distributed, often by stewards, to union members so that they can determine whether their representatives vote in their interest. Usually resolutions adopted at union conventions form the basis for determining the issues on which the candidates are judged. A "yes" vote on one issue may be considered a "right" vote, while on another it may be labeled a "wrong" vote. For example, voting "yes" on a bill raising Social Security benefits would be labeled a "right" vote while a "yes" vote to repeal the Davis-Bacon Act would be listed as a "wrong" vote.

Effective political action requires an effective voter registration campaign. As shown by the figures in Table 2, three important factors—family income, age, and race—influence participation in the electoral process. The higher the family income, the more likely people are to register and vote.

Table 2. Percent Voting in 1980 Presidential Election by Family Income, Age, Race, and Spanish Origin

	All Races 18 years and older (%)	All Races 18–24 yrs. (%)	All Races 55–64 yrs. (%)	Blacks 18 years and older (%)	Spanish Origin 18 years and older (%)
Under $5,000	39.4	25.5	50.2	46.9	21.2
$5,000–$9,999	48.8	27.3	60.4	45.2	24.1
$10,000–$14,999	54.8	36.4	69.3	50.8	28.6
$15,000–$19,999	60.3	42.6	74.8	54.6	34.3
$20,000–$24,999	67.2	43.5	80.1	64.0	36.0
$25,000 and over	73.8	52.5	86.2	68.7	51.8

Source: Bureau of Census, U.S. Department of Commerce (November 1980).

In part, family income is associated with age because one's income tends to go up as one grows older. Voter participation increases sharply with age: those between 55 and 64 years vote at the highest rate, while those between the ages of 18 and 24 are least likely to vote. Members of minorities have low voter participation rates. Since the labor movement consists of workers in the low or middle income groups as well as a significant number of young people and minorities, unions make a major attempt to stimulate political participation.

The apathy expressed by American society toward the electoral process is also evident among union members. Since their membership is also subject to substantial turnover, unions are engaged in a never-ending registration campaign. Unions first seek to identify the unregistered union member. This task can be accomplished more efficiently through the central labor body than by an individual local union. When voter registration information is made available to the local unions, it will then often be the responsibility of the steward to urge the union member to register.

Because there is no guarantee that those who register will vote, local COPE committees make a major effort on election day to get out the vote. Poll watchers keep careful track of those who have not voted. This information is conveyed to volunteers manning a telephone bank who then phone the "no shows," urging them to vote. Volunteers find baby sitters and organize car pools, making it easier for homemakers and retirees to vote. If the election produces a winner, the inevitable victory party follows, involving more people. The steward may be asked to participate in any of these activities or to recruit others to do so.

The national COPE committee endorses presidential candidates, and the state and local COPE committees endorse candidates at their respective level. Sometimes endorsements, particularly at the local level, result in heated debates because personal friendships may be viewed as more important than issues. Endorsement implies financial help. The local union COPE committee or the steward, or both, have the responsibility for obtaining voluntary contributions of $1 to $2 per member per year.

Voluntary contributions are sought because the Taft-Hartley Act forbids campaign contributions from union dues to any candidate for the Presidency, the House of Representatives, and the U.S. Senate. Some state laws prohibit contributions out of the dues dollar to candidates for state office as well. If labor-endorsed candidates are to wage successful campaigns they need financial support, available only through voluntary contributions. In the past, collecting the COPE contributions was the steward's most difficult task, so a number of unions resorted to selling raffle tickets. The COPE collection may become easier in the future because new federal election laws permit workers to authorize a checkoff deduction from their pay for political contributions.[13] This can be accomplished in one of two ways. Either a checkoff for political contributions can be negotiated as is any other contract provision, or in cases where an employer has already established a corporate political action committee that checks off for management personnel or stockholders, the employer must set up a similar method for union members.

The steward will now have the responsibility of circulating and convincing the workers to sign the voluntary political checkoff. Since the union seeks to have a broad base of small contributions, the amount checked off will be small. The Paperworkers union is seeking a checkoff of one penny a calendar day. The Steelworkers union seeks 2 cents per day; other unions are asking 50 cents a month and some are asking 5 cents per week.[14] These contributions will enable labor to compete more effectively with the industry and right-wing groups which have organized numerous political action committees for supervisors and have raised large sums of money for political contributions to candidates of their choice.

Organization and Unionization of Workers

Contract clauses stating the conditions under which workers in a bargaining unit must join the union are called "union security" clauses. They range from no requirement to join (*open shop*) through a variety of intermediate stages to a full *union shop* under which an employer is free to hire whomever he wishes, but then all workers in the unit must join after a period of time, usually 30 days (7 days in the construction and garment industries), and remain union members. The *closed shop*, which required an employer to hire those who were already union members, was outlawed by the Taft-Hartley Act in 1947. Closed shops were prevalent primarily in the construction, longshoring, and shipping industries.

The weakest form of union security, when it stands by itself, is the *checkoff* of union dues. Under such a clause, workers may sign a written authorization to have their dues deducted from their pay. Under federal law such authorizations are revocable annually or at the expiration of the agreement, whichever comes first. The checkoff can be used in conjunction with any of the other forms described below.

---

[13]Federal Elections Campaign Act Amendments of 1976, 2 U.S.C. 441, §112.
[14]AFL-CIO COPE, *Check-It-Off for COPE*, No. 11-C, Washington, D.C., n.d.

A second form of union security is the so-called *maintenance-of-membership,* popularized by the War Labor Board during World War II. This form requires those who become members to remain members for a fixed period of time, usually the duration of the contract.

The strongest form of union security permissible under federal law is the *union shop,* described above. In the public sector particularly, but also in some cases in the private sector, the *agency shop* has developed. It requires those workers in a bargaining unit who choose not to join the union to pay an "agency fee," roughly equivalent to union dues. The rationale behind this clause is that, since by law all workers in a bargaining unit must receive the same wages and benefits as union members and must be represented by the union equally with nonmembers, nonmembers should pay their fair share of the freight.

The courts have muddied the waters here by attempting to deduce what proportion of union dues are spent for collective bargaining purposes and reducing the agency fee to that amount. The idea is to exempt nonmembers from paying for political or legislative activities. Some unions have added to the confusion by allowing agency fee payers to participate in union activities normally reserved to members, such as contract ratification and even strike votes. Modified forms of the union and agency shop are sometimes negotiated. They exempt from coverage current employees but require all new hires to either join the union or pay a service charge.

Section 14 (b) of the Taft-Hartley Act allows states to enact more restrictive curbs on union security than those in the federal law, the only area in the labor relations field in which federal law is "pre-empted" by state law. As a result of this provision, 20 states have enacted misnamed "Right to Work" laws prohibiting any form of union security except the checkoff (see Table 3, page 32). Included in this ban is the agency shop. These laws provide no employment guarantees.

Right to work laws are promoted by the National Right to Work Committee, an organization dedicated to the destruction of trade unionism which currently finances many of the court cases challenging union expenditure of agency fee funds.

If a union negotiates a union shop, it need not seek to get workers to join the organization since the contract assures that they must become members. But the steward retains the obligation to see that the new worker is familiar with the policies and accomplishments of the union. This is frequently referred to as "unionizing" those al-

---

Table 3. **"Right to Work" States**

Alabama	Nevada
Arizona	North Carolina
Arkansas	North Dakota
Florida	South Carolina
Georgia	South Dakota
Iowa	Tennessee
Kansas	Texas
Louisiana	Utah
Mississippi	Virginia
Nebraska	Wyoming

Source: Donald P. Rothschild, Leroy S. Merryfield, and Harry T. Edwards, *Collective Bargaining and Labor Arbitration* (Indianapolis: Bobbs-Merrill Co., 1979), p. 515.

---

ready in the organization. Therefore the steward, aware of a new employee, should introduce himself or herself and explain that he or she is available for assistance concerning problems that may arise on the job. The steward should present the worker with a copy of the union contract and explain that it contains the benefits the union has negotiated over the years. Many unions are lax on this point. Management is permitted and even encouraged to distribute the contract and may give the impression that the benefits described are solely a result of its generosity.

A short history of the local union or a one-page flyer comparing working conditions and wages before and after the union arrived is another useful piece of material the union steward can give the new employee. Exhibit 1 is an example of a one-page welcoming flyer. Either item can be prepared by an education committee or stewards council. But whatever kind of information is available, the steward should make contact with the new worker as soon as possible to show that an ongoing organization exists that is concerned with the welfare of the workers it represents.

If no union shop exists, then the steward plays an important role in organizing. Since the steward is in daily contact with people in the workplace, he or she is best able to answer their questions and effectively argue the union's cause. Where the agency shop exists, the steward should make every effort to get the agency fee payer to become a union member. Such action will lessen the possibility of lawsuits challenging the amount of the service charge, and joining the union will permit the worker to enter the mainstream of union activities by being eligible to vote, run for office, and serve on committees.

Exhibit 1. Sample Welcoming Flyer

Welcome New Member

Welcome to Local 000 of the _____ International Union. We want you to know what your union has accomplished since it was organized in 1950. Be an active member, attend the local union meetings and take part in all our activities. Help to make the organization a better one. Because of the support of the membership, here is what your union has won since 1950.

Wages	1950	1982
Average Hourly Earnings	$1.34	$7.50
Escalator Clause	0	Wages go up 1¢ per hour for each .3 of a point increase in the Consumer Price Index.
Fringe Benefits		
Pension	0	$12.00 credit per year of service.
Hospitalization	0	Blue Cross-Blue Shield
Paid Holidays	6	10 (3 times straight rate for holidays worked)
Vacation with pay	1 week after 3 years 2 weeks after 5 years	1 week after 1 year 2 weeks after 3 years 3 weeks after 10 years 4 weeks after 15 years
Job Security		
Grievance system	Stalling by company	Time limitations and binding arbitration
Seniority	Department	Plantwide
Promotion	Based on ability with company sole judge.	Based on seniority if worker has ability to perform job.
Working Conditions		
Safety	0	Joint company-union safety committee
Rest Periods	0	15 minutes in morning and afternoon.
Call-in Time	0	4 hours

If you have any questions concerning your rights, contact your steward _____.

Help build a better union. Attend your membership meeting at the Union Hall, _____ Street. Fourth Monday of every month at 8:00 p.m.

Participation of Membership

Unions face the same problem as every other organization seeking to get a high percentage of its members to attend the normal business meeting. Most business meetings consist of rather routine matters which simply cannot be made exciting and therefore draw a small turnout. Meetings that include election of officers, strike votes, or contract ratifications are exceptions but it is, of course, impossible to schedule "big business" of this kind for each monthly meeting. Although the union can never hope to get a large majority of its members to attend meetings on a regular basis, it should not be content with doing nothing.

The steward can play an important role in helping to increase attendance by posting meeting notices and personally reminding members of the meeting to be held. Even more effective is an offer by the steward to drive members to the meeting. Speaking personally to those members who are known to have a special interest in an agenda item will also help. Even though few members may appear at the meeting, the steward on the following day, either during a rest break, lunch period, or after work, should summarize for members the main business accomplished.

Why Workers Become Stewards

Altruism or Prestige. Workers become stewards for various reasons. Many accept the assignment because they want to help those with whom they work. This attitude can be expressed best by the phrase, "I am my brother's keeper." They realize the need for organized self-defense against the employer and that this can be accomplished through the successful processing of grievances. Helping others is the reason thousands of Americans serve in various capacities in voluntary organizations, whether they are fraternal, veteran, or social service groups.

At the same time, union officers or stewards representing others gain prestige in the eyes of those same persons because of the power involved. They have the right to meet formally with management to discuss problems and to request specific information. The successful handling of grievances demonstrates their leadership ability and further enhances their prestige with fellow workers. It may also lead to increased status in the eyes of union officers, who may as a result ask for the steward's advice concerning local union problems.

Career Opportunities. Others may look upon the job of steward as entry into a union career. Almost all officers of industrial unions at both the local union or international union level at one time served as stewards. Initially serving as a steward may lead to becoming a member of the local union executive board and from there to being elected local union president, perhaps followed by a staff appointment with the international union. Others who become stewards may not, at the time of assuming the post, look upon trade unionism as a career. After working as a steward, however, they may decide that this is a desirable career direction. Many unions have a policy of hiring from their own active membership all international union staff for organizing and servicing except for those few jobs that require a specialized knowledge not obtainable through participation in the organization.

Becoming a steward may provide an entry into the ranks of management. Some employers have a policy of promoting the most effective stewards out of the bargaining unit and into their ranks either for the deliberate purpose of weakening the union or because management realizes that the qualities of leadership that make an effective steward may also make an effective management representative. The union in effect serves as a training agent for the employer.

A perennial debate among union members is whether the supervisor with a union background is easier to deal with than one without. Some argue that a good union member retains his attitude toward the workers at least partially and therefore the union worker will receive better treatment. Others argue that the former union representative, in order to prove that he is loyal to management, will be particularly hard-nosed to prove that he has cut his former ties, and that the higher the management position attained by the former union representative, the greater will be the hostility displayed by union members.

Sometimes management hires the local union president as the personnel director in the same workplace. Resentment is then expressed against the individual on the grounds that he or she "sold out" and is now utilizing the skills that were developed at the union's expense against former comrades. Although it sometimes happens that union representatives go over to management, almost never does one who worked for management in a labor relations capacity wind up with a union.

Personal Grievances. Another reason workers become stewards is because they have a personal grievance they want processed, or they feel that they were unfairly treated and are determined to give management a hard time. If resolving a personal grievance is the only motivation for accepting the assignment, this steward may rapidly lose interest in the job and prove to be ineffective. On the other hand, improvement may result if the individual was motivated to take the job because the previous steward was unwilling or unable to effectively handle the complaints of the work force.

Political Ideology. In the past, workers have also become stewards for political reasons. Usually they were influenced by communist or socialist ideologies that called for the replacement of capitalism by an economic system based on production for use rather than profit. They looked upon the labor movement as a vehicle for changing society and felt the position of steward was of key importance in converting workers to their philosophy because of the steward's daily face-to-face contact with the work force.

These political views are in sharp contrast to those held by the majority of American workers who do not believe in changing the system but only in reforming it. Selig Perlman, the labor historian, in *The Theory of the Labor Movement*, has pointed out that historically, American workers have been motivated by job consciousness.[15] He maintained that they recognized the scarcity of jobs. Since the closing of the western frontier denied them the option of moving westward and obtaining land cheaply, it became necessary to organize unions to obtain a monopoly of labor and to concentrate on wages and workshop problems rather than changing the economic system. Most American workers do not object to the profit system as such, but they do argue vigorously about how the profits should be divided.

Personal Benefits. Personal benefits attached to the steward's job sometimes motivate persons to seek that position. Under many contracts, a steward holds *superseniority* and cannot be laid off as long as he can perform any of the jobs of those he represents. The National Labor Relations Board has ruled, however, that the steward cannot be awarded superseniority with respect to promotions.[16] The test of legitimacy for superseniority is whether it benefits the workers whom the steward represents or the steward as an individual. Superseniority for layoffs was upheld because all the workers benefit if a trained person knowledgeable about the contract remains on the job, whereas superseniority for promotions benefits only the individual steward.

Serving as a steward may mean relief from a dull, repetitive job while suffering no loss in wages, since management usually pays the

---

[15]Selig Perlman, *The Theory of the Labor Movement* (New York: Augustus M. Kelley, Pubs., 1928).

[16]*NLRB v. Teamsters Local 338,* 531 F2d 1162, 91 LRRM 2929 (CA 2, 1976), *enforcing Dairylea Coop., Inc., Inc.,* 219 NLRB 656, 89 LRRM 1737 (1975).

union representative for time spent processing grievances. Other tangible benefits to which the steward may be entitled include the waiver of union dues as well as additional overtime opportunities, since some contracts require that the steward be present whenever any overtime work is scheduled for those the steward represents.

The Selection of Stewards

Election. Most unions select their stewards through the election process. This procedure is followed because workers are apt to have more confidence in someone they have a part in selecting. Grievances, particularly in the public sector, may be regarded by workers as personal matters rather than problems of the bargaining unit, and thus grievances may not be filed unless workers have trust in their steward. The steward is usually elected only by those he or she represents, although in some situations the steward may be elected by the membership at large.

Appointment. Some unions appoint stewards. They hold that the officers are entitled to have persons in positions of authority who agree with their policies. This raises the question as to whether the steward is a representative of the union as an institution or a representative of the workers in his or her department.

Abuse of the election process is another argument for the appointment system. Because steward elections are often handled very informally, a nomination is made and then the ballot is closed in a way that may result in the election of an unqualified person. Some unions require that those persons seeking the job of steward attend a training program before the election while others require such attendance after the individual is elected.

In construction unions, the appointment process is used since the workers often are not on a job long enough to determine who they want to represent them.

The Dual Nature of Stewardship. One of the most difficult tasks faced by the steward is adjusting to the different roles required of him or her when serving both as a hired hand of the company and as a union representative. As a worker, the steward is expected to carry out orders and work assignments without questioning them. As a steward, however, he or she meets with representatives of management as an equal and not only may, but must, question any decisions felt to be wrong. The transition from a master-servant relationship to that of one of equal status sometimes results in much personal anxiety for the individual involved.

Most active union members also participate in other organizations. As such, they function in different roles. In some groups they serve as leaders and in others as rank-and-file members. The adjustment required in changing roles in the workplace, however, is often more difficult to make because of the economic power in the hands of management. Therefore, the union must make every effort to protect those stewards who stand up to management. A major cause of wildcat strikes is management's efforts to discipline a steward, an action that workers perceive as an attempt to weaken the union.

Removal. Who has the authority to remove a steward who is not performing his or her duties? The grounds and procedures for removing a steward should be spelled out in the local union's bylaws. In some organizations a petition with the signatures of a majority of the workers the steward represents is sufficient for removal. In other organizations, the executive board or local union meeting has that authority. More often, however, although the bylaws may contain procedures governing the removal of officers, no similar provisions for stewards are included. As a result, no action takes place until the term of the steward runs out and he or she is replaced at the next election or by a new appointment. It is important that the bylaws spell out both the reasons and procedures for the removal of a steward, particularly if there are active caucuses in the union. This will guarantee the steward's right to due process and the membership's right to competent representation.

Summary

We have seen that the union representative has many responsibilities, the most important of which deals with the processing of grievances, a subject to be discussed in later chapters. Other duties discussed include:

(1) Being informed on a wide variety of labor legislation at least to the extent of knowing where and how to get detailed information concerning them;

(2) Acting as a transmission belt between the workers whom he or she represents and the leaders of the organization;

(3) Supporting programs such as the AFL-CIO Community Services Program designed to ensure that union members get their fair share of services from the wide variety of community agencies which they contribute to;

(4) Supporting such programs as the AFL-CIO Committee on Political Education which has the responsibility of informing union members about political issues and which helps to elect friends of the labor movement to office;

(5) Organizing at the local workplace if no union security provision exists in the contract or unionizing those who are already union members; and

(6) Getting workers to participate in their organization by urging them to attend union meetings and to serve on committees.

Workers become stewards for different reasons. Many do so out of the desire to help others. Some look upon the position as a potential entry into an eventual full-time union career while some hope that management will recognize their leadership qualities and promote them. Others may seek the post because they have one or more personal grievances they want settled. In the past, workers sometimes become stewards out of ideological reasons, hoping that this post would enable them to exert political influence. Sometimes the desire to obtain superseniority in respect to layoffs motivates a worker to seek the post of steward.

The number of persons interested in becoming stewards varies among workplaces. In some instances, particularly in large unions, strong competition exists. Most unions have a steward election, feeling that a worker is more apt to have confidence in someone he or she helps to choose. Other unions, particularly in the construction industry, find stewards appointed by the business agent or by another union officer.

Although their roles may vary from one workplace to another it is apparent that no union can function effectively without dedicated and informed stewards.

Review and Discussion Questions

1. What are some of the federal and state laws with which a steward should be familiar?

2. How does the Davis-Bacon Act affect construction workers?

3. What is the steward's role as a communicator?

4. How many states have right to work laws? What are these laws designed to do? Where do they exist?

5. Why do unions oppose the use of lie detector tests at the workplace?

6. Why are unions involved in politics?

7. Explain the major forms of union security?

8. What are some of the ways stewards can "unionize" the workers they represent?

9. How do the method of selection and duties of a steward in an industrial plant differ from that of a steward in the construction industry?

10. Why do workers seek to become stewards?

Key Words and Phrases

access to personnel files
agency shop
checkoff authorization
Committee on Political
   Education
community service programs
Consumer Credit Protection
   Act
Davis-Bacon Act
double-breasted employer
election of steward
employee assistance
   committees
Employee Retirement Income
   Security Act
equal employment
   opportunity laws
Fair Labor Standards Act
Freedom of Information Act
garnishment
Labor's League for Political
   Education
Labor's Non-Partisan League

lie detector (polygraph)
   tests
maintenance-of-
   membership
Occupational Safety and
   Health Act
open shop
Political Action
   Committee
political checkoff
relocation allowances
removal of steward
right to work laws
severance pay
Social Security Act
steward
superseniority
unemployment insurance
union security clauses
union shop
wage payment laws
workers' compensation

3

Definition of a Grievance

The definition of a grievance is important to the process of contract administration because it determines the types of disputes eligible for the grievance procedure. In the early stages of collective bargaining, management—sometimes worried about its ability to retain its right to manage—will seek to restrict access to the grievance procedure. As the collective bargaining relationship matures and the two parties learn to live together, opposition lessens and ultimately in many workplaces any complaint dealing with the workplace becomes grievable.

Some definitions restrict a grievance to a violation of the contract or to disputes over its interpretation. Management may seek this kind of definition:

> A grievance is a complaint in which it is claimed that either party has failed to comply with the terms of this agreement and which involves either a charge of a violation of this agreement or a dispute concerning the interpretation or application of this agreement.

Even with this narrow definition that restricts a grievance to a contract-related matter, an experienced steward usually can find some language in the agreement on which to base a legitimate complaint.

Unions prefer a definition that permits them to grieve any complaint arising out of the workplace, regardless of whether the specific issue in dispute is included in the contract. They argue that if the problem arises out of the workplace the worker is entitled to have it settled through the grievance procedure. A clause such as the following permits such action:

> The term grievance shall mean any dispute or controversy between the management and one or more of its employees or between the management and the union.

This clause does not restrict the definition of a grievance, but permits the union to file a complaint in any of these eight areas:

(1) A violation of the contract or a dispute over its interpretation;
(2) A violation of federal or state law;
(3) A failure of management to deal with an area of its responsibility;
(4) Unfair treatment by management;
(5) A violation of an arbitrator's decision;
(6) A national security discharge;
(7) A dispute over work rules; and
(8) A violation of a past practice.

Violation of Contract/Dispute Over Interpretation

In the early stages of the collective bargaining relationship, grievances are frequently filed charging violation of the contract. As the relationship matures and as the parties realize each is not out to destroy the other, this type of grievance decreases in number.

Grievances, however, over the interpretation of a contract continue to be common, because it is impossible to foresee and provide contract language for every problem that will arise over a two- or three-year period. Furthermore, unclear contract language is sometimes negotiated deliberately because the two parties cannot agree on how to handle a problem. The hope is that a mutually agreeable solution can be found in the future or that an arbitrator's decision eventually will clarify the matter.

Additional factors may result in disputes involving interpretation. The contract may be silent on a subject. Then, management may argue that the subject falls within its inherent rights, while the union may insist that there is an established past practice. Grievances also arise when two or more clauses deal with the same subject. For example, the term "calendar days" may be used in defining the period within which a grievance must be filed initially, while "working days" may be used to designate the period within which the foreman must respond to the steward in the first step of the grievance procedure. If a third clause, dealing with the period in which new job openings must be posted uses the term "five days," does this clause mean five "calendar days" or five "working days"? The issue may be further complicated if part of the force works around the clock while others work a standard five-day shift.

Violation of Federal or State Laws

Today an increasing number of grievances charge the violation of federal or state laws. In part this is because new legislation, such as the Occupational Safety and Health Act, grants workers new rights on the job. When government agencies display a lack of speed or enthusiasm for enforcement, unions resort to the grievance procedure for remedy. Although progress through the grievance procedure may appear slow to the union member who wants immediate action, it is faster than resorting either to the courts or the appropriate administrative agency.

Many of the laws with which a steward should be familiar, referred to in Chapter 2, may be the basis for a grievance. As the concept of equal opportunity employment is expanded, so are the number of grievances filed in this category. Federal law, and in many cases state laws as well, require equal pay for substantially equal work. Since the phrase "substantially equal" does not mean identical work, value judgments are involved as to when equal pay is required. If not determined through the grievance procedure, the problem will be determined eventually in the courts.

For example, men and women are employed by a supermarket. During six hours of the day they both split their time between the checkout counter and stocking shelves. For the last two hours of the shift, however, the men help unload produce trucks while the women continue on the other assignments. The men receive a higher wage rate based on unloading the trucks. The women file a grievance. In this case the court ruled that although the jobs were not identical they were substantially equal, and therefore the women are entitled to equal pay. The court may have found the jobs not substantially equal if the men had unloaded trucks for three, four, or five hours instead of two hours each day.

Equal pay for equal work is further complicated because some women's groups and some unions are proposing that pay scales should be based on the comparable worth of the job. They argue that work of a clerical nature, historically done by women, receives lower pay. They question this policy, stating that there is no good reason to pay these jobs at a lower rate if, for example, they are of comparable worth to those performed by blue-collar workers.

Determining comparable worth is not an easy task. Presumably the purpose of a job evaluation system is to perform that task by ranking jobs in relation to each other based on such factors as skill, education, effort, and reliability. Evaluating completely different jobs, such as that of typist and pipe fitter, is much more diffi-cult, however, than comparing a clerical pool typist with a secre-tary, or a pipe fitter with a construction laborer.

If the term "comparable worth" is interpreted to mean the so-cial worth of the job to society, the entire traditional hierarchy of job relationships may be subject to change. For example, the migrant agricultural laborer performs work related to one of the three basic primary needs of every society—food, shelter, and clothing. How should his or her wage compare to the director of a state-run lot-tery? The implications of a pay policy based on comparable worth have even greater ramifications than those currently raised by wom-en's groups.

Management Failure to Deal With Its Responsibilities

The failure of management to deal with its responsibilities may result in grievances. Such grievances arise primarily from com-plaints about working conditions. Union contracts do not require a worker to be supplied with lighting of specific wattage or a work-place with a minimum and maximum temperature. It is assumed, however, that management, undertaking the responsibility of oper-ating the workplace, also assumes the responsibility of providing a healthy and safe work environment. Other grievances in this cate-gory may concern proper rest rooms, showers (depending on the na-ture of the work), and lunchroom facilities.

Unfair Treatment

Unfair treatment by management may also be the subject of a grievance. In this context "unfair" means discriminatory treatment by management in areas other than those covered by equal employ-ment opportunity legislation. For example, two women are em-ployed in a clerical pool with the same job classification and the same pay rate. One woman takes dictation from a machine while the other constantly types charts of figures in columns. The second one argues that typing charts is more difficult because both the typ-ing and proofing require more care. She says she is being treated unfairly and that either she should get more money or the typing of charts should be rotated between the two women with the same job classification.

A complaint based on unfair treatment of this sort should not be confused with an unfair labor practice. Unfair labor practices relate only to specific employer activities prohibited either by the Taft-Hartley Act or appropriate state law. In general these laws prevent the employer from penalizing workers for union activity. The example cited above could be the basis for an unfair labor practice charge against the employer only if it can be shown that the woman was given the charts to type as punishment for union activity. Absent such evidence, unfair treatment cannot be the basis for an unfair labor practice charge.

Violation of an Arbitrator's Award

Management may violate an arbitrator's award for several reasons. If management is determined to give a union a hard time, it may ignore the arbitrator's decision. The union does have recourse, as follows:

(1) It may take to arbitration management's refusal to comply with the previous decision.
(2) It may go into federal or state court for an enforcement order if the case involves a private employer (and into a state court if a public employer is involved).
(3) It may file an unfair labor practice charge.

Any action the local union takes should be done in careful consultation with its international union representative or its business agent. In one case it may make sense to go into court for an enforcement order depending on the issue and the judge involved as well as the status of the court docket. In another case the better approach may be the unfair labor practice route, particularly if the union seeks to establish a precedent.

In some instances management may argue that it will not obey the arbitrator because the decision is either unclear or requires management to take impossible or unrealistic action. Then it may be necessary to ask the arbitrator to explain or expand upon the original decision.

National Security Discharge

The issue of national security is raised during a period of international crisis. As tensions with the Soviet Union increased during the Cold War, demands increased for the establishment of loyalty and security programs within both government and private industry. In 1947 President Truman established the first loyalty program governing federal employees. Under pressures generated by the late Senator Joseph McCarthy and the hysteria arising out of the Korean War, this program was expanded, and political beliefs and associations became the grounds for barring citizens from employment by the federal government.

Because subversives were barred from federal employment or restricted as to where they could work, similar programs were extended to private employers with defense contracts.[1] Government agencies and employers placed heavy pressure on unions in these industries to exclude from coverage of the grievance procedure those workers discharged for "security" reasons. Unfortunately a number of unions agreed to such provisions. One study of such discharges indicates that some employers would accuse a militant union member of being a security risk and the individual would be discharged, often without even being able to confront the accuser.[2] The United Auto Workers in particular made every effort to defend those of its members discharged for such reasons.

Even where such discharges were not excluded from the grievance procedure, the accused often had little recourse if and when his case got to arbitration. Arbitrators typically ruled that if the U.S. Supreme Court upheld security discharges they saw little reason to do otherwise. It was only after President Eisenhower appointed Earl Warren chief justice of the U.S. Supreme Court that the various loyalty and security programs were rolled back. Arbitrators in cases of this kind again are following the decisions of the Supreme Court and now reinstate security discharges.

Security discharges are not a problem at this time, but an increase in world tensions between the great powers could again create difficulty for unions interested in protecting the rights of freedom of association and due process for their members.

Disputes Over Work Rules

There is a great deal of misunderstanding among union members as to the authority of work rules established by management. Management unilaterally has the right to establish work rules, if they are reasonable and do not conflict with either the contract or law. Management has the right to enforce these rules as a means of

---

[1] Harry Fleischman, Joyce Kornbluh, and Benjamin Segal, *Security, Civil Liberties, and Unions* (Washington, D.C.: AFL-CIO, 1956), pp. 12–13.
[2] *Ibid.*, pp. 9–11.

maintaining discipline or efficiency at the workplace. Work rules may forbid gambling; possession of weapons; drinking or use of drugs; leaving the workplace before quitting time; profane language; fighting; horseplay; excessive absenteeism or tardiness; abuse or destruction of company property; loitering in rest rooms; or immoral conduct. Sometimes work rules are spelled out in great detail together with the penalties for violating them.

Even if the contract requires discussion of work rules with the union, management still has the sole right to implement them. But changes in long- and well-established work rules may be challenged on the basis of past practice. When work rules are changed, management has a responsibility to inform the workers by the method it usually uses to communicate. This may be accomplished by posting the changes on the bulletin board or the time clock or by the supervisor speaking to workers individually.

The union has the right to grieve a work rule on several other grounds. It can be grieved as unreasonable, because it is not related to a legitimate objective of management, but is arbitrary or discriminatory. An example of an unreasonable rule might be to require that a standard form of clothing be worn on the job when it is not needed for identification, as with police officers.

The following is an example of an arbitrary rule. Some years ago the owner of a plant who had retired from active management returned for an inspection and was horrified to note that workers were smoking on the job, for this conflicted with his views of morality. He immediately ordered the plant manager to issue a work rule ending all smoking. The result was a wildcat strike that ended only after the new rule was withdrawn.

Stewards should be aware that work rules also may be challenged on grounds that they violate the contract. The union may challenge a work rule at the time it is issued and need not wait until a worker files a grievance. The union may also grieve if the penalty was not applied uniformly to all offenders.

Past Practice and Management Rights

Past Practice. The most difficult grievance for a steward to process is a violation of a past practice because the burden of proof that the practice exists is on the union. The past practice argument is most effective when the contract is silent or unclear on the subject of the grievance. Past practice may be the basis for a grievance on a wide variety of subjects: working conditions (such as washup time and coffee breaks); definition of jobs and classification lines that may affect wages; layoffs; promotions; subcontracting; and benefits such as a bonus or Christmas turkey. One definition of a past practice is as follows:

> A practice is a reasonably uniform response to a recurring situation over a substantial period of time, which has been recognized by the parties implicitly or explicitly as the proper response.

It is important for a steward to understand that a problem handled once in a given way does not establish a past practice. The problem must have been handled in a similar way over a substantial period of time. For example, workers have been quitting work ten minutes early to wash up. This has continued every day for the last two years, so that the time span would meet the test of "a recurring situation over a substantial period of time." On the other hand, in that same two-year period the employer used the maintenance crew only once to repaint water stains and oil slicks on the walls of the plant. If this job was subcontracted the next time, it is doubtful that a union grievance charging a violation of a past practice would be upheld since the practice had occurred only once. Additional occurrences over a longer span of time would be required to establish a past practice.

Explicit recognition of the past practice requires that both parties agree either orally or in writing how a problem should be handled. More often than not, implicit agreement is involved. To illustrate, in the washup example cited above, management was aware of what the work force was doing because everyone engaged in the practice daily over a two-year period. If management had neither ordered the work force to end the washup practice nor disciplined anyone for it, the union would argue that an implicit agreement existed because management had never objected and therefore had given implied consent. But lax enforcement of an existing rule fails to establish a valid past practice since there is no acceptance, either implicit or explicit.

The past practice argument may arise under three separate circumstances:

(1) Where a clear practice exists that is in conflict with equally clear contract language;
(2) Where a clear practice exists but the contract is silent or unclear; and
(3) Where the practice itself is unclear and the contract is also silent or unclear.

Clear Practice Conflicts With Clear Contract Language. Most arbitrators agree that where clear contract language exists, the contract must apply despite a practice that may have developed over a period of time. Either party has the right to request the other to comply with the terms of the agreement. For example, the contract may state that the overtime rates are to be paid on all hours worked in excess of eight per day and 40 per week. Because a company is in financial trouble the union may waive the overtime rate on a daily basis until such time as the company recovers. If after a year business picks up, the union would be justified in requesting the resumption of overtime pay. A few arbitrators rule that a past practice supersedes clear contract language, claiming that practices engaged in by the parties themselves are more meaningful than the language to which they originally agreed, particularly if it bridges several contracts.

Clear Practice Where Contract Is Silent or Unclear. The past practice argument is most complicated where the union charges that a legitimate past practice exists and the contract is silent or unclear. Management responds by arguing the *residual rights theory.* This theory states that management retains any rights not specifically modified by the union contract. Management may seek to implement this theory in one of two ways: by negotiating a detailed management rights clause that specifically lists all the rights it seeks to retain or by negotiating a broad general management rights clause. Some managements prefer the detailed clause on grounds that then there can be no argument over what rights they retain. Here is an example of a detailed clause:

> Except as otherwise provided in this agreement, the management retains all the rights and functions of management that it has by law, the exercise of which shall not be subject to arbitration.
>
> Without limiting the generality of the above statement, these rights include:
>
> (1) Direction of the work force including the right to hire, suspend, discharge for cause, transfer, relieve employees from duty because of lack of work, or other legitimate reasons.
> (2) The determination of products to be produced or services rendered.
> (3) The location of the business including the establishment of new units, and the relocation of and closing of old units.
> (4) The determination of the management organization of each producing unit and the selection of employees for promotion to supervisory and other managerial positions.

(5) The determination of discipline, control, and use of plant property.
(6) The determination of financial policies including accounting procedures, as well as the prices of goods sold and customer relations.
(7) The scheduling of operations and the number of shifts.
(8) The right to enforce plant rules and regulations now in effect and which may be issued from time to time.

It is further agreed that these detailed enumerations of management rights shall not be deemed to exclude any other management prerogatives that may not have been specifically enumerated.

Other managements prefer a broad general clause because they fear that a failure to list specific rights in a detailed clause may deprive them of some of their authority. An example of a broad general clause is the following:

Except as expressly limited by the terms of this agreement, management retains the sole and exclusive right to operate its plant and direct its work force and take any action affecting any or all of its employees without consultation with the union.

The theory of management's reserved rights has been described by one author as "management acts, the union reacts,"[3] meaning that management seeks to retain the status quo while the union seeks to alter the conditions of employment. The history of collective bargaining indicates that a management right today may become a bargainable item tomorrow.

In general, however, unions concede that in every industry certain "areas of managerial decisionmaking are not shared with the union."[4] These rights, which may vary from workplace to workplace, belong exclusively to management and do not enter collective bargaining. The most common of these are the right to determine the product to be produced, the price of the product, the method of producing the product, and the material to be used. There have, however, been some unions—particularly those in construction—that have successfully challenged management's exclusive right to make determinations in these areas.

---

[3] Paul Prasow, "The Theory of Management Reserved Rights Revisited," *Industrial Relations Research Association 26th Annual Winter Proceedings*, ed. Gerald G. Somers (Madison, Wis.: IRRA, 1973), p. 74.
[4] *Ibid.*

In addition, management has a number of procedural rights which it may implement unilaterally. These relate to its authority to direct the work force. Management has the right to initiate action for this purpose while the union has the right to challenge any such action. Most of the items listed in a detailed management rights clause fall into the category of procedural rights. Therefore, the union can challenge them either on the basis that other contract clauses limit their application or on the basis that management seeks to implement them in an unreasonable manner. For example, the right of management to discharge workers is modified when the contract states that such action may be taken only for "just cause."

An employer seeks to incorporate a strong management rights clause into the contract to remind the union that management retains the administrative right to initiate an action. Such a clause also notifies the union that the employer seeks to prevent the union from muscling into areas over which it wishes to retain control.

Unions oppose management rights clauses because they fear their inclusion may discourage unions from protesting management's decisions on subjects listed in that section of the contract. The union may also be concerned that management will seek to exclude from the bargaining process all benefits about which the contract is silent, using the argument that management retains sole rights in those areas not covered by specific contract language.

In addition to seeking a narrow definition of a grievance and a strong management rights clause, the employer may also try to limit the union's ability to process grievances by restricting the types of grievances going to arbitration.

The following clause would prevent an arbitrator from hearing a grievance charging a violation of a past practice when the contract is silent:

> Matters or subjects not specifically incorporated in the terms of this contract shall not be subject to arbitration.

Because a union seeks to process all legitimate workplace complaints through the grievance procedure, it will vigorously oppose this limitation to the scope of arbitration.

Although a grievance based on a violation of past practice is often complicated, the union usually can win when the contract is silent or unclear if it can establish that a clear practice existed.

Zipper Clauses. Zipper clauses are currently being advocated by employers, particularly those in the public sector, in an attempt to recapture management's rights. A zipper clause may seek to:

(1) Restrict the processing of grievances to disputes involving the violation or interpretation of specific sections of the contract, thereby eliminating grievances based on a violation of a past practice;

(2) Retain as a management right all matters not specifically covered by the contract; and

(3) Prohibit the union for the duration of the contract from requesting midterm negotiations on issues not covered by the contract.

A typical clause follows which would make it difficult for a union to file a past practice grievance, because it "zips up" the contract and excludes all complaints not specifically related to it:

> The two parties to this agreement jointly and separately agree that the agreement embodies all applicable provisions relating to employees covered. Only those provisions or procedures relative to wages, hours, or other working conditions which are included as contract terms shall be valid and have effect.

Usually the union can request the employer to open negotiations during the term of a contract on those issues on which the contract is silent and which were not raised by either party at the last negotiation. This next clause might prevent the union from doing so:

> The parties acknowledge that during the negotiations which resulted in this agreement each had the unlimited right and opportunity to make demands and proposals with respect to any subject matter not removed by law from the area of collective bargaining, and that the understandings and agreements arrived at by the parties after exercise of that right and opportunity are set forth and solely embodied in the agreement.
>
> Therefore, management and the union, for the life of this agreement, each voluntarily and unqualifiedly waives the right, and each agrees that the other shall not be obligated, to bargain collectively with respect to any subject referred to or covered in this agreement or with respect to any subject or matter not specifically referred to or covered in this agreement, even though such subjects or matters may not have been within the knowledge or contemplation of either or both of the parties at the time they negotiated or signed this agreement.

This clause is particularly objectionable from a union's standpoint because the last paragraph prohibits the union from pursuing, during the term of the contract, an issue that may have arisen after the contract was negotiated.

For example, a warehouse operation that owns its own trucks is silent on the subject of subcontracting. The employer knew before the last negotiations were completed that he planned to subcontract the trucking operation after the union signed the contract. When he announces the discontinuance of the trucking operation, the union charges a violation of a past practice. The employer responds by arguing that he need not negotiate on this matter, since the zipper clause excludes those subjects that "may not have been within the knowledge or contemplation of either or both parties at the time they negotiated...."

The union's counterproposal to management's demand for a broad zipper clause prohibiting midterm bargaining might be this clause:

> It is agreed and understood between the parties that this agreement is limited to and embraces only such matters as are specifically set forth in this agreement and all other matters shall be subject to further negotiations.

The inclusion of such a clause permits the union to open negotiations on any subject not covered by the contract. Any new contract language resulting from midterm bargaining also will be subject to the grievance procedure.

A zipper clause does not eliminate all past practices automatically. A number of arbitrators have ruled that if a practice existed over several contracts it serves as a bridge between them and cannot be eliminated by including a broadly phrased zipper clause. Instead, the zipper clause must refer to the specific practices in order to eliminate them.

Unclear Practice Where Contract Is Silent or Unclear. Because unions seek joint determination of conditions of employment, they often try to obtain benefits through the grievance procedure that they were unable to win at the bargaining table. Thus a union may file a grievance charging a violation of a past practice where the practice itself is unclear and the contract is silent or unclear. A practice may be unclear for a number of reasons: the same problem may have been handled in different ways; confusion may exist as to whether or not management made an effort to discourage or end the practice; or the practice may not have occurred over a substantial period of time. In such situations the union's claim will usually be denied since the burden of proof falls on the union to prove that the practice exists.

Sometimes when a contract is silent or unclear, a union will seek to negotiate a clause that formalizes a practice. If the union is unsuccessful and later submits to arbitration a grievance concerning the legitimacy of a practice, the arbitrator will rule against the union on the grounds that he or she lacks authority to grant the union what it was unable to negotiate. Therefore, the union should be cautious in negotiations when raising issues over practices which are known to be well established.

Benefits vs. Gratuities. The outcome of a grievance charging violation of a past practice may be determined by whether the matter in dispute is judged to be a "benefit" or a "gratuity." The employer must negotiate the discontinuance of a "benefit" while it can end a "gratuity" unilaterally. Benefits include working conditions, washup time, paid vacations and holidays, severance pay, and paid leave for time not worked, such as jury pay, military duty pay, and election pay.

Items commonly considered to be gratuities are Christmas turkeys and parties, bonuses, picnics, employee discounts, and check cashing facilities. Any of these items, however, may be found to be a benefit depending on how they conform to these guidelines:

(1) Does the practice concern a major condition of employment?
(2) Was the practice established unilaterally?
(3) Was the practice administered unilaterally?
(4) Did either party seek to incorporate the practice into the contract?
(5) What is the frequency and repetition of the practice?
(6) Is the practice of long standing?
(7) Is the practice specific and detailed?
(8) Do the workers rely on it?

A year-end bonus might fall into either category depending on the circumstances. A bonus would be considered a "gratuity" if the employer, when making it available, announced it was a gift, that it wasn't guaranteed annually, and that it was dependent on economic conditions. The employer could then terminate the bonus unilaterally and a grievance charging a violation of a past practice would lose. On the other hand, it would be termed a "benefit" if the union could show that the employer had proposed the bonus in lieu of a fringe benefit; the workers relied on its payment as a continuing practice; the bonus had been paid for a number of years; and it amounted to a substantial sum. Under these circumstances, a grievance charging a violation of a past practice is likely to be upheld.

Subcontracting. In recent years, a number of union grievances have raised the past practice argument over the issue of subcontracting. Subcontracting can take one of two forms: sending out of the workplace some work formerly done there or bringing outside employees into the workplace to perform tasks normally done by members of the bargaining unit. Here is an example of the former: A company producing automobile door handles decides to farm out the plating operation to another company. An example of the latter form of subcontracting occurs when the employer who previously used the maintenance crew to do touch-up painting within the plant decides to bring in an outside painting contractor to do the same work.

In both examples management may argue either that subcontracting is a management right or that it represents a more efficient method of getting the job done. The union may challenge the action, charging a violation of a past practice or that members of the bargaining unit are laid off as a result of others doing their work.

Borderline Grievances

Sometimes a steward, after examining a worker's complaint under the eight-point guideline for determining the existence of a grievance outlined at the start of this chapter, will still not be sure that the complaint is legitimate. This type of complaint is called a borderline grievance. A steward may be unsure for several reasons: because he or she is new on the job and lacks experience; because the problem has not arisen previously; or because two or more contract clauses appear to conflict.

In any case, the steward should discuss the complaint with the union representative who has the authority to determine if a grievance exists. This individual will vary from union to union depending on its structure and bylaws. Therefore the union bylaws should state clearly who has such responsibility. Is it a chief steward, the grievance committee, the union's executive board, the local union president, the business agent, or the international union representative? Without such clarity, chaos can result if one steward contacts a chief steward for an interpretation while another steward seeks out the union president. Furthermore, if no clear channel exists, the worker with the complaint may be encouraged to contact different union representatives until the worker gets the desired answer; this will hinder the orderly handling of grievances and blur the lines of authority.

An example of this occurred in a local union which held bargaining rights for several companies under one contract. Three business agents were responsible for handling grievances, but were not assigned exclusively to any one company. As a result, both workers and stewards shopped around until they found a business agent who agreed with them. Since the business agents were all elected by the membership at large, they were not averse to pulling the rug out from under each other if such action appeared to be politically profitable. To prevent this leapfrogging, the employees and stewards of each company were eventually assigned to a specific business agent.

If doubt remains after the proper channels have been followed, the grievance should be filed and processed at least through the first step of the procedure. The steward is the worker's representative. Therefore, any doubt about the legitimacy of the grievance should be resolved in the worker's favor rather than that of management.

Unjustified Complaints

One of the tough decisions a steward must make occurs when a worker comes with a complaint that obviously is not a grievance. For example, the contract reads that in order to collect holiday pay, an employee must work the last scheduled workday before the holiday and the first scheduled workday after the holiday. The worker did not work the last scheduled day, but argues that eight hours of overtime was worked during that week. In this case, the steward has three options available:

(1) Explain to the worker that no grievance exists because overtime hours do not qualify as time worked on the last scheduled workday before the holiday, and therefore, the situation does not meet the contract requirements.

(2) Placate the worker by filing the grievance and simply going through the motions while processing it.

(3) Refer the worker, if he or she insists that the grievance be filed, to the person in the union authorized to decide if the complaint is legitimate.

Most unions take the position that a steward should not process complaints that lack merit. They feel that clogging the grievance procedure by filing complaints that cannot be won will slow down the processing of good grievances. In addition, management may decide that a steward who files such complaints does not know the difference between a good and bad complaint. Therefore, management may adopt a tough attitude on all complaints, hoping that the steward will lose prestige in the eyes of the workers, because he or she is unable to reach any settlements.

Despite the fact that unions do not want weak or unreasonable complaints processed, they are often handled for a variety of reasons. The steward may be inexperienced and not know the contract well enough to make intelligent decisions. This shortcoming can be corrected through experience or formal training. Or the steward may want to be a good guy and never say "no," or the steward may have political aspirations within the union and seek support by taking on management on all issues.

On the other hand, an opposition candidate for union office, in order to embarrass those in power, may demand that the steward process an unjustified complaint. If the steward refuses to process the grievance, the candidate will charge the steward with discriminatory treatment, explaining to all that this is the same kind of treatment they can expect if they are not part of the "gang in power." When the grievance is lost, the opposition can then charge that the loss proves the incompetency of those in office. Faced with this dilemma, the steward may process the grievance as the lesser of two evils.

Stewards may support unjustified complaints because they believe the law requires such action regardless of the merits of the complaint.[5] Collective bargaining laws, whether at the federal or state level, do require the union holding exclusive recognition to

---

[5] For example, some stewards believe that the Landrum-Griffin Act requires such action. Landrum-Griffin, however, deals not with the handling of grievances, but only with internal union affairs in the following five areas:

(1) A bill of rights of union members that guarantees freedom of speech within the union and notification of any attempt to raise union dues or assessments;
(2) The filing of financial reports with the U.S. Department of Labor;
(3) The regulations governing the placement of local unions under trusteeship;
(4) The election procedures for union officers; and
(5) The fiduciary responsibility of union officers and stewards.

Nowhere does the Landrum-Griffin Act deal with the role of the steward in handling grievances or with collective bargaining.

perform a duty of fair representation for all employees in the unit. The steward retains the right to refuse to process a grievance if it is felt that the complaint lacks merit. The steward may not, however, pick and choose the complaints he or she wishes to handle. If in the steward's judgment the complaint is valid, the grievance must be filed and processed vigorously even if the worker is not a union member. Unless the job is done without discrimination, both the steward and the union may be charged before the appropriate administrative agency with a failure to provide fair representation. This can result in an assessment of damages to the union. More will be said about this subject in a later chapter.

Summary

If no contract language limits its definition, a grievance may charge: a violation of the contract or a dispute over its interpretation; a violation of federal or state law; a failure of management to deal with an area of its responsibility; unfair treatment by management; a violation of an arbitrator's decision; a national security discharge; a dispute over a work rule; or a violation of a past practice.

Furthermore, a management rights clause does not automatically eliminate the union's right to grieve on issues not specifically covered in the contract, because most of the rights listed in such a clause deal with procedural rights shared between the two parties rather than with exclusive rights. Shared rights are areas in which management can initiate action but to which the union can react by grieving. Nor do zipper clauses automatically eliminate past practice grievances if the practice has bridged several contracts.

Key Words and Phrases

benefit	security discharge
borderline grievances	subcontracting
clear practice	unclear practice
comparable worth	unfair treatment
contract interpretation	unjustified complaints
gratuity	violation of arbitrator's
grievance	award
management rights clause	work rule disputes
past practice	working conditions
residual rights theory	zipper clause

Review and Discussion Questions

1. Does a union seek a broad or narrow definition of a grievance? Why?

2. How can a union justify filing a complaint about a subject not specifically covered in the contract?

3. What alternative methods of enforcement are available to a union if management refuses to comply with an arbitrator's decision?

4. What arguments can a union make to challenge disciplinary action charging a violation of work rules?

5. Why is it difficult for a union to win a grievance charging a violation of a past practice?

6. What are zipper clauses, and how do they affect contract administration?

7. How does a benefit differ from a gratuity?

8. Who should have the authority in a local union to determine whether a complaint is a grievance and should be processed?

9. How should a steward deal with a worker who demands that a complaint which is obviously not a grievance be processed?

4

Purpose of the Grievance Procedure

The basic purpose of the grievance procedure is to settle disputes arising out of the workplace. If no grievance procedure existed, an alternative method for settling disputes over violations of the contract or its interpretation, violations of past practices, or charges of unfair treatment would need to be found. Otherwise, these problems would remain unsolved. Today, though, virtually all contracts in both the private and public sector contain grievance procedures ending in arbitration.

Most grievances are filed by the worker or the union against management, although in a few cases management may resort to the grievance procedure. Therefore, workers have the most to gain from a process that permits them to talk back to management. William F. Whyte, an authority in the human relations field, refers to the grievance procedure as

> a social invention of the greatest importance for our democratic society. . . . It is a means whereby the lone individual and the work group can take up their problems with people who are pretty close to those problems in the plant itself.[1]

Whyte's emphasis on democracy is important. A contract without a grievance procedure is the equivalent of a nation state without an independent judicial system through which constitutional rights can be enforced. The example of the Soviet Union illustrates this concept. That country, at least on paper, guarantees a variety of democratic rights to its citizens that they are unable to exercise, since they have no access to an independent judiciary.

---

[1]William F. Whyte, "The Grievance Procedure and Plant Society," in *The Grievance Procedure* (East Lansing, Mich.: Michigan State University Labor and Industrial Relations Center, 1956), p. 11.

The incorporation of a grievance procedure into the contract and management's agreement to have its actions subject to review and revision, if found to be arbitrary, indicate that management has accepted the union as an institution.

In addition to bringing industrial democracy into the workplace, the grievance procedure serves as:

(1) A systematic method for handling complaints;
(2) A channel for the bargaining agent to protect the bargaining unit;
(3) A method for interpreting the contract;
(4) A support system of the union for the individual;
(5) A source of information for management about workers' complaints; and
(6) A substitute for the strike.

To Handle Complaints

The grievance procedure provides a systematic method for handling complaints because it defines the process and then proceeds to spell out the appeal steps if the problem remains unsettled. The absence of such a method may make equitable and speedy handling of complaints impossible. The absence of a grievance procedure may create additional problems: workers may seek to deal with the management representative they feel has the most clout and thereby undercut the person with the responsibility to act; the management person contacted may pass the buck by stating the problem does not fall within his or her jurisdiction; or workers may seek out the union representative with the most authority to handle their complaint. If settlements are reached, the union may find that they conflict sharply with each other, and as a result, the union may be forced to justify to the membership why one worker received a better grievance settlement than another.

To Protect the Bargaining Unit

The grievance procedure also serves as a channel for the union, which is the bargaining agent, to protect the workers who compose the bargaining unit. The contract is held in the name of the union because the majority of the workers selected it as their representative. The union has the responsibility to ensure that workers receive the rights and benefits to which they are entitled under the contract. Thus the union often will file grievances, even though the individual with the complaint may prefer to drop the matter. Unless the union vigorously processes all violations of the contract, the employer may be encouraged to whittle away benefits one by one until the contract becomes an empty shell.

To Interpret the Contract

The grievance procedure provides a method for interpreting the contract and as a result expands the scope of the negotiated agreement. Today, one-year contracts are the exception rather than the rule. As their duration increases, it becomes harder to foresee every problem that will occur over the two, three, or more years of the contract. The grievance procedure becomes the avenue by which the gaps are filled when the contract is silent or unclear.

A union may agree to ambiguous language for several reasons. Sometimes a union does so because agreement has been reached on the major issues, and it wants to submit the document for ratification to a membership which has been complaining. Other reasons for unclear language include: inexperienced negotiators who may not understand the precise difference in the meaning of various words and phrases; unfamiliarity with the issue being negotiated; contributions to the language of the clause by several people, each seeking to emphasize his or her own ideas; or changed conditions in the workplace which are no longer adequately dealt with in the contract.

At other times, a union may prefer unclear language because it is unsure about how a particular problem should be handled. By the time a grievance is filed, however, the union will either have clarified its position or will leave the decision to an arbitrator. If dissatisfied with the arbitrator's decision, the union can seek to resolve the issue at the next contract negotiation.

Management may prefer unclear language for some of the same reasons. Furthermore, it may know that if it pushes for the language it wants, the union's negotiating committee may not recommend the package for ratification. Therefore, an employer, too, may seek to obtain through the grievance procedure what it was unable to gain through negotiations.

To Support the Individual

The grievance procedure places the power of the union behind the individual with the complaint. Under Section 9(a) of the Taft-

Hartley Act, individuals have the right to process their own grievances. In practice, however, this right may have little meaning since
individual workers may lack know-how, money, and power. All too
often, the workers who insist on the legal right to handle their own
grievances wind up on the doorstep of the union hall asking for help
when they discover that expertise is needed to successfully process
grievances.

In the past, nonunion workers sometimes were assured by the
employer that they had the right to bring grievances to the attention
of management. If they exercised that right, they soon discovered
that they were labeled troublemakers and were thereby discouraged
from pursuing complaints. If they managed to present their cases
effectively, they found that as individuals they lacked power to enforce a favorable decision. In the minds of most people, power in
labor relations is usually associated with the collective bargaining
process rather than the contract administration process. Yet, many
times, winning or losing a grievance is ultimately determined by the
aggressiveness of the union, the solidarity of its membership, its ability and willingness to use the arbitration process, or its willingness to
resort to pressure tactics (see Chapter 1). In the unionized workplace, the organized power of the work force is used to back up the
individual, thus insuring that the complaint is treated on its merits.

To Inform Management

Some workers automatically regard management as being better informed about labor relations than their stewards. This may not
be true, however, because union representatives may spend more
time on labor relations than do their management counterparts. In
this respect, an effective grievance procedure can be just as valuable
to an employer as it is to the worker. A sensitive management may
learn several things. A large number of grievances filed against one
supervisor may indicate a lack of basic skills in handling people;
complaints about piece rates or department quotas may show that
unrealistically high production projections have been made, a situation over which the supervisor may have no control. Because processing grievances is a cost item to management, it may respond by
providing supervisors with special training in human relations or the
handling of grievances. If no improvement takes place in respect to
the number of grievances filed, the supervisor may be transferred or
eventually discharged if unable to perform this important part of the
job.

The kinds of grievances filed also tell management what problems are of concern to its work force. Through grievance records, management can foresee those sections of the contract in which the union may seek language changes at the next negotiations. Management knows that changes will be requested in areas where a number of grievances were lost by the union. Meanwhile, it may be able to forestall wildcat strikes or slowdowns if it responds to complaints affecting a large number of the workforce. For example, a work stoppage may result if, during very hot days, numerous complaints are made about the lack of ventilation. Although grievance handling represents a cost item to management, it may be even more costly to do nothing when workers have legitimate complaints.

To Provide Alternatives to the Strike

If contracts did not contain grievance procedures, a substitute method for handling complaints would need to be developed. There appear to be several alternatives: the use of the regular courts, the creation of special labor courts, or the use of the strike weapon. Generally, unions in this country have been opposed to the use of the judicial system because at best judges have been unfamiliar with labor issues and at worst have been hostile to unions. Although labor courts have been employed in many European countries, unions in the United States prefer to settle grievances without the intervention of government and the increased legalism that can result.

The U.S. Supreme Court ruled in 1960 that binding arbitration, as the last step in the grievance procedure, was a substitute for the right to strike. In return for binding arbitration, the union usually agrees to a no-strike clause for the duration of the contract, the violation of which may subject the union to a damage suit under Section 301 of the Taft-Hartley Act. In recent years, the right to strike over grievances has been advocated by younger members in several large unions, such as the United Auto Workers and the United Steelworkers. The opponents of arbitration charge that the process is too slow and too costly, that it prevents the union from exerting its economic power, and that both the arbitration process and its decisions are becoming overly legalistic.

Open-End Grievance Procedures. Two unions—the Teamsters and Region 7 of the relatively small Allied Industrial Workers (AIW)—have had extensive experience with open-end grievance procedures that permit the workers to strike on any grievance. In the early 1940s both these unions adopted this policy as a result of radical leadership which felt that arbitration represented a compromise with capitalism, an economic system they felt should be replaced. In the case of the Teamsters, Farrell Dobbs was responsible. He was a member of the Socialist Workers Party (a Trotskyite offshoot of the American Communist party) who successfully organized truck-drivers in the Minneapolis area and from whom James Hoffa learned bargaining strategy.

It was Hoffa, a conservative trade unionist, who used the open-end grievance procedure to build his power in the Central States Teamster Council, the midwest district of that union.[2] Under this type of procedure, grievances begin at the local union level and, if not settled, ultimately reach the Joint Area Committee, composed of equal numbers of management and union representatives with the chairmanship rotating between the two parties. If this body cannot agree on a grievance settlement, then the union is free to strike. In practice, a threat to strike is usually sufficient to get employer agreement, because the union wields far more economic power than any individual employer. Therefore, the right to strike on grievances is beneficial to the union, particularly in the trucking industry.

This grievance procedure, however, does not automatically benefit the individual union member. When Hoffa was Teamster president, this power was used to obtain favorable settlements of grievances based on factors other than the merits of the case. The union, in the person of its president, used its power to engage in horse trading.

Under the open-end grievance procedure, no grievance serves as a precedent. As a result, one worker might win a grievance and six months later another member with an identical complaint might lose his. What factors account for the different settlements? One answer may be that the union officers will reverse their position because they hope to convince the employers to concede on an issue that they currently feel is of greater importance. In short, the grievance of the individual is submerged by what is perceived to be the benefit of the group.

Union Politics. In other cases, union politics may be responsible for horse trading. Grievance settlements may be used to persuade local union officers that if they want to win their members' grievances, they ought to "stay in line." This argument can be persuasive since the task of explaining the disposition of grievances falls on local

---

[2]Estelle D. James and Ralph C. James, *Hoffa and the Teamsters* (Princeton: D. Van Nostrand Co., 1965), pp. 167–185.

union officials. Sometimes the union concedes a grievance of a type it previously won in order to go easy on a company which may be in poor financial shape or which cooperated with the union on a matter considered to be of strategic importance.

Unlike the Teamsters, Region 7 of the Allied Industrial Workers never had the great overall economic strength of the Teamsters necessary to dictate grievance settlements to an employer. Yet it wielded great power in some cases. A number of its contracts were with plants that supplied parts to the major auto makers. The mere threat of a strike sent corporate shivers through these companies, because they knew their business contracts might be terminated if, as a result of a grievance strike, they failed to make a delivery date. In addition, the union proved skillful in holding back unsettled grievances or, in the language of the union, placing them in the deep freeze and then dumping them on management during contract negotiations.

Over the last 15 years the grievance procedures in many AIW contracts have changed and most of them now terminate in arbitration. What are the reasons for this shift? Many of these companies were purchased by major corporations which would not and will not negotiate a contract permitting grievance strikes. An example is the Motor Wheel Corporation of Lansing, Michigan, which produces brake drums, wheels, and related parts and employs about 2,500 workers. In 1964 it was purchased by the Goodyear Corporation. Several years later in negotiations with the union, the new owner insisted an arbitration clause was a must item. Despite a lengthy strike, the union was forced to accede to the company demand.

What then can be said about the prospect of substituting the right to strike for arbitration in the grievance procedure? It would be a powerful weapon for a union that is stronger than any single employer or of any probable combination of employers. It is unlikely, however, that any other union officers would have the same freedom to wheel and deal on grievances as do Teamster officials.

Nothing destroys the workers' confidence in the grievance procedure faster than the knowledge that their grievances have been traded off. Although unions emphatically deny engaging in this practice, the evidence indicates that most have done so at one time or another. The temptation to drop a grievance in return for management's concession on a point considered to be of major importance represents a form of "plea bargaining" in the workplace that is hard to resist. The immediate short-term gain for the union, however, may be eroded over the long haul when workers realize that their grievances are subject to union politics.

The fixed nature of some workplaces enables union members to follow the progress of their grievances and, if necessary, appear at the union office or union meeting with regularity and "raise hell." The settlement of grievances based on union politics would cause an uproar as well and result in suits charging the union with failure to provide its members with fair representation. Truck drivers—on the road and therefore away from their home base—find it difficult to do likewise.

The same set of value judgments must be made whether the strike or arbitration is to be the last step in the grievance procedure. Before going to arbitration, the union must decide whether or not it can afford the cost and what benefit it can expect to gain. Small local unions are sometimes deterred from going to arbitration because the cost of one case might bankrupt them. Larger unions may hesitate if they feel the benefits received will not justify the cost. A grievance may charge management with violating the overtime provision by failing to offer two hours work resulting in a total claim of $15–$30. Some unions would not arbitrate this issue even if they felt they were sure to win, since they could not justify an expenditure of several hundred dollars or more. Such a decision must be consistent with past practice, however, so that it is not discriminatorily applied.

A union, before it decides to strike over a grievance, must also make some judgments. Can it convince the work force to strike, causing a loss of wages for the entire group? If the members strike once, can they be convinced to strike on a second or third grievance, particularly if only a few are affected by the issue?

Experience indicates that the strike weapon works best in settling grievances when the bargaining strength of both parties is relatively equal. This is more likely to occur when both parties know and understand the limits beyond which neither can go without expecting retaliation. Management knows that if it stonewalls on grievances the union will strike, and the union knows that if it raises unjustified complaints management is prepared to take a strike.

Small bargaining units might consider negotiating the right to strike on grievances, since the cost of arbitration may be a real obstacle in attaining justice. The union should not underestimate potential management opposition to such a clause, however.

In theory the grievance procedure should render justice for big and little problems alike. In practice, however, a value judgment must be made whether to take a grievance to arbitration or to a strike, what to give and what to take.

Theory of Grievance Procedure

The grievance procedure is based on the theory that the representatives of the union and management at the level at which a problem occurs should seek to solve the matter. If they are unsuccessful, representatives with more authority on both sides are brought in until eventually top management and top union officials meet. If the problem is still unresolved, then an impartial third party in the form of an arbitrator is used to make a final and binding decision.

The number of settlements made at the first level depends on the authority delegated to the immediate supervisor. In some places the supervisor serves only as a courier, taking the grievance to a higher level and then reporting to the union the decision reached there. This downgrading by management of its own representative does not improve the status of its immediate supervisor among those being supervised.

In other places, the immediate supervisor has the authority to settle complaints about such matters as pay shortages, the assignment of overtime work, and the modification of minor disciplinary actions. If so, a high percentage of grievances are settled at this level. Sometimes the immediate supervisor, resentful of pressure from both higher management and the union, may choose not to exercise such authority. In the past the supervisor may have had wide leeway to run the department. With the advent of the union, industrial relations departments have been created or, if already in existence, given additional power. An industrial relations department demands standardization of work rules and practices so that the union cannot play one department against another. Thus the firstline supervisor is no longer permitted to make rules but is required to work under rules formulated at a higher level.

In addition, the supervisor discovers that his or her decisions are challenged by the workers through the grievance procedure or by various pressure tactics. Pressured by higher management as well as the union, the supervisor may adopt an attitude of "a plague on both your houses," and strike back at both tormentors by refusing to settle grievances. This creates problems for the union by requiring it to appeal every grievance. It also creates headaches for management because the time of additional personnel is taken up by matters that the supervisor might have settled.

The inability or unwillingness of the supervisor to settle grievances may lead to other problems. The union in its frustration may start to process grievances at a higher step. In turn management may refuse to discuss the complaint there, arguing that the contract clearly states where the complaint must begin.

A union is concerned with the number of stewards it may have; without a sufficient number, grievances cannot be handled effectively. It seeks to model its steward system after the management structure, so that a steward is matched with each immediate supervisor. Ideally, the steward should represent about 25 workers, but this goal is often the exception rather than the rule. This number permits a steward to be familiar both with the workers' job assignments and their personalities. Knowing who is timid, militant, or a chronic complainer may better enable the steward to evaluate a complaint.

The Grievance Process

Most contracts provide that complaints should be filed first with the immediate supervisor. Some contracts permit grievances to be initiated at a higher step if they involve discharges, policy grievances filed by the union concerning contract interpretation, or complaints involving a group of workers. These problems usually lay outside the authority of the immediate supervisor and therefore would be a waste of time to file at that level.

When the steward and immediate supervisor fail to settle a grievance, the grievance procedure calls for representatives with more authority, such as the chief steward and the second level supervisor. If these parties are unable to agree, the process of referring the grievance to representatives with more authority is continued. The union representatives may be a committee variously named the grievance committee, bargaining committee, or shop committee. Its members may be elected by the membership at large, elected by the stewards, or composed of the chief stewards. Management at this step may be represented by its industrial relations or labor relations department.

If no agreement is reached, top representatives of both the union and management meet. For the union, this may again involve the grievance committee, joined by the international union representative or the business agent, depending upon the union's structure. In a single-plant operation, management may be represented by the president or the president's designee, and in a multi-plant company it may be represented by someone from corporate headquarters.

When the grievance is not resolved at this level, it is apparent that settlement cannot be reached internally. It is now time for an impartial third party—an arbitrator or umpire—to enter the scene.

An arbitrator is a person employed to hear one or more grievances at the same hearing, while an umpire handles all grievances reaching this level for the duration of the contract.

Below is a chart of a typical grievance procedure used in most workplaces (other than construction), showing the progression of the complaint from the point that the steward and supervisor become involved until it terminates in arbitration. The grievance is filed initially at the first step and then proceeds until the representatives of the two parties reach agreement. If they are unable to agree, an arbitrator, as an impartial third party, is employed to make a final decision. The number of steps in the grievance procedure depends on the size of the work force or the type of goods and services produced. A contract covering a small number of workers may call for arbitration after only one level of meetings between union and management representatives. In such a situation grievances are handled informally with only a few reduced to writing. Grievance procedures in contracts covering construction workers also have fewer steps for reasons that will be discussed later in this chapter.

Most grievance procedures contain two types of time limitations. One type relates to the number of days within which the grievance must be filed; the other places time limitations on labor and management decision making—management must answer the grievance within a stated time period, as must the union if it chooses to appeal management's decision.

Table 4.   Grievance Procedure

Step	Union Representative	Management Representative	Management Time Limit (days)	Union Time Limit (days)
1	Steward	Immediate Supervisor	2	2
2	Chief Steward	General Supervisor	5	5
3	Grievance Committee	Labor Relations	10	10
4	Grievance Committee & Int'l. Union Representative or Bus. Agent	Top Management	15	30
5	Arbitration*			

*Arbitrator to issue decision within 30 days after completion of hearing.

It is of key importance that the steward understand the number of days within which the grievance must be filed. Here are examples of three different contract clauses, each providing for a different time limitation:

(1) An employee or the union shall file a grievance within 30 days after the date the situation occurred that caused the grievance.

(2) An employee or the union shall file a grievance within 30 calendar days after the date the situation occurred that caused the grievance.

(3) An employee or the union shall file a grievance within 30 days after the date the situation occurred that caused the grievance or within 30 days after the parties should have known of its occurrence.

The first clause states that a grievance must be filed within 30 days, but it is unclear whether this means 30 calendar days or 30 working days. If the workplace covered by the contract operated only Monday through Friday, 30 working days would permit a longer filing period than would 30 calendar days. The second clause defines the type of day by stating calendar days. The third clause may provide for a filing period longer than 30 days if the worker is not aware when the grievance first occurred. In this instance, management may, however, challenge the claim as to when the worker should have known there was a grievance.

The time span during which a grievance may be filed generally ranges from 24 hours to 30 days or more, and sometimes no limitations exist except on grievances involving backpay where the employer's liability may be limited to 30 days. Most unions seek to negotiate the longest possible period within which to file because often workers are not aware that they have a legitimate complaint until they talk to others about their problems. This may not take place until two union members are socializing after work, a week or more after the event happened. After discussing the problem, the worker may then decide to talk to the steward. A short filing period can result in losing grievances if the steward is sick or unavailable to the worker.

If the contract provides for 30 days within which to file a grievance the union should not wait until the deadline. Grievances should be filed as soon as possible so action to settle them can begin. The purpose of a reasonable time period is to ensure that grievances are not lost on the technicality of failure to file on time.

In addition to a time limit within which a grievance must be filed, many contracts also spell out time limits on each step of the grievance procedure. Management must respond at each step of the procedure within the time limit indicated. Without this restriction, management could frustrate the purpose of the grievance procedure by not acting.

For the union, time limits spell out the period within which it must decide whether to appeal management's decision to the next step. The union seeks to negotiate as short a period as possible on management's responses, but a longer time limit with respect to its appeal rights. Management attempts to do the opposite. As a result the negotiated procedure usually contains the same limit for each party at each step of the procedure.

At the first step, the time limit for decision is usually short, ranging from a day to a week. As the grievance moves to a higher level, the time limits are lengthened, since the higher level representatives are not as readily available. Furthermore, only the most important grievances reach the third or fourth step and both parties need adequate time to prepare their arguments.

Under most contracts, a failure by a union to meet the time limits results in the loss of the grievance. For example, the 1982 UAW-General Motors agreement states:

> Any grievance not appealed from a decision at one step of this procedure in the plant to the next step within five working days of such decision, shall be considered settled on the basis of the last decision and not subject to further appeal.[3]

Typically, however, management's failure to comply with its time limits does not result in an automatic loss of the grievance. Instead, the union has the right to appeal immediately to the next step, as stated in this contract between Michigan State University and the Michigan State University Clerical and Technical Union, representing clerical and technical employees:

> Failure of the employer to render a decision on a grievance within the specified time limits shall permit its appeal by the grievant to the next step.[4]

---

[3] Agreement between General Motors Corporation and International Union, United Automobile, Aerospace and Agricultural Implement Workers of America (AFL-CIO), 1982–1984, p. 27.

[4] Agreement between Michigan State University and the Michigan State University Clerical and Technical Union, 1980–1983, p. 51.

This double standard results in the loss of the grievance by the union when it fails to meet the time limits, but no comparable penalty applies to management when it does likewise. To prevent this, some unions negotiate clauses that treat violations of the time limits by both parties in the same manner. A contract negotiated by Local 705, Retail, Wholesale and Department Store Union, and the H. J. Heinz Company states:

> Failure of the company to comply with the time limits provided in steps (1), (2), (3), (4), or (5) . . . shall be considered an affirmation of the request contained in the grievance, thus disposing of the grievance. Failure of the union to comply with the limits provided in steps (1), (2), (3), (4), or (5) . . . shall be considered as an acceptance of the last answer given by the company, thus disposing of the grievance.[5]

This clause can speed up the grievance process as well as ensure equitable treatment for the union, since the loss of the grievance applies when either party violates the time limits. Neither side may unilaterally extend the time limits, although it is often done by mutual agreement. Such extensions are granted for several reasons: the international union representative may be tied up in critical negotiations elsewhere; the plant manager may be sick; or, both sides may agree that more time is needed to investigate the facts.

Principles for an Effective Grievance Procedure

Grievance procedures, whether for blue-collar or white-collar employees, are based on the same following general principles.

Both labor and management must understand and accept the grievance procedure.

Understanding implies that all concerned know the steps in the procedure, the time limits, and the respective representatives responsible for processing complaints. Acceptance of the grievance machinery depends on qualified representatives whom the workers feel can effectively represent them with management. In order to guarantee effective representation, superseniority must be negotiated to ensure the availability of qualified personnel when layoffs take place. Only necessary information should be requested, and the

---

[5]Agreement between H. J. Heinz Company and Local 705, Retail, Wholesale and Department Store Union (AFL-CIO), 1982–1985, p. 20.

grievance forms must be understandable. Language on the forms, such as "Contention of Claimant," should be replaced with "Nature of Grievance" or "Reasons for Complaint." The quality of the information needed to win grievances is more important than the quantity of information.

Grievances should be handled promptly and on their own merits.

The truism, "Justice delayed is justice denied," summarizes the worker's reaction to a long, drawn-out process. Delay is particularly serious when discharge or serious disciplinary action is involved. In either case, it is difficult for the individual to make decisions about the future. Should a job search be undertaken while a decision is being reached? What are the chances of finding another job if the grievance is lost? Faced with financial loss, the worker is also under severe emotional and psychological pressure. Delay caused by postponement of meetings due to the absence of the appropriate union or management representative, inability to agree on an arbitrator, or the failure of the arbitrator to render a prompt decision, may destroy confidence in the grievance system. Prompt settlement of grievances may be impossible if the union does not undertake the responsibility of screening the complaints; overloading the grievance procedure may succeed in burying the good grievances along with the bad. Workers who are convinced that the decision to process a grievance is based on political considerations rather than on merit may take out their frustrations by engaging in wildcat strikes.

All grievances should be processed through the same procedure.

Under some contracts, particularly in the public sector, grievances involving disciplinary action and promotions must be processed through a separate system. As a result, both the steward and the worker may be confused as to where a complaint should be filed.

All complaints eligible for the grievance procedure should be eligible for arbitration.

If a contract has a broad definition of a grievance but restricts the type of complaints that may be arbitrated, then management can refuse to settle at any step of the grievance procedure. This leaves the union no alternate source of settlement. There is no good reason why a complaint eligible for the grievance procedure should not be eligible for impartial third-party settlement.

A few unions as a matter of policy seek to exempt from the arbitration process grievances that they feel are too important or that fall in areas about which an arbitrator, unfamiliar with the industry, may lack knowledge. For example, the UAW in its contracts with General Motors, Ford, and Chrysler reserves the right to strike legally over grievances involving health and safety or production standards.

General Electric management, on the other hand, refuses to arbitrate certain types of grievances. The GE contract with the International Union of Electrical Workers (IUE) provides for "involuntary arbitration" of any discipline or discharge and any alleged direct violation of the contract. "Involuntary" means that either party may take the case to arbitration, and the other party must accept the arbitration process.[6]

"Voluntary" arbitration under this same contract means that both parties must agree before the matter can proceed to arbitration. Examples of matters that come under voluntary arbitration are changes in manufacturing methods, subcontracting, changes in incentive rates, wage rates in general, and insurance and pension claims. When the parties disagree as to which category a grievance falls in, the issue goes to the arbitrator who decides it on its merits.

The union representative should have the right to be present at each step of the grievance procedure.

Although the Taft-Hartley Act and most state public employment collective bargaining laws permit workers to process their own grievances, the union should insist on its right to be present at the time of settlement so it can determine if the settlement conforms to the contract. In addition, the union should be careful to write into the grievance procedure the right of the international union representative or the business agent to participate formally in settling grievances.

The contract should specify which union and management representatives will meet at each step.

For example, instead of listing "union representative" at step one and step two, the contract should read "Step One: Steward," "Step Two, Chief Steward," etc. Likewise, the management representative should be clearly identified. In this way, everyone concerned will understand who has the responsibility at each step of the grievance procedure.

---

[6] Agreement between General Electric Company and the International Union of Electrical, Radio and Machine Workers (AFL-CIO) and its affiliated GE-IUE (AFL-CIO) Locals, 1982–1985, p. 63.

The union, as well as the worker, should have the right to file a grievance.

A union has this right under the law unless the contract restricts it to employees. It is important for the union to retain this prerogative, since there are occasions when a member may not be willing to file a grievance and the contract can be enforced only by the union itself taking action. Sometimes a union seeks to file a policy grievance in its own name either because it wishes to get an interpretation of a contract clause or because the grievance affects a group of employees, making it impractical to file a large number of individual grievances.

Grievance Procedures in the Construction Industry

Both the collective bargaining process and contract administration in the construction industry differ from that found elsewhere.[7] In the construction industry, employment is seasonal and temporary, with workers moving not only from one job site to another, but from employer to employer as well. The worker's primary identification lies with the craft union rather than the employer because of the short duration of any one job. Often the worker's skills were acquired through a common apprenticeship program conducted by the union. This shared educational experience provides construction workers with a broad variety of skills that require minimal supervision despite dangerous and difficult working conditions.

Unemployment is common in this industry, with an unemployment rate double that found elsewhere, because of the sensitivity of the construction industry to downswings in the overall economy. High interest rates affect not only residential construction but commercial and industrial construction as well. Businesses, like individuals, cut back on expansion when interest rates—i.e, the price of money—soar. Even under the best economic conditions, high frictional unemployment, or that unemployment created when workers are between jobs, continues to exist in the construction industry.

Changing technology also affects career opportunities among the crafts. Over the years, equipment operators, electricians, and

---

[7]D. Quinn Mills, "Construction," in *Collective Bargaining: Contemporary American Experience*, ed. Gerald Somers (Madison, Wis.: Industrial Relations Research Association, 1980), pp. 49–97.

pipe fitters have had an increase in work, while carpenters, bricklayers, plasterers, painters, and lathers have seen a decline.

Members of the 17 craft unions that operate in the construction field are not employed to the same degree in all branches of the industry. The basic trades, consisting of carpenters, operating engineers, laborers, cement masons, teamsters, and bricklayers, are heavily involved in residential and commercial construction. The mechanical trades such as plumbers and pipe fitters, electricians, boilermakers, sheet metal workers, and structural iron workers are more involved in heavy construction and power plants.

Unique Aspects of Collective Bargaining in the Construction Industry. Collective bargaining for building construction workers is typically conducted at the local level. A craft union negotiates a contract with an employer association that covers the geographic area from which the labor force is drawn. This pattern in building construction, however, does not exist everywhere. In some communities, contracts are negotiated not by a craft but by a council representing all the crafts and the corresponding contractors' associations.

Other divisions of the construction industry have developed different models. National agreements are usually negotiated for pipeline construction because a project may cover a number of states. The number of national contracts is growing because of an increasing number of traveling contractors with jobs in many parts of the country. Under these contracts, the employer agrees to utilize only organized subcontractors and to meet local wages, fringe benefits, and working conditions. In return, the national union agrees to settle disputes that may arise between its local affiliates and the employer. At the same time, the national contractor is usually permitted to continue work at other sites when a local union calls a strike against local employers within a certain geographical area. Sometimes a large project is covered by special provisions in which the national union agrees to concessions in local working conditions in order to discourage the contractor from hiring nonunion workers.

Development of Grievance Procedures. The unique characteristics of the construction industry have resulted in a pattern for processing grievances different from that of manufacturing or service industries. For many years, grievances in construction were handled by direct action. The business agent met with the contractor and, if no settlement was reached, the job site was shut down until the problem was resolved.

The way in which construction unions deal with grievances has changed in recent years. The Taft-Hartley Act allows unions to be sued for damages for breach of contract, and some craft unions have paid substantial penalties over the years. Strikes over grievances also were a factor in convincing some contractors to hire nonunion workers with the expectation that they then would have uninterrupted production. As a result, craft unions modified their handling of grievances by negotiating formal grievance procedures closely modeled after those in other industries.

The activities of a steward in a craft union and those in an industrial setting differ substantially. Because construction jobs are generally of limited duration, the first person reporting on the job usually becomes the steward. If several report at the same time, the business agent makes the appointment. A number of craft unions now provide special training to some members so they are better equipped to assume the assignment of steward when they appear on the job.

In the past, the craft union steward in construction played a limited role in handling grievances. He generally called a violation of the contract to the attention of the foreman, particularly if it involved actual work. If the problem was not immediately corrected, the steward contacted the business agent, usually a full-time representative of the local union elected by its members to negotiate and enforce the contract. The steward rarely attempted to process a grievance, because he served as a representative of the business agent rather than the worker.

The same general principles governing grievance procedures elsewhere apply in the construction industry, but they are implemented in different ways. Grievance procedures in construction contracts contain fewer steps. On both sides persons closest to the problem become involved. Although not specifically spelled out, usually they are the steward and the craft foreman in step one, followed by the business agent and the general foreman or the contractor in step two. In part, this results from a simplified management structure, which usually consists of a craft foreman, a general foreman, and the contractor. Therefore, no need exists for a four- or five-step procedure. Furthermore, speedy handling of grievances is essential because of the seasonal and temporary nature of most construction jobs. Time limits are also of shorter duration than found elsewhere. The time period in which a grievance must be filed is typically five days and the time limits in which management and the union must respond to each other are also shorter.

If a settlement cannot be reached in the initial steps of the grievance procedure, a joint labor-management committee consisting of equal numbers of union and employer representatives attempt settlement. Here is an example of a typical construction grievance procedure negotiated by the Laborers' International Union of North America (LIUNA):

> In the event a dispute occurs . . . an earnest effort will be made to settle such dispute between the contractor and/or his representative and the union. If the dispute cannot be resolved in two (2) working days by this method, either party can then refer the matter to the Joint Grievance Committee. . . .
>
> The Joint Grievance Committee shall be composed of four (4) members, two (2) from the Employers and two (2) from the Union. . . .
>
> All complaints . . . shall be referred to the Joint Grievance Committee. . . . If the committee within two (2) working days . . . is unable to decide the matter before it, the members of the Committee shall choose a fifth member. Should the Committee be unable to agree on the fifth member within two (2) days, the Director of the Federal Mediation and Conciliation Service shall be requested to supply a list of five (5) arbitrators from which the union and the Association shall alternately strike two (2) each, with the remaining one (1) to become the fifth member. The decision of said Committee shall be determined by a majority of its members and shall be rendered within five (5) days after such a submission. Said decision shall be final and binding upon the parties. . . . [8]

Construction union contracts differ most often on whether an impartial third party or a joint labor-management committee should render the final decision. Although the Laborers' contract above provides for a five-person arbitration board, the ultimate decision will be determined by whether the person selected from the FMCS's list supports the position of the union or of management. The trend among construction unions is to negotiate third-party arbitration.

The Council on Industrial Relations. The International Brotherhood of Electrical Workers (IBEW) and, to a lesser extent, several other craft unions utilize a joint labor-management committee as the final decisionmaker on grievances. The excerpts from this grievance procedure negotiated by IBEW Local 131 show that no significant differences exist between it and that found in the Laborers' contract cited above except that the Council of Industrial Relations (CIR) makes the final decision:

---

[8] Agreement between Michigan Chapter, Associated General Contractors of America and Local 998, Laborers' International Union of North America (AFL-CIO), 1980–1982, pp. 29–30.

All grievances or questions in dispute arising out of this Agreement shall be adjusted by the duly authorized representatives of each of the parties to this agreement. . . .

In the event that the duly authorized representatives are unable to adjust any matter upon mutual agreement of all parties within forty-eight (48) hours, they shall refer the same to the Local Labor-Management Committee along with copies of the written grievance and answer. . . . There shall be a Local Labor-Management Committee of three (3) representing the union and three (3) representing the employer.

All matters coming before this Committee shall be decided by a majority vote. Four (4) members of the Committee, two (2) from each of the parties hereto, shall be a quorum for the transaction of business, but each party shall have the right to cast the full vote of its membership and it shall be final and binding on both parties. . . .

Should this committee fail to agree or to adjust any matters referred to it after a full submission of the same, such shall then be referred to the Council on Industrial Relations for the Electrical Construction Industry of the United States and Canada. The decision of the Council shall be final and binding on both parties.[9]

The Council on Industrial Relations (CIR) was organized in 1920 by the IBEW and the National Electrical Contractors Association (NECA) for the purpose of stabilizing labor relations in the electrical field of the construction industry.[10] The aim was to eliminate strikes over both "interests" and "rights," eliminate employer lockouts, and fix minimum qualifications for employment. "Interest" disputes take place when impasses are reached in negotiating the original terms of the contract; disputes over "rights" deal with the violation or interpretation of the previously determined language of the contract.

A number of principles have been adopted to implement decisionmaking in this joint effort to develop a better relationship: sudden wage changes and retroactive pay are discouraged because of the employer's contract commitments made in an accepted bid; contracts are to contain a grievance procedure to settle disputes; and

---

[9] Agreement between Kalamazoo Division, Michigan Chapter, National Electrical Contractor's Association and Local 131, International Brotherhood of Electrical Workers (AFL-CIO), 1978–1980, p. 3.

[10] Donald J. White, "The Council on Industrial Relations for the Electrical Construction Industry," *IRRA 24th Annual Winter Proceedings*, ed. Gerald G. Somers (Madison, Wis.: Industrial Relations Research Association, 1971), pp. 16–24.

restrictions of output are considered harmful to the industry. The employer, on the other hand, is expected to recognize and deal with the union and to honor a contract on a continuing basis.

The Council on Industrial Relations itself is a national committee composed of six union and six NECA representatives. Since outside neutral third parties are never employed, it is the final appeal board on grievances. All of its decisions are based on unanimous action.

The Council on Industrial Relations in a sense operates locally as well as nationally. A local labor-management committee consisting of three employers and three union representatives is part of every local union agreement. This committee seeks to settle all contract disputes through majority vote. The settlements are reported to the appropriate IBEW vice-president and the regional director of NECA by the local committee. This committee plays an important function because local IBEW contracts forbid strikes over disputes involving both interests and rights whereas most other construction unions permit strikes over interest questions and in some cases on rights as well.

Over the years, resolutions critical of the CIR have been introduced at IBEW conventions. These criticisms charge that (1) CIR interferes with local union autonomy, since local unions cannot withdraw from CIR without its permission; (2) CIR represents a form of compulsory arbitration, since all disputes over contract negotiations must be referred to it for final settlement; and (3) grievances are lost at the final appeal level unless the CIR management representatives unanimously approve them, whereas the use of arbitration would not require the employer's support. Despite these criticisms, it is unlikely that the Council on Industrial Relations will be eliminated or significantly modified in the foreseeable future, since these criticisms usually have been voiced by younger members who do not hold positions of power in the union.

Types of Grievances in the Construction Industry. The construction industry also differs in the types of grievances that predominate. Those over seniority, promotions, and incentive systems do not exist. Most construction grievances fall into the areas of:

(1) Premium pay
(2) Staffing of equipment
(3) Ratio of journeymen to foremen
(4) Employers' obligation to supply tools
(5) Time at which wages are to be paid

(6) Employers' refusal to accept workers referred from the hiring hall
(7) Jurisdiction

Premium pay applies not only to overtime hours, weekend work, and holidays, but also to hazardous work and the use of hazardous materials. Grievances about overtime pay arise because contract clauses may be open to different interpretations. For example, one clause of an IBEW contract reads, "All work performed outside of the regularly scheduled working hours and on Saturdays, Sundays and . . . holidays . . . shall be paid at double the regular rate of pay." Another clause in the same contract states: "All overtime work required after the completion of a regular shift shall be paid at one and one-half times the shift hourly rate." Unclear are both the definition of "regularly scheduled hours" found in the first clause and the definition of "regular shift" found in the second clause. Therefore, it is unclear when the payment of double time or time and a half is required.

Historically, the pyramiding of overtime was a problem in the construction industry. That is, on some jobs the worker received time and one half for Saturday, when those hours were in excess of 40 per week, and in addition received double time pay because the contract stated work done on that day required that rate. Most construction contracts prohibit this practice by the inclusion of this type of clause: "There shall be no pyramiding of overtime rates and double the straight time rate shall be the maximum compensation for any hours worked."

Grievances result if employers fail to make premium payments when hazardous materials are used or hazardous working conditions exist. For example, a carpenter's contract might provide that "employees handling material coated with creosote or toxic preservatives shall receive 35 cents per hour above the journeyman's rate and 75 cents per hour for employees working on a two-point swing stage, using acid bonding material in laying bricks, or performing the sand blasting of masonry." Other craftsmen may receive premium pay for doing high work on towers or for working on bridges. Arguments often occur in these cases over the amount of time spent in the hazardous situation or the height at which a worker qualifies for high pay.

Staffing provisions exist in many construction contracts that specify either the number of workers who must be employed or that restrict the type of work they may do. Whether and under what circumstances a foreman can engage in the work of the trade being supervised is regulated by the contract and is often the basis of a grievance. In other situations a worker may not become a contractor while a member of the union.

Some contracts require that workers 50 years of age or older, if available, must constitute one-third of all those jobs employing three or more journeymen. Employers often prefer younger workers and their attempts to ignore this clause result in grievances.

Staffing provisions may also govern the number of workers required to run a compressor or, with bricklayers, "a masonry unit set by hand weighing thirty-nine pounds must be set by at least two bricklayers working in pairs."

Closely related to the staffing provisions are clauses dealing with the *ratio of apprentices to journeymen.* It may range from one apprentice per journeyman to a high of ten per journeyman. If construction is booming, more apprentices will be taken into the program than during a period when work is slack. Employers may seek to employ fewer apprentices than the contract requires if the job requires a high level of skill. If the reverse is true, the employer may exceed the apprenticeship ratio in order to save on labor costs since apprentices are paid a lower wage rate.

Two clauses from a typical bricklayers' contract illustrate how grievances may arise over the *employer's obligation to provide tools and equipment.* The first might read:

> The employer shall provide every bricklayer with a respirator where dusty conditions prevail; safety goggles on work which endangers or impairs the eyes; and shall take suitable precaution to allow employees to be warned of danger in due time where gas exists.

This clause is unclear as to the type of equipment required as a warning device against gas. A similar problem arises in this clause: "When bricklayers are working on heated surfaces, the Employer shall supply wooden shoes or an acceptable facsimile." A dispute may occur over the type of shoe that will serve as a suitable substitute.

Numerous grievances occur in construction concerning the *times wages are to be paid.* Different procedures govern the payment of wages to those on the payroll who have completed the workweek, those who have quit, and those who have been discharged. If the deadlines are not met, the employer is assessed penalties which in some cases are substantial. An employer who is not able to pay the work force on time may be an employer unable to pay at any time, therefore requiring the union to take action.

Grievances also involve the *union's referral system.* Many construction unions have an exclusive system which requires the employer to hire workers through the union hiring hall. The employer usually retains the right to reject them if it is felt that they cannot perform the work. If the union is unable to supply the workers within a stated period of time, which may range from 24 to 48 hours, the employer is free to hire off the street.

Even when the union has the exclusive right to refer, it is required by law to do so free of discriminatory treatment based on union membership. In order to provide as much work as possible for its membership, a union will sometimes negotiate priority groups for referral. These referrals are based on qualifications that are not directly related to union membership but are most likely to be met by union members. Typically, the highest priority group will hold these qualifications:

(1) A specified number of years experience in the branch of the construction industry in which they are seeking employment;

(2) Residency in the geographic area constituting the normal labor market;

(3) Passage of a standard examination for the appropriate branch of the trade; and

(4) Employment for a specified period of time under the local union contract.

Each additional priority group contains fewer requirements. If the contract contains four priority groups, workers in the two lowest categories are unlikely to be referred unless the construction industry is booming.

Grievances over jurisdiction occur when one union charges that the employer assigned the work of its craft to another union. Jurisdiction disputes tend to increase in number and bitterness when work is slack, since each craft union seeks to preserve work for its membership. These disputes, often resulting in strikes, have been a major reason for public antagonism toward unions.

The AFL-CIO Building and Construction Trades Department has tried to eliminate jurisdictional disputes by creating a National Board for Jurisdictional Awards. The National Board for Jurisdictional Awards has ceased to function temporarily while the AFL-CIO Building and Construction Trades Department and the Associated General Contractors attempt to resolve their differences about its responsibilities. Its decisions, called "agreements of record," are binding on those international unions that sign them, as well as the contractors they represent. Agreements of record are found in the Green Book, the official guide governing work assignments.[11] In reaching its decisions, the National Board for Jurisdictional Awards examines previous awards made by it and its predecessors, some of which go back 50 years or more.

In addition to the Green Book, a Grey Book contains "attested agreements."[12] These decisions, signed by only two international unions, are confirmed by the chairman of the National Board for Jurisdictional Awards and have the same standing as "agreements of record." A third category is called "agreements not attested." They are not recorded in the Green Book or Grey Book, but are recognized as valid by those unions signing them. Technically they are not binding on the contractor, but it is recommended that the contractor consult representatives of the unions involved before making any work assignments. These agreements may be changed without going through the National Board for Jurisdictional Awards.

Procedural agreements also exist. They do not define work jurisdiction but do outline procedures to be followed by unions in settling local disputes.

It is important that the union stewards be familiar with jurisdictional agreements since they have the responsibility for making sure that the craft receives the work to which it is entitled.

Grievance Procedures in a Nonunion Workplace

In recent years there has been a substantial growth in grievance procedures (often called "complaint systems") in nonunion workplaces, particularly in large companies.[13] The motivation in most cases is to deter union organization. Not all nonunion companies, however, think it is a good idea to introduce such a system, because it may put the company in a "no-win" situation.

If the worker loses the grievance, the system is denounced as being a kangaroo court. If management concedes the grievance, the company's objective of convincing its work force that a union is not needed may be destroyed because management is forced to admit that it does make mistakes or acts in an arbitrary fashion. This

---

[11]Building and Construction Trades Department, AFL-CIO, *Agreements and Decisions Rendered Affecting the Building Industry* (Washington, D.C.: AFL-CIO, 1975).

[12]Associated General Contractors of America, *National Jurisdictional Disputes (not printed in the "Green Book")* (Washington, D.C.: Associated General Contractors of America, 1974).

[13]Fred Foukes, *Personnel Policies in Large Non-Union Companies* (New York: Prentice-Hall, 1980).

may lay the groundwork for concerted action on the part of the employees.[14]

These procedures suffer from some obvious deficiencies, particularly the absence of any "contract" to be applied or interpreted. The usual lack of an outside third-party terminal procedure (such as arbitration) is also a major drawback for the worker.

It has even been proposed that legislation be adopted to provide "due process" in nonunion workplaces through a grievance procedure leading to outside, third-party arbitration. However beneficial this might be to nonunion workers (and despite its potential to provide full employment for arbitrators), it is unlikely to surmount management opposition in the Congress or in state legislatures.[15]

Summary

The grievance procedure has introduced a form of industrial democracy into the workplace. The collective strength of workers is pooled for administering the contract just as for negotiating its original terms. The grievance procedure serves as:

(1) A systematic method for handling complaints;
(2) A channel for the bargaining agent to protect the bargaining unit;
(3) A method for interpreting the contract;
(4) A method of support by the union of the individual;
(5) A source of information for management about workers' complaints; and
(6) As a substitute for the strike.

Regardless of whether the worker is a blue-collar or white-collar employee, the same principles apply for an effective grievance procedure: both labor and management must understand and accept the grievance system; grievances should be handled promptly and on their own merits; all grievances should be processed through the same procedure; all grievances eligible for the grievance procedure should also be eligible for arbitration; a union representative should be present at each step of the grievance procedure; the contract should specify which representatives of union and management meet

---

[14]Richard L. Epstein, "The Grievance Procedure in the Non-Union Setting: Caveat Employer," *Employee Relations Law Journal*, 1, no. 1 (Summer 1975), pp. 120–127.

[15]Jack Stieber and John Blackburn, eds., *Protecting Unorganized Employees Against Unjust Discharge* (East Lansing, Mich.: Michigan State University School of Labor and Industrial Relations, 1983), p. 123.

at each step of the grievance procedure; and the union as well as the worker should have the right to file a grievance.

Construction unions, too, are negotiating grievance procedures closely paralleling those found elsewhere. At one time the strike was used to settle disputes in this industry. With the passage of the Taft-Hartley Act and the inroads made by nonunion contractors, complaints are increasingly settled by union and management representatives. Even though construction contracts contain fewer steps, the grievance is first handled by those closest to the problem, with arbitration as the final step in many cases.

Key Words and Phrases

agreements not attested	jurisdictional dispute
agreements of record	national agreement
ambiguous contract language	National Board for Jurisdictional Awards
arbitration	nonunion grievance procedures
arbitrator	
binding arbitration	open-end grievance procedures
Council on Industrial Relations	policy grievance
frictional unemployment	premium pay
Green Book	pyramiding overtime
Grey Book	umpire
involuntary arbitration	voluntary arbitration

Review and Discussion Questions

1. What are some purposes of a grievance procedure?

2. Why do union and management sometimes agree to ambiguous contract language?

3. How can a grievance procedure be beneficial to management?

4. What are some of the arguments for and against the right to strike on grievances?

5. How do grievance procedures in an industrial plant differ from those in the construction industry?

6. Explain the theory of the grievance procedure.

7. What kind of time limits should a union seek to negotiate in respect to the grievance procedure?

8. How are disputes over work jurisdiction settled in the construction industry?

9. What is meant by the phrase, "The grievance procedure has introduced a form of industrial democracy into the workplace"?

5

Processing Grievances

As pointed out in Chapter 2, the steward has many jobs. The most important is processing grievances. The enormous amount of time and energy poured into this is illustrated by estimates that there are over 400,000 stewards in the American labor movement. In the General Motors Corporation alone, stewards process about 300,000 grievances annually.

A contract, no matter how carefully drafted, cannot cover every question that is likely to arise during its term. Nor can future problems be foreseen, such as problems arising out of new technology or changes in the financial status of a company or government agency. Even when the written agreement covers a subject, the language may be imprecise, resulting in questions of interpretation. Therefore, a grievance procedure is necessary if workers are to be protected. The life of the steward would be less complicated if the goal of this author were to be realized:

> The employee must want to read and understand the agreement. He must be challenged by a contract so interesting that he wants to read it and understand its application in the day-to-day operations of the shop.[1]

As contracts become more technical and legalistic, workers are less likely to understand them and as a result will rely more on the steward for assistance. This chapter deals with the "how-to" aspects of grievance handling that will help the steward perform more effectively. Consideration is also given to analyzing problems and developing strategies for settling complaints.

---

[1]C. Wilson Randle and M. S. Wortman, Jr., *Collective Bargaining: Principles and Practices,* 2nd ed. (Boston: Houghton Mifflin, 1966), p. 212.

Grievances

Types of Grievances

Under the typical contract the union can be involved in three different types of grievances: an individual grievance, a group grievance, and a policy grievance.

Individual Grievance. An individual grievance involves one person and may be based on any one of the reasons discussed in Chapter 3. These range from violations of the contract to charges of unfair treatment.

Group Grievance. A group grievance involves two or more people having the same complaint. Typically such a grievance involves incentive rates, job classifications, changes in the work schedule, or coverage under various fringe benefits.

Policy Grievance. A policy grievance is filed on behalf of the union and may involve workers in more than one department or even the entire unit. This type of grievance may seek an interpretation of contract language or, where the agreement is silent, it may charge the violation of an established past practice. A policy grievance, however, does not normally involve the steward, because it is usually filed at a higher step in the grievance procedure. Here is an example of a provision providing for a policy grievance from the national agreement between General Motors and the UAW:

> An issue involving the interpretation and/or the application of any term of this Agreement may be initiated by either party directly with the other party. Upon failure of the parties to agree with respect to the correct interpretation or application of the Agreement to the issue, it may then be appealed directly to the Umpire.... [2]

Depending on the language of the contract, management may also have the right to file a grievance. Here is an example:

> Any grievance which the corporation (GM) may have against the union in any plant shall be presented by the Plant Management involved to the Shop Committee of that plant. [3]

Unless the contract provides otherwise, the employer does not have access to the grievance procedure and the union will strongly

---

[2] Agreement between General Motors and the United Auto Workers (GM/UAW), 1982, p. 43.

[3] *Ibid.*, p. 42.

resist management's efforts to use it. Even though management may have the right to initiate action, its use of the grievance procedure will be rare. It may do so if it seeks to hold the union responsible for failure to stop a strike or end a slowdown; or when the contract states that the union will cooperate in reducing absenteeism, and management feels it has not complied; or when the union publicly discredits the company. Actions against which the employer will grieve are usually found in the "Union Responsibility" clause.

Management may in fact lose some of its rights by insisting on access to the grievance procedure. Some arbitrators have ruled that when management charges a union with violating a no-strike clause, it must take the complaint to arbitration rather than sue the union for breach of contract.

Subject Matter of Grievances

Grievances cover a wide range of subjects. In many workplaces disciplinary action, ranging from reprimand to discharge, is a major cause of grievances. Other important subjects include:

(1) *Pay.* Examples of such disputes might involve a worker, paid less than others doing the same work, who requests an individual wage adjustment; a group of workers which is improperly classified and wants to be upgraded; workers who have experienced loss of pay because of improper wage calculations; workers hired under an incentive system which is too complicated to understand; and workers who experience a cut in piece rates when production increases.

(2) *Supervision.* Here, disputes commonly arise because the supervisor plays favorites; the supervisor picks on some individuals; the supervisor ignores complaints; management discriminates because of union activities; time-study rate-setters appear in the workplace without warning; there are too many rules and regulations.

(3) *Seniority.* Typically, grievances over seniority occur because workers are unfairly deprived of accumulated seniority; workers do not receive credit for all seniority; the seniority clause is improperly interpreted; or violations of the seniority clause occur.

(4) *General Working Conditions.* Employees may file grievances because toilet, shower, and lunch room facilities are inadequate; parking facilities are inadequate and are not

patrolled; or health and safety problems exist, such as dampness, noise, fumes, excessive heat, cold, and toxic substances.

(5) *Other Problems.* The improper assignment of overtime, the failure of management to post notices, and the existence of arbitrary shop rules also generate grievances.

Conditions may exist which in themselves may not be grievable but contribute to the overall potential for grievances within the workplace. Among these are a management which stalls on grievances or impedes the process; a supervisor who has no authority to settle grievances; and the failure of management to discipline supervisors guilty of harassment.

Complaints That Are Not Grievances

The success of the steward in handling grievances is determined in large part by the steward's ability to obtain the necessary information. The complaint must first be screened to see if it is a clearcut grievance, a borderline case, or if it completely lacks merit. Sometimes a worker has a legitimate complaint which is not a grievance because management is not responsible for the problem.

For example, a worker is laid off at noon and goes to register for unemployment insurance. He arrives at 4:30 P.M., a half hour before the scheduled closing time. The claims taker tells him to return tomorrow, because he is locking up early to go fishing. The next day the worker sees his steward and says that he wants mileage compensation for the additional round trip he was forced to make. Although the worker has a complaint, it is not a grievance, because his employer is not responsible for the actions of the state employee. Therefore, the matter must be resolved through a different channel.

The steward is also faced with complaints that lack merit both within and outside the grievance procedure. For example, a contract states that employees must work the scheduled workday before and after a holiday in order to be eligible for holiday pay. The holiday falls on Friday and Martha Jones fails to show up on Thursday. She does not receive holiday pay and tells her steward that she wants eight hours of overtime worked earlier that same week to be substituted for the day she was absent. The contract contains no provision for this substitution, and this complaint therefore lacks merit as a grievance. The steward who processes such a grievance will lose the respect of management. In addition, the same steward will most likely find that the workers consider him or her a soft touch and, hoping to benefit from any horse trading of grievances which might take place later, they will bring similar complaints to the steward.

Should the steward contact management before the grievance is submitted at the first step? Sometimes workers feel that such action will compromise their grievance. Many times, however, time and effort can be saved if management is asked a few questions before the grievance machinery is used. For example, a worker, denied a promotion under a contract where seniority is the determining factor, claims to be senior to the worker who got the job. The contract reads: "The senior employee shall be promoted if he has sufficient ability to do the job." Smith, hired January 2, 1975, says that Jones, who was promoted, did not come on the payroll until May 1, 1975. The supervisor points out, however, that Jones had worked February 8 through December 31, 1973 before being laid off and that the contract provides for the retention of seniority for two years. Therefore, under the contract Jones is entitled to the promotion based on previous work experience of which the grievant was unaware.

The difference between winning or losing a grievance may depend on the completeness and accuracy of the information on the fact sheet. Common sense should be used to decide which facts make the strongest case. Facts must be relevant; that is, they must be related to the problem under discussion. *Hearsay* (second hand) evidence is discounted because the original source cannot be questioned concerning the accuracy of the evidence. The answer is to find witnesses who have first-hand knowledge of the problem. Likewise, *opinions* are not facts and therefore have little bearing on the issue unless the party qualifies as an expert witness in the field.

Getting the Facts

Various types of information are required to process a grievance. Some of this information will be available through the local union. The union grievance file, for example, may contain similar grievances from which the steward can determine how such a complaint was settled. Other workers, witnesses, and the union contract may be of help.

The Union Contract. The union contract is the primary source of information for the steward. The fact-finding process can be impeded, however, if the steward cannot readily find the relevant information in the contract. Every contract, whether a national or local agreement, should have a table of contents and an index, so the user can find various subjects. A table of contents lists only the number of each article and its title with the page number on which the article begins. An index is of the utmost importance, because the title of the article does not always describe its content. For example, many postal employees are unaware that their national agreement contains a definition of an emergency because the definition appears under the heading "Management Rights."

If necessary, a local union can easily prepare its own index. To do this, the preparer begins by taking 26 sheets of paper and labeling them A through Z. Then the preparer, reading through the contract, lists each subject mentioned with the page number on which it appears under the appropriate letter. For example, the word "steward" may appear several times throughout the contract, i.e., under the heading "Grievance Procedure" on pages 8 and 9; under the heading "Union Rights" on page 9 where the number of stewards is listed, as well as the circumstances under which they are to receive lost time; and under the heading "Seniority" on page 18 where superseniority is defined. In the final index, the entries for the word "steward" would appear as follows:

Steward(s)
 in grievance procedure, role of 8–9
 number of 11
 payment for lost time 11
 superseniority of 18

Government Agencies. Government agencies are another source of information. If the grievance involves health or safety it may be necessary to obtain those standards that apply to the type of work involved. Unions in private employment can obtain such standards from the nearest federal Occupational Safety and Health Administration office, unless they are covered by an approved state plan. If so, unions in both the public and private sector can usually obtain the pertinent standards from their state department of labor.

Public Records. Sometimes management will cite a law, a court decision, or some other document as its basis for taking a certain action. The union should request a copy of the document in order to judge for itself the validity of management's claim. The union may not agree with management's interpretation and therefore decide to process the complaint further.

Both the Taft-Hartley Act and state public employment collective bargaining laws require the employer to provide necessary and relevant information to the union, not only for the purpose of negotiating the contract, but also for the processing of grievances. Information available from management includes payroll, production, attendance, medical, and disciplinary records, as well as seniority lists and work rules. If management refuses to honor such a request, the remedy for the union is to file an unfair labor practice charge with the appropriate administrative agency. Federal unions often can obtain information quicker through the federal Freedom of Information Act than by filing an unfair labor practice charge. Some states have their own freedom of information laws through which public employee unions can do likewise.

Circumstantial Evidence. Sometimes circumstantial evidence may be useful. For example, several persons in a workplace using a variety of cleaning solvents develop a skin rash. New cleaners introduced recently at the workshop were certified to be safe by the manufacturer. Although the labels do not indicate that the new cleaners contain any known hazardous substances, the union could request that their content be analyzed to see which of the solvents, if not all, are responsible for the rash. Since the workers did not develop rashes when using the old solvents, circumstantial evidence indicates that the new ones are responsible.

Use of the Grievance Fact Sheet

The first thing a steward should do when approached by a worker with a complaint is to get out a fact sheet, which should not be confused with the grievance form although both may require most of the same information. (A sample grievance fact sheet is shown on pp. 95–96.) The purpose of the fact sheet is to assist in gathering as much information as possible about the worker's complaint. Not only should it contain information about the grievant, but also about witnesses and the appropriate management representatives. Only by analyzing all the information can the steward determine what evidence is most useful. If the first step of the grievance procedure calls for an oral meeting, the fact sheet should be filled out and reviewed beforehand. At the oral meeting the steward may obtain additional information that should be added to the fact sheet.

One of the most difficult jobs of the steward is conducting the initial interview with the worker. The worker may be upset and assume that the steward knows all or part of the story and thus may fail to describe the entire picture. Or, a worker with a grievance involving disciplinary action may have had previous infractions and may hold back information or shade the truth in order to present the best case. The best approach for the steward is to ask the griev-ant to describe the problem, then listen carefully and take notes. After the worker finishes the story, the steward should summarize the grievance as he or she understands it, being prepared to make the necessary corrections or additions. If there were witnesses to the incident, their names should be obtained and they should be inter-viewed. Their statements should be reduced to writing, and the wit-nesses should be asked to sign them. It is absolutely essential that this be done as soon as possible because memories are faulty and the testimony of witnesses in an arbitration hearing may not be required for a year or more. Interviewing witnesses when the grievant is not present also gives the steward a better opportunity to evaluate the complaint.

Exhibit 2. Sample Grievance Fact Sheet

> **Grievance Fact Sheet**

Who Is Involved?

Worker
  Name_____ Classification_____
  Seniority Date_____ Department_____
  Shift_____ Supervisor_____
  Clock Number_____
Management
  Name_____ Department_____
Witnesses
  Name_____ Department_____
  Name_____ Department_____
  Name_____ Department_____
Other Participants
  Name_____ Department_____
  Name_____ Department_____

Why Is This Complaint a Grievance?

Violation of Contract: Article_____ Section_____ Page_____
Violation of Law: Federal_____ State_____ Local_____
Violation of Work Rule_____
Unfair Treatment (Give specific examples)_____
_____
_____
Violation of Arbitrator's Decision_____
Violation of Past Practice_____
_____
Other_____
_____
Worker's Story_____
_____
_____
Witness(es)' Story (Get signed and dated statements)_____
_____
_____

Sample Grievance Fact Sheet—Contd.

When Did Grievance Occur?

Date Grievance Occurred_____
Date Worker Contacted Steward_____
Date Grievance Filed_____

Where Did Grievance Occur?

Aisle_____
Department_____
Building_____
Parking Lot_____
Other_____

What Settlement Will Make Grievant Whole?

(Adjustments necessary to place grievant in position he or she would have been in if the grievance had not occurred.)

_____
_____

Factual Information That May be Needed

Arbitrator's Decisions _____   Medical Records _____
Disciplinary Record _____   Memo of Understanding _____
Federal, State, Local Law _____   Other _____
Grievance File _____   Past Practice File _____
Job Bid Sheet _____   Seniority List _____
              Work Rule _____

Disposition of Grievance

With Whom Was Grievance Discussed?

	Name	Title	Date
Step 1			
Step 2			
Step 3			
Step 4			

What Answers Were Received?

Step 1 _____
Step 2 _____
Step 3 _____
Step 4 _____

Settlement Reached

Grievance Won_____
Grievance Lost_____
Complaint Rejected_____

Was Worker Informed of Reason(s) for Rejection?

Orally_____   Date: _____
In Writing_____   Date: _____

Each of these points is illustrated in the hypothetical case that follows. Here is the information the steward obtained after interviewing the grievant, James Perdue:

> The grievant, James Perdue, is a Class B machinist with 10 years of seniority on the job. He is married and his wife just recently had a fifth child. Perdue is finding it difficult to support his family on his present pay and has been nervous and on edge because of this. Recently a Class A machinist's job opened and management gave the job to Ben Blue. The promotion clause of the contract reads: "In making promotions, seniority will apply if after a 15-day trial period the employee can perform the new operation satisfactorily." Perdue claims Blue has only eight years seniority, and a check of the seniority list confirms this. After stewing over the matter for 10 days Perdue went to see his foreman, Steve Fitch. They got into an argument over the promotion and a fight erupted. Perdue then received a 60-day disciplinary layoff for fighting at the workplace.
>
> Perdue claims that he did not start the fight and provides the names of three witnesses who will verify his story. He says the foreman is a liar and cannot be trusted and that everyone in the department agrees with him. As a settlement Perdue requests immediate promotion, since he never received the original trial period; a 60-day disciplinary layoff for the foreman since he started the fight; and transfer of the foreman to another department or shift.
>
> Upon checking further the steward obtains additional information. All the other machinists who were interviewed agree that the foreman was asking for a fight and if they had been involved, they would have done the same thing. Until seven years ago Perdue and Fitch were backyard neighbors and they had engaged in a running feud about who was responsible for cleaning up the rotten apples that fell off Perdue's tree into Fitch's yard. Roscoe Tilly, another machinist, told one of Perdue's witnesses that his neighbor overheard the foreman tell the plant superintendent that Perdue would get a promotion "only over his dead body."

Before the steward can take up the complaint with management, he must first determine exactly what the grievance is. In this case two separate but related grievances exist: the failure to promote Perdue and the disciplinary layoff of Perdue. Now it is necessary to separate the relevant information from that having no bearing on the case.

It is a fact that Perdue's wife had a fifth child, but this is not relevant to the promotion issue because management is paying the agreed-upon rate for the job. Management is not responsible for Perdue's inability to support his family. This fact, however, may be related to the reason for the fight between Perdue and Fitch. The fact that the seniority list shows that Perdue has more seniority than Blue is the steward's best argument in favor of Perdue's getting the 15-day trial period. The steward's best evidence in the disciplinary case is the testimony of the three witnesses if they confirm Perdue's version of what happened.

The three witnesses state that the foreman struck the first blow. It is important, however, that the steward get additional information regarding the fight. What precisely preceded the fight? Did Perdue threaten the foreman with a piece of pipe, or did the foreman give Perdue a hard shove knocking his head against a concrete wall? Self-defense is a legitimate response when attacked. But the degree of force used in defending one's self should not exceed the threat to one's safety. For example, being pushed does not justify shooting the aggressor.

Perdue's view of the foreman is an opinion and has little bearing either on the promotion or the disciplinary issue. It does tell the steward, however, that a great deal of hostility has existed between the two men. Likewise, the statements of the other machinists represent opinions rather than facts. Furthermore, what a person says and what he or she does in a conflict may bear no relationship to each other. These statements have little direct bearing on either the promotion or disciplinary issue unless the men can provide a justification for their statements.

The running backyard feud between Perdue and Fitch has nothing directly to do with the promotion dispute, unless the foreman decided he could get back at Perdue by denying him the promotion. The relationship between these two events will be hard to prove. The feud may have been one of several matters contributing to the fight, but again this is difficult to substantiate. Roscoe Tilly's statement is hearsay and is of no value. He is reporting what someone else said to a third party. The remarks allegedly made by the foreman could be used only if the person who heard them was available to testify.

Perdue's proposals for settlement need examination. His demand to be promoted immediately without serving the trial period violates the contract and therefore will be rejected by management. Furthermore, the union cannot require management to take disciplinary action against the foreman because he is not in the bargaining unit. Management may discipline the foreman if it chooses, but it is unlikely that this will happen. Since the purpose of the grievance procedure is to make the worker whole again, other remedies need to be implemented. The union should request:

(1) Reinstatement with full backpay and the removal from Perdue's personnel file of any reference to the disciplinary action.

(2) A trial period as a Class A machinist for Perdue and, if he completes it successfully, promotion and backpay to the date when he was passed over.

Before the steward takes up Perdue's grievance, he should check the grievance fact sheet against the "five W's"—Who, When, Where, Why, and What. This is information essential to every grievance. The process of checking the facts is a quick one, if a form such as the one on pp. 95–96 is utilized.

The "Who" part of the fact sheet identifies the parties to the grievance. In this case there are a number of participants: James Perdue, the worker filing the grievance; Ben Blue, who received the promotion; Steve Fitch, the foreman; and several witnesses to the fight. The steward already has the grievant's name and seniority date and knows that Perdue is a machinist. Depending on the size of the work force, the steward may also need to know Perdue's clock number, department, and shift. Steve Fitch should be listed on the form as the management representative, and Ben Blue's name and identifying information should appear under "Other Participants." The steward must also obtain the names of the witnesses as soon as possible.

The "Why" part of the fact sheet refers to the reasons why the complaint is a grievance. This is the heart of the case. The steward should review Chapter 3 to make sure he or she understands all of the actions taken by management that may be the basis for a grievance.

In Perdue's case one grievance involved the violation of the promotion clause of the contract; the other dealt with unfair treatment by management. The steward should remember that it is possible to have a legitimate grievance without being able to point to the violation of a specific clause of the contract.

The "When" part of the fact sheet refers to the time element. In this grievance, as well as most others, more than one date is needed to properly process the complaint. The steward knows the date on which he interviewed the worker but lacks information regarding the dates on which the grievances occurred. On what day should Perdue have started his trial period? On what day did the fight take place? Since both of Perdue's grievances involve backpay, the missing dates are crucial in determining that amount.

The "Where" part of the fact sheet refers to the exact place where the grievance took place. This factor plays no role in Perdue's promotion grievance but may be important in reaching a decision on the disciplinary matter. Exactly where did the fight take place? Where were the witnesses in respect to the combatants? Did the witnesses view the fight from the same vantage point?

The "What" part of the fact sheet refers to the remedy requested by the grievant. The steward found that Perdue's request for settlement included demands with which management need not comply, but he failed to ask for those to which he is entitled. The settlement demands should include everything necessary to make the worker whole again.

Clarifying the Grievant's Role

Before approaching management the steward should reach a clear understanding with the grievant on several points. No statement should be made giving the worker the impression that the grievance is an open-and-shut case. On the other hand, the steward should be careful not to create such a negative impression about the chances of winning that a person hesitant about filing a complaint decides to drop it. They should agree on the approach to management both as to the substance of the arguments and the tactics to be used. Typically, the grievant accompanies the steward when the grievance is discussed at the first step. The steward should make it clear that the steward is the spokesperson and that the grievant should speak only when requested to do so by the steward. Sometimes management will direct follow-up questions to the grievant hoping that the response will differ from the steward's. If the steward is unable to control the grievant, the steward may find it advisable to recess to clarify the grievant's role.

The Steward and the Supervisor

The steward should keep several points in mind when meeting with the immediate supervisor. Some of these are easier said than done. The steward should be calm but forceful in approach and make sure of equal treatment. If the grievance is discussed in an office and the supervisor is seated, the steward and the worker should sit down. If no chairs are available, they should request them. To remain standing places them psychologically in an inferior position. The steward should not make idle threats; this can cause the steward to lose credibility with management. Controlled anger, however, may be necessary as a tactic to demonstrate that strong feelings exist on the matter.

It is helpful if the steward knows in advance whether the supervisor has the authority to deal with the grievance. Can the supervisor authorize the payment of overtime to a worker who was improperly denied the opportunity to work? Can the supervisor replace someone who was improperly promoted? If not, then the steward should confine the discussion to asking questions that may provide additional information, rather than arguing the case. The steward must go through the formality of processing the complaint at the first step even though the supervisor must take every complaint to a higher authority for an answer. Otherwise management can argue that the contract was not complied with and refuse to process the complaint. The steward should not go over the head of the supervisor whether or not that person has the authority to handle the problem. The supervisor, if ignored, may simply exert authority in other ways.

Time Limits

Most grievance procedures contain time limits at each step that require both management and the union to respond within a stated period of time. The steward should not agree to time extensions unless there is good reason to do so. The worker wants the grievance settled immediately, and any delay contributes to the feeling that the union is lax in enforcing the contract.

Horse Trading

A steward may be tempted to "horse trade" on grievances for several reasons. Management may offer to settle a grievance for the steward's friend in return for the steward dropping the grievance of a political foe, or management may be willing to concede on an important grievance such as a discharge if the union waives its claim for a few hours of overtime pay. In either case the steward would be in trouble with constituents if they felt their grievances were not being processed on their merits. The steward may also be in trouble under the law, as we shall see in a later discussion of the duty of fair representation. Despite these dangers, unions—although they deny it—horse trade when they feel they can get the better of the deal.

Every effort should be made to settle the grievance at the lowest step possible, because the higher it goes the more apt management is to take a strong stand so as not to appear to desert its representatives. Nevertheless both the steward and the worker should realize that the grievance is not automatically lost if it is turned down at the first step.

The Grievance Process

One of the ways to view the grievance process is to follow a case through the process on a step-by-step basis. By returning to the hypothetical Perdue grievance and following the case through the grievance process, one can acquire an overview of the entire process. While the biases are pretty obvious and the outcome predictable, an examination of Perdue's case can also help to clarify the roles each of the protagonists must play in the grievance process.

The Oral Step

Probably the best tactic for the steward to use when discussing the Perdue promotion grievance with the foreman for the first time is to ask, "Why didn't Perdue get the trial period?" This question puts the foreman on the defensive since he is required to explain his action. The more the steward can get the foreman to talk, the more successful he or she will be in getting a feel of the case. In discussing the promotion the steward may also gain some insight as to why the fight occurred. During the first meeting with the foreman, the primary duty of the steward is to obtain information rather than to debate the issue.

The only new information that will be obtained by the steward at the oral step is the foreman's reason for denying Perdue the 15-day trial period to qualify for the new job. For the sake of argument, we will assume that the foreman said Perdue was not qualified.

The Written Grievance

The contract in the Perdue case provides that a grievance which is not settled at the oral meeting must be reduced to writing. A Grievance Form is used for this purpose (see p. 103). Before completing the form, the steward should examine Perdue's production

record, even if this information is not formally included in the grievance, and review the information on the grievance fact sheet covering the five "W's"—the Who, When, Where, Why, and What of
the grievance.

Every grievance procedure requires that the complaint be reduced to writing, at one stage or another, in order to:

(1) Reduce the number of unfounded complaints:
(2) Provide a record of past settlements, thus reducing the
    possibility of conflicting decisions regarding the same
    issue;
(3) Force the union to be more specific about the complaint;
(4) Require a written response by an authorized management
    representative. This makes it hard for management to re-
    pudiate a settlement on the grounds that an authorized
    party was not involved.

Exhibit 3. Sample Grievance Form

Grievance Form

Local Union No. ____

Grievance No._____ Date_____
Employee's Name_____ Clock No._____
Department_____ Shift_____
Seniority Date_____ Classification_____
Nature of Grievance_____
_____
_____
_____
_____
_____

Settlement Desired_____
_____
_____
_____
_____

Signed_____ Signed_____
              Employee   For The Union
Management Action_____
_____
_____
_____

Date_____ Signed_____
                                                  For Management
Copies:
1. Management
2. Union Office
3. Steward
4. Worker

There may, however, be reasons that both the foreman and the steward do not want to see grievances written. For example, in return for meeting the monthly production quotas, a firstline supervisor may agree to waive the enforcement of work rules that the employees find objectionable. If no written records exist, it is unlikely that top management will be aware of lax enforcement. The steward, on the other hand, will not want the workers in other departments to learn about the concessions obtained because, if they want the same, management may respond by eliminating the favorable treatment for everyone.

As a matter of policy a union should request its stewards to follow several key principles involving both style and content when reducing a grievance to writing.

Style. Usually the grievance is written at the first or second step of the grievance procedure. The steward rather than the worker should write the grievance in order to standardize language in the third person. For example: "Perdue was denied a promotion" rather than "I was denied a promotion." Since the steward is not as emotionally involved, he or she will be less inclined to write at length and can exclude material which may be irrelevant. In some cases, a chief steward or some other union representative may be assigned the responsibility for writing all grievances.

For its content to be easily grasped, the grievance should be written in short, concise sentences. Writing is no more difficult than talking with a pencil. In most cases, if a steward can say it, he or she can write it. A sharp pencil is needed to get clear copies. The grievance form should be filled out on a hard surface because most such forms consist of several copies. For this purpose a steward can use a clip board with the grievance pad. One can be purchased at any office supply store. If possible, the forms should be composed of "no carbon required" paper so that separate sheets of carbon paper are not needed.

The format of the grievance form is a negotiable item. It should be no larger than an 8½" × 11" sheet, lined for easier writing with an adequate amount of space for each of the "five W's." The "Why" and "What" information should be under two separate headings, "Nature of Grievance" and "Settlement Desired" for example. When negotiating the grievance form, the union should try to avoid the inclusion of the clause "Contract Section Violated." Such a clause may intimidate a steward from filing a grievance unless a specific reference to the subject of the complaint in the agreement is found. It was pointed out in Chapter 3 that under most contracts legitimate grievances exist even though no specific violation of the contract can be cited.

Content. The steward must remember that not all of the information on the fact sheet should be automatically transferred to the grievance form. This is particularly important in respect to the "Why" portion of the grievance form, entitled "Nature of Grievance." Here the actions of management that constitute the grievance should be clearly stated. The arguments of the union should not be included.

There are several reasons for listing only the bare bones of the grievance. The union seeks to settle the grievance at the lowest level possible. This is accomplished best when the emphasis is placed on oral, face-to-face meetings rather than on written documents. Otherwise, the processing of grievances becomes an exercise in paper shuffling with very little face-to-face discussion between the two parties. Furthermore, if the union is wrong on one of its points, regardless of how minor, management will seek to use this error to discredit the rest of the union's argument. The steward may also inadvertently supply information that weakens the case.

Many grievance forms do not have a separate section for the "What" part of the grievance—that is, what the union wants in the way of remedy. In those cases the steward must be sure to include the settlement request under "Nature of Grievance." Some stewards simply write, "The employee to be 'made whole' again." This request may not be enough for a grievance that goes to arbitration, because an arbitrator may not be aware of all of the adjustments required to make the worker whole again and, therefore, may order as a remedy only those items which are obvious.

Other stewards will enumerate those adjustments that they feel are needed. Some arbitrators take the position that they will not award benefits over and above those originally requested when the grievance was reduced to writing. Therefore the best procedure for the steward to follow is to request all the specific adjustments that come to mind and then conclude with "as well as all other benefits required to make the grievant whole again."

The Perdue grievance can be written simply as follows:

Nature of Grievance

The promotion clause was violated. On April 19, 1981, Ben Blue, who had less seniority than James Perdue, was improperly given a trial period for a Class A Machinists job and subsequently promoted.

Settlement Desired

(1) Perdue to receive trial period and upon successful completion to be promoted.
(2) Perdue to receive retroactive pay from date he should have received trial period and all other benefits required to make him whole again.

Distribution of Grievance Form

It is important for the union to plan for the distribution of the copies of the grievance form. This process will vary among unions because of differences in structure. Where single-plant bargaining exists, a procedure such as the following is common: the original copy goes to management; the steward retains a copy; the shop committee or the union office receives a copy, as does the employee. Where companywide bargaining exists, the regional office, the director of the national collective bargaining department, or company counsel may also receive copies. Apparently, none of the national unions have standardized procedures for their local unions regarding the maintenance of grievance records.

The Grievance File

There are immediate practical reasons for a union to have an up-to-date grievance file, as well as important historical considerations. Unions often argue cases on the basis of precedent, especially when similar grievances occur during the same contract period. Arbitrators will also be guided by precedent, particularly when identical cases occur under the same contract. Therefore a good filing system of grievances is essential to the union.

One interesting study summarizes some of the historical information that is available through a union's grievance file.[4] The file can provide insight into the conditions that the workers have found objectionable and the intensity of their dissatisfaction. The file may also explain which individuals or groups, based on race, sex, or job, file grievances and so give clues as to the internal politics of the union. These records also indicate the union's success in dealing with management on the issues that concern its members.

---

[4]*The Appraisal of Labor Union Records,* Archives of Labor and Union Affairs (Detroit: Wayne State University, undated), p. 3.

Rights of the Steward in the Grievance Procedure

The steward as a representative of the union has certain rights which differ from those of the members.

Access to Workplace. The steward is entitled to access to the workplace to the degree necessary to investigate and process grievances. Therefore, there are occasions when leaving the job or department is justified. Some contracts require that the steward first obtain "permission" to do so. "Permission" in this context means that management is to be notified so that it may take the necessary steps to prevent interference with production. "Permission" means only that management may determine *when* the steward may leave the job, not *whether* it can be done. For example, a steward on an assembly line operation may be required to wait until replaced by a relief person so that production is not interrupted. Management, however, cannot indefinitely prevent the steward from processing the grievance by refusing to make a relief person available.

Time Off for Processing Grievances. Today, most stewards are paid by the employer while processing grievances during working hours (where they are not compensated, the union pays the lost time). At one time this practice was controversial because Section 8(a)(6) of the Taft-Hartley Act states that it is illegal for a union "to cause or attempt to cause an employer to pay or deliver ... any money or other things of value ... for services which are not performed." Although the steward is paid for services not considered part of his job as an employee, all parties now agree that the steward is rendering "services" not only to the union but also to the employer, because the prompt settlement of grievances benefits both parties. Therefore, these lost time payments do not violate the law.

The number of hours for which a steward may be paid for handling grievances is a matter for negotiation. Some agreements spell out the maximum hours allowed. The UAW agreement with General Motors states:

> The total amount of time which may be used in any week by committeemen [stewards] for the purpose of adjusting grievances, meeting with Management ... shall not exceed the following: Monday through Friday 30 hours, Saturday 6 hours, Sunday 6 hours.[5]

---

[5]GM/UAW, 1982, p. 18.

The International Union of Electrical Workers' contract with the General Electric Company is much more restrictive. It reads:

(a) (E)mployees . . . will be paid by the company . . . while engaged in the following activities on Company premises:

(1) During each month, the number of weeks in each General Electric fiscal month multiplied by 1½ hours per week for these stewards . . . while engaged in processing grievances at Foreman level. . . .[6]

The next clause, typical of public employment, found in a contract between the Michigan State University Employees Association and Michigan State University, does not limit grievance-handling time by citing a maximum number of hours.

Association representatives may be granted reasonable released time for investigating and/or adjusting grievances, or at the request of the employer for other matters pertaining to this agreement.[7]

The structure of the steward system is also negotiable. Ideally the union prefers one steward for every 25 employees. Usually the steward system is based on management's organizational structure with one steward matched with each immediate supervisor. As a result stewards represent varying numbers of workers. Some contracts, however, specify the number of workers each steward represents. The UAW-General Motors contract states:

The union shall be represented in each bargaining unit as follows: in the ratio of not to exceed one district committeeman for each two hundred and fifty employees covered by this Agreement except that in plants of five hundred or less employees there may be three committeemen. . . .[8]

The agreement between the International Association of Machinists and the Douglas Aircraft Company provides for greater representation:

The union shall be entitled to Representatives in the approximate ratio of one Representative for each eighty-five employees in the Bar-

[6]Agreement between General Electric Co. and the International Union of Electrical, Radio and Machine Workers, 1982, p. 50.

[7]Agreement between Michigan State University and Michigan State University Employees Association, 1980, p. 53.

[8]GM/UAW, 1982, p. 12.

gaining Unit . . . and assigned so as to give effective representation to employees.[9]

Superseniority. Sometimes union members object to contract language granting superseniority to stewards and officers on the ground that it is a form of fictitious seniority providing special benefits to those covered by its provisions. Unions negotiate such clauses to ensure that experienced union representation will be available at all times for contract administration. Without such a provision an entire steward system might be wiped out during large-scale layoffs because stewards often do not have the highest seniority.

Beginning in 1975 the NLRB issued decisions defining a legitimate superseniority clause. It ruled that such a provision is legal for purposes of layoffs and recalls, because the provision assures the continued presence of a steward to process grievances and thereby benefits the entire work force. Superseniority may also be negotiated for other union officials who are involved directly in processing grievances and administering the contract.

Additional superseniority provisions that the NLRB has found proper include (1) providing the stewards with preference for overtime and weekend work, and (2) barring stewards from being transferred to another shift on the grounds that those working are entitled to have union representation at all times.

But the NLRB found several situations to which superseniority may not be applied. A steward may not be promoted on the basis of superseniority, because this action benefits the individual personally rather than the membership. It also decided the superseniority may not be granted to union officials such as trustees and sergeants-at-arms not involved in the grievance process. In one case the union and the company were required to make whole the wages of two senior employees who were laid off while these minor union officers had been retained.

The Board will uphold superseniority clauses that benefit the work force but will reject those that provide only a personal advantage to the officers or stewards.

Open Discussions With Management. The steward has greater leeway than does the average worker in discussions with management because the steward acts as an official representative of the union. A worker's vigorous discussion with management might be

---

[9]Agreement between Douglas Aircraft Co. and the International Association of Machinists and Aerospace Workers, 1978, p. 12.

considered insubordination; the same activity on the part of the steward may be viewed simply as aggressively processing the complaint. In some workplaces the steward may use both harsh and profane language on occasion. A steward may not be penalized for filing what management considers an excessive number of grievances or for being overly persistent in pushing them. The steward, may, however, be disciplined for purposely filing untruthful grievances, such as a fabricated charge of sexual harassment against a supervisor. This action should be distinguished from those cases where in good faith the steward files a grievance and later learns that the information supplied was inaccurate.

Potential Problems for the Steward

The Steward's Dilemma

There are times when the steward is faced with a no-win situation. Regardless of what action is taken, management or the steward's constituents, or both, will be dissatisfied. Here is an example:

The six workers on the 11:00 P.M. to 7:00 A.M. shift in Building No. 1 took their lunch break at 3:00 A.M. Four of them engaged in horseplay, tossing around a large scrubbing brush. Pete Smith, one of the workers, got fancy and flipped it behind his back. The brush hit the wall and broke an expensive wall clock, containing a barometer, thermometer, and hydrometer, valued at about $300 dollars. The clock stopped with the hands at 3:15 A.M. The steward was present but took no part in the horseplay.

This morning the foreman, Mel Young, calls steward Mike Petrie into his office. He asks Mike to help him find the man who threw the brush and says he has made up his mind to fire him, if he can put his finger on him. Young tells Mike that he will give everyone on the night shift, including Mike, a 10-day disciplinary layoff if he does not get the name.

The foreman is a reasonable man. He is friendly toward the union and fair. But he has told the men repeatedly that he will not tolerate horseplay. This is the third time in a few months that damage in the building has resulted from horseplay by this same group. The men were reprimanded then, but no one was laid off or fired. The plant manager has raised hell with Young wanting to know why he is unable to properly supervise his employees and hinting that he may be in trouble if the problem occurs again. The agreement gives management the right to lay off or to discharge for this offense.

Pete Smith says he is not about to confess, because he was reprimanded twice before and knows he will be fired. Besides, the other guys were also tossing the brush around, he says, and they were just lucky that they did not break the clock. Smith says the steward is a no good so-and-so if he rats on him.

Jim Longo says he does not know why he should be laid off for ten days, since he was on the other side of the lounge reading his *Playboy* magazine while the horseplay went on. Longo says not only will he not contribute to pay for the clock, but he will not agree to accept a written reprimand either.

The steward's decision as to what to do would be a lot easier if he could get the workers to agree on a common course of action. There is, of course, no way of knowing whether the foreman will accept payment for the clock in place of disciplinary layoff if the group agreed that such action seemed least objectionable.

The dilemma would not have arisen if there had been no horseplay. This raises the question of whether the steward has a responsibility to intervene. There is general agreement among unions that the steward should not act as an arm of management in enforcing workplace discipline. On the other hand, unions feel that the steward should warn fellow workers about actions that may result in disciplinary penalties. Although the steward cannot turn in those workers who violate shop rules, the steward should explain to them that they are headed for trouble if they do not straighten out and that the union may not be able to help. Similar counseling by the steward may be required for workers with alcohol or other drug-related problems, when they interfere with workplace performance.

Importance of Contract Language

Periodically, a worker will confront a steward and want to know why his grievance was lost, when a friend, who had an identical problem and who works in another plant, won his grievance. The steward will then need to explain that the same problem may have different answers depending on the contract language governing the workplace.

Promotion clauses are a good example. The formula governing the relationship between seniority and ability varies from contract to contract. The union seeks to emphasize seniority as the basis for promotions because determination of seniority is value free. Employment records can quickly settle the question of which worker has the most seniority. Determining ability, however, requires subjective value judgments that may not be based on objective criteria, with the decision often made on the basis of whom management likes best rather than who is best qualified for the job.

The following seniority clause, or a modification of it, is the most common in union contracts today: "In making promotions, seniority shall apply if ability is equal." The worker with the most seniority will receive the promotion only if he or she has as much ability as anyone else who applies for the job. Because limited promotional opportunities exist at many workplaces, some arbitrators will place the burden of proof on management to show that the senior employee does not have equal ability. These arbitrators may require management to provide a trial period for the senior employee even though the contract does not provide for one.

The union would have an easier time winning a grievance for the senior employee if the contract read, "In making promotions, seniority shall apply if the employee has sufficient ability." "Sufficient ability" is easier to prove than "equal ability." For example, it is easier to demonstrate that a dozen or more professional football quarterbacks have sufficient ability to perform their job on a regular basis than it is to determine who has the most ability.

Excessive Number of Grievances. A hard line by management on every grievance will result in the filing of every complaint by the union regardless of how trivial. The conflict escalates when the union, forced to go to arbitration, loses a substantial number of cases. Membership disillusionment with the system can lead to wildcat strikes or other pressure tactics which the union leadership may not be able to control.

Inexperience with the collective bargaining process on the part of either or both parties may result in an excessive number of grievances. Poor investigation on the part of the steward or a supervisor's lack of familiarity with the contract may be responsible.

New technology can create grievances. A shakedown period may be required before a determination can be made as to what constitutes a fair day's pay for a fair day's work. For example, a worker employed previously doing one machining operation on an engine block now is in charge of a multicolored control panel that operates a transfer machine performing many functions. Does the increased responsibility justify a higher rate of pay? Another example is an assembly line which in the past turned out 85 compact cars per hour and now assembles subcompacts that require fewer parts. How many workers should be required to assemble how many cars during an hour?

Incentive systems breed their own forms of grievances. Style changes in the garment industry require the continual setting of new rates which may be contested. In other industries grievances result from incentive systems so complicated that workers have difficulty in understanding how their pay is determined.

Obviously, actions taken by management will directly affect the number of grievances filed. Grievances resulting from the introduction of new technology may be regarded as unavoidable by management. Others, however, may not be so readily justified. Management can conceivably force a grievance to arbitration if it wishes to pass the buck as a result of conflict within its ranks. For example, production personnel may want to eliminate work practices they feel hinder efficiency. The industrial relations department, however, may feel that turmoil will result if the work practices are eliminated with no corresponding concessions from management. Therefore both factions agree that the problem should be passed on to an arbitrator.

A union, like any other institution, often has ulterior motives for the actions it takes. Grievances may be filed to obtain justice for an individual, to deal with the internal politics of the union, or to place pressure on management in regard to matters other than those covered by the grievance.

The Right of the Individual to Present a Grievance

Section 9(a) of the Taft-Hartley Act poses special problems for unions in enforcing the contract, and it will therefore be discussed in some detail. The act states:

Representatives designated or selected for the purposes of collective bargaining by the majority of the employees in a unit appropriate for such purposes, shall be the exclusive representatives of all the employees in such unit for the purposes of collective bargaining in respect to rates of pay, wages, hours of employment, or other conditions of employment: *Provided,* That any individual employee or group of employees shall have the right at any time to present grievances to their employer and to have such grievances adjusted, without the intervention of the bargaining representaive, as long as the adjustment is not inconsistent with the terms of a collective bargaining contract or agreement then in effect: *Provided further,* That the bargaining representative has been given opportunity to be present at such adjustment.

It is clear that, when a union obtains exclusive recognition, management may negotiate and process grievances with representatives of no other organization. An employee cannot have a representative of another union or an individual from outside the workplace (such as an attorney) process the complaint without receiving specific authorization from the union. Section 9(a), however, states that an individual worker may present a grievance and the union representative has no right to be present during the discussion.

Such actions by a member pose problems for the union. Management may seek to drive a wedge between the union and its membership by encouraging an individual to present a complaint in an effort to undermine confidence in the union. If management succeeds in this attempt, it may make a settlement with the individual which violates the agreement.

Although the individual has the right to present a grievance, Section 9(a) has been interpreted to give management a corresponding right to refuse to deal with the individual if it so chooses because the grievance procedure is owned by the union, not the worker. The union can deal with this problem in several of the following ways:

(1) Negotiate language that requires the steward and the worker together to meet with the supervisor at step one. Such a clause prevents an individual from processing a complaint.

(2) Persuade management to bar the individual from processing a grievance as a matter of policy if management is unwilling to agree to formal contract language. It is advantageous for management to know that when it deals with the union the settlement is final; if management deals with the individual its decision may be challenged if the union feels that the adjustment violated the contract.

(3) Persuade members of the bargaining unit of the importance of filing all complaints through union representatives.

(4) Always have a representative present when management settles a grievance with an individual, as provided for in Section 9(a).

Management has a responsibility to inform the union of its right to be present at the time the adjustment is made. Failure to do so may be the basis for an unfair labor practice charge or a grievance. By convincing its members to go through the union for all grievances, the union will avoid having a settlement made behind its back that violates the contract.

The Right to Union Representation at Investigatory Meetings

It is clear that a worker is entitled to union representation at any meeting at which the union discusses a grievance challenging an action already taken by management. What has not been clear until recently was whether a worker was entitled to union representation at an investigatory meeting at which management sought information for the purpose of deciding if disciplinary action should be taken.

The current policy was established by the NLRB in its *Weingarten* decision upheld by the Supreme Court in 1975.[10] A member of the Retail Clerks Union (now the United Food and Commercial Workers Union) was called in by management for the purpose of determining whether she had paid $1.00 for a box lunch rather than the full price of $2.98 required of all employees. She requested union representation at the meeting, which was denied, and the union filed an unfair labor practice charge with the NLRB.

The Board ruled that management's refusal to permit union representation violated Section 8(a)(1) of the Taft-Hartley Act which states that it is an unfair labor practice for an employer "to interfere with, restrain, or coerce employees in the exercise of the rights guaranteed in Section 7." Those rights are "to form, join, or assist labor organizations, to bargain collectively through representatives of their own choosing, and to engage in other concerted activities for the purpose of collective bargaining or other mutual aid or protection...." The Board ruled that failing to permit union representation violated the "concerted activities" referred to in Section 7. It concluded that a worker is entitled to union representation at any meeting that the worker reasonably believes will result in disciplinary action. A prior argument or incident, the location of the meeting, or the person with whom it will be held may create reasonable grounds to fear discipline. The Supreme Court in upholding the NLRB said:

> There has been a recent growth in the use of sophisticated techniques—such as closed circuit television, undercover security agents,

---

[10]*NLRB v. J. Weingarten, Inc.*, 420 US 251, 88 LRRM 2689 (1975).

and lie detectors to monitor and investigate the employees' conduct at their workplace ... often as here ... an investigative interview is conducted by security specialists; the employee does not confront a supervisor who is known or familiar to him, but a stranger trained in interrogation techniques.[11]

The Court further stated that it is the worker's own responsibility to request union representation and if it is not requested the worker cannot claim later to have been denied the right to be represented. If the steward is requested but is not available, management need not postpone the meeting until the steward is available. The recourse of the worker is to request another union representative. The Court also found that the employer does not have an obligation to justify its action and is free to continue an investigation employing methods other than interviewing the worker. The employer has three options if a worker requests union representation at a meeting where the worker reasonably believes disciplinary action may result: grant the request, end the interview, or offer the worker the choice between continuing the interview alone or having no interview at all. The worker's *Weingarten* rights are limited because the employer has no duty to bargain with the union representative who attends the investigatory meeting. The union representative may be restricted to assisting the employee, by clarifying the facts, or suggesting other employees who may have knowledge. This policy contrasts with a formal grievance meeting where the management representative must bargain with the union representative.

There are some meetings with management at which the worker does not have a right to union representation because it is not reasonable to believe that the meetings will involve possible disciplinary action. These include situations where management is giving instructions, conducting training, or correcting faulty work techniques.

The NLRB later ruled that the worker not only has the right to union representation at an investigatory meeting that he or she reasonably believes may result in discipline, but also has the right to consult with a union representative before attending any investigative session.[12] Otherwise management will again be in violation of Section 8(a)(1). The Board however, has ruled that a union representative need not be present at a meeting when the employer an-

---

[11]*Ibid.*
[12]*NLRB v. Climax Molybdenum Co.*, 227 NLRB No. 154, 94 LRRM 1177 (1977).

nounces a disciplinary decision that was made earlier based on information obtained previously.[13]

Because the *Weingarten* decision provides limited rights to a worker, what should union policy be in this area? The membership should be urged to request union representation if there is the slightest reason to believe that the purpose of the meeting may involve disciplinary action. If management states that no disciplinary action will result from the meeting, then the worker is not entitled to union representation. If disciplinary action is taken, an unfair labor practice can be filed. Either the union representative or the worker can request the right to confer with the other person prior to the meeting. When meeting with the worker, the steward should obtain as much background information as possibly to fully understand the issues that are discussed. At the meeting with management the steward may act just as at any grievance meeting unless specifically told not to bargain. This is important because management may, if it chooses, waive its legal right not to bargain. In either case the steward should make a careful record of the questions asked and the answers given.

The Steward and the Union

Free Speech Rights of Stewards. In order to effectively represent workers, a steward must be able to express himself freely on issues concerning them. The steward, although an agent of the union, has some leeway to disagree with union policy and still retain his or her position. This is an important issue because the steward whose opinions conflict with those of the officers may be reflecting views of those he or she represents as well as the steward's own views. Here are two cases that deal with this subject.

A shop steward of a utility workers' local union was removed after he organized a membership meeting to discuss the danger of low-level radiation. Because not enough volunteers were willing to perform short-term maintenance work at a nuclear power plant, other union members, including some who objected to the assignment, were required to perform it. The union officers and the union's safety consultant maintained that no radiation hazard existed. The union's executive committee found the steward guilty of willfully harming the union. The steward, while his appeal was

---

[13]*Baton Rouge Water Works Co.*, 246 NLRB No. 161, 103 LRRM 1056 (1979).

pending, and with support from those he represented, filed suit in federal district court under the Labor-Management Reporting and Disclosure Act (LMRDA), asking for an injunction to prevent his removal.

The judge stated that the issues were whether the steward's opposition to the union's programs or policies prevented him from acting effectively as its representative or whether his removal would prevent him from exercising his free speech rights under Title I of LMRDA. The judge found that the union's trial committee, in finding the steward guilty, charged that the steward and an antinuclear group were working together to close down the nuclear plant. No evidence, however, was introduced at the hearing showing the steward personally advocated this position. Therefore, the judge ordered the immediate reinstatement of the steward. It appears that the judge was saying that if the steward advocated closing down the plant, which would have resulted in a loss of jobs, the union was justified in removing the steward from his post. Because he was only seeking information on the effect of low-level radioactivity, he could not be removed.[14]

In another case a year earlier, the Court of Appeals for the Second Circuit ordered the reinstatement of a steward who strongly opposed some of the policies of his union's leadership.[15] The executive committee of a local union of the Communication Workers of America (CWA) removed the steward, because he condemned the negotiating tactics of the leadership; advocated a national strike, if Bell Telephone failed to agree to a 32-hour work week at 40 hours pay; and also circulated a petition to the membership calling for the same action. The court found that the steward effectively carried out his duties as steward, that he explained the policies of the leadership with which he disagreed, and that he implemented all programs as directed. The judge writing the decision stated that the union is not prevented from requiring stewards to follow "reasonable rules designed to assure that they will cooperate in implementing the [union's management] policies or programs and in spreading its views or from removing a representative who fails to do so, provided the local does nothing to inhibit the representative from exercising his right under LMRDA as a member to criticize the local's management or policies."

---

[14]*Ostrowski v. Utility Workers Local 1-2*, 104 LRRM 2343 (SD NY, 1980).

[15]*Newman v. Local 1011, Communication Workers of America*, 597 F.2d 833, 101 LRRM 2265 (CA 2, 1979).

Since this steward carried out the normal duties of the job, his opposition to the policies of the leadership was not considered harmful to the organization and he was ordered reinstated.

These cases show that stewards are permitted to criticize union policies as long as they continue to fulfill the duties of their position.

Dual Union Power Structure. The steward plays a vital role in the day-to-day operations of the union but is rarely mentioned in the organization's constitution.[16] Usually that document makes no mention of the steward's qualifications for the job, rights and duties, relationship to the members and the officers, or the role of the stewards' council.

As a result of trial and error, some of these questions have been answered, but many have not. The steward's relationship to management is much clearer than the connection to the union, particularly a large one.

In smaller unions there tends to be only one power structure consisting of the officers, executive board, and stewards. The same persons tend to have the responsibility of both carrying out the duties of the union and dealing with management. In larger local unions, however, dual power structures operate. In addition to the officers and executive board, a shop committee exists which has the responsibility of dealing with management on shop problems. Committee members may be elected by the membership at large, or the stewards may select its members from their own ranks, or the officers may appoint them. The power of the shop committee, or the grievance committee as it may be called, stems from the fact that it determines which grievances will be appealed to the higher steps of the grievance procedure. Members of this committee often receive more lost time than do the officers.

The steward also has responsibilities to the union's officers and to the shop committee. While the steward is expected to communicate the union's view on political and legislative issues to the workers, he or she is expected to transmit to the officers the concerns of the workers. At the same time the steward has ties with the shop committee through the grievance procedure. When these dual power structures are controlled by competing caucuses, the steward is once more placed in the middle. The officers expect loyalty; at the same time the shop committee will in no uncertain terms point out its role in the grievance process.

---

[16]Al Nash, *The Union Steward: Duties, Rights, and Status* (Ithaca, N.Y.: Cornell University, 1977).

Conflicts occur between the officers and the shop committee for various reasons. Sometimes the issue is one of power: which body shall be the dominant group in the local union? At other times conflict takes place because problems are viewed from different perspectives. The shop committee may feel that working conditions are the major issue for which the union should fight in the upcoming negotiations. The international union on the other hand may want a coordinated campaign to improve pension benefits. Generally, the local union officers have closer ties to the international than does the shop committee and therefore would be more likely to push for pensions. As a result, sharp conflicts can develop within the local union with organized caucuses carrying on the debate. Although both groups compete for the steward's allegiance, neither wants to see the steward establish a strong independent power base.

Fractionalized Bargaining. Fractionalized bargaining is an informal method of handling grievances that operates outside the grievance procedure set forth in the contract.[17] It can develop when a part of the work force exerts bargaining power great enough to obtain gains for itself that the union is unable to obtain for the work force as a whole. This power is based on either the unit's skill or the key role it plays in the production process. Although this situation may develop in a bargaining unit of any size, it is more likely to occur in large ones where a dual power structure exists and where the stewards are less likely to be as closely controlled by the union officers as they typically are in smaller unions. The steward in this position may be either a leader of the group or simply a follower. In either case priority is given to the specialized interests of this work group rather than to those of the unit as a whole.

The basic tactic of fractionalized bargaining is to pressure the immediate supervisor to grant concessions. If that person does not have the necessary authority or refuses to exercise it, pressure is applied to higher levels in the management structure until some benefit is obtained.

A victory for one group may be a defeat for another group in the union. For example, eliminating a wage inequity is another way of saying that the traditional wage alignment in the workplace is altered. Those who get the increase will be happy while others may not be. Fractionalized bargaining occurs over issues of concern to

---

[17]James W. Kuhn, *Bargaining in Grievance Settlement* (New York: Columbia University Press, 1961), pp. 84–110.

individual work groups, such as the proper classification of groups for determining the equalization of overtime, the reduction of hours of work rather than layoffs, the extension of trial periods for setting piece rates, or a change of shifts for a limited period of time for employees on the same job.

There are pros and cons to fractionalized bargaining. Decentralizing the bargaining process may make it more responsive to the needs of the workers. Often the steward and firstline supervisor are better able to make these decisions than a centralized industrial relations department with little direct day-to-day contact with the workshop floor. The supervisor may as a result regain some of the authority taken away when management decided to set up a centralized labor relations policy. The morale of the workshop group may be improved if it is able to make changes that directly benefit it. Sometimes the union will use the success in one department to force management into granting the concessions to the entire work force.

Fractionalized bargaining has disadvantages as well. The strongest work group may exercise a dictatorship of the elite, with more power than the union has as a whole. As a result the authority of both the union and management may be undercut, leading to a form of workplace anarchy. Informal tactics, sometimes involving disruption of the work process, may be used in such a workplace. Wildcat strikes are the most visible. Often a union will denounce the strikers as "radicals," "Trotskyites," "Communists," "disrupters," "extremists," or "irresponsible elements." Under some union constitutions members engaging in wildcat strikes may be expelled. Other forms of disruption include slowdowns that result in excessive overtime costs, refusal to work overtime, holding union meetings during working hours, showing a supervisor's errors to higher management, displaying ignorance when receiving instructions, fouling up special orders, misleading the time-study man, and flooding the grievance procedure with complaints.

Management, of course, has countertactics to employ. Shop rules may be strictly enforced and individuals disciplined or, in wildcats or slowdowns, group discipline may be utilized with particularly harsh penalties for the leaders. Ringleaders may be assigned undesirable jobs or given poor quality material that will cause their earnings to drop. Entire departments may be eliminated by moving that operation to another plant of the company, or the work involved may be subcontracted. Unless the basic issues responsible for the turmoil are resolved, it is unlikely that disciplinary action in itself will bring stability to the workplace.

Steward Council Meetings. There are several reasons most local unions should set up a regular steward council meeting to provide opportunity to discuss problems related to the grievance procedure. The steward council meeting is a place where the steward may obtain general background information. Since there is a wide turnover among stewards, this constant sharing of information is important.

The meeting time for a steward council meeting should be carefully chosen. How often should the steward council meet? In sizable organizations a monthly meeting may be appropriate; in a smaller organization where stewards are apt to be in daily face-to-face contact, quarterly meetings may be sufficient.

It is desirable to divide the meeting time between discussing grievances and training stewards on broader issues. The meeting provides an opportunity to discuss ways of best handling current shop problems, but it should not be confined to that.

A new steward, unsure as to whether a complaint is a legitimate grievance, can obtain advice from more experienced persons. The meeting may be used to discuss the progress of grievances; settlement at the third step between the shop committee and the industrial relations department; grievances scheduled for arbitration; or the effect of an arbitration decision on several of the grievances that were recently filed. The training program on the other hand should provide stewards with an understanding of the union's problems, both inside and outside the shop, and provide skills to deal with them.

Historically the local union meeting was regarded as a place at which the membership could obtain information regarding union activities. It is doubtful, however, whether this institution will play this role again because of the number of interests competing for members' attention. Regardless of the devices used by a local union, increased attendance is unlikely at these meetings over a long period of time, because the average union member is not interested in the day-to-day business operations of the union. Attendance is high only when "big business" such as strike votes, contract ratifications, or union elections are held. Because it is impossible to schedule this kind of activity for every meeting, it is unlikely that local union membership attendance will be high. Therefore, techniques other than the local union meeting are essential to inform the membership. The steward council meeting often becomes more important in this respect than the local union meeting. Unless the stewards are informed, it is unlikely that the members will be informed, because in most cases they turn to these representatives of the organization for information concerning its activities.

If a new contract has been recently negotiated, time should be spent at the stewards' meeting explaining the new clauses so that every steward understands the union's interpretation. Another important function at a steward council meeting is the analysis of past grievances in preparing for upcoming contract negotiations. Where has the contract been weak from the union's point of view and how can the language be strengthened?

Political activities may also be discussed at the meeting. How many union members are registered to vote and how best can the union convince the nonregistrants to do so? Collecting political contributions also requires careful planning to be successful. Another important purpose of a steward council meeting is to update the stewards' knowledge of various federal and state laws. Each year amendments or court decisions are made that may considerably alter the original legislation. For the stewards to be up to date, experts in these areas should be brought in periodically to summarize new developments. In particular, the union's duty of fair representation should be carefully explained so that the stewards are aware of their responsibilities in this area.

New labor films can be shown at steward council meetings, followed by discussion and comments. These films are available through the AFL-CIO, international union film libraries, and often from the nearest state university. The steward council meeting should be carefully integrated with any local union education program for which the education committee may be responsible. The stewards play an important role in the overall education program of the union. Unless they are convinced of a program's worth it is unlikely that any recruiting will be done because the steward, more than any other union representative, has contact with the people at the workplace.

Obviously the grievance meeting should be a place where the steward is informed on the progress of grievances the steward has initiated. This information can then be communicated to the grievant. The steward council meeting not only provides the steward with information needed to process grievances, but it also provides information that can be carried back to the members.

Summary

Once the collective bargaining agreement has been negotiated, the processing of grievances is the union's single most important function. Because it is a neverending process, special attention must be devoted to this activity by every organization. The three basic types of grievances may involve different representatives in reaching a settlement. Individual grievances will be processed by the steward. Group grievances involving more than one individual may also be handled by the steward. Policy grievances filed on behalf of the union usually involve matters related to the interpretation of the contract and are handled by persons with more authority in the organization.

Grievances in the private sector and in many places in the public sector cover virtually all problems arising out of the workplace. In order to process them successfully the union must obtain the facts. The use of a grievance fact sheet enables a union systematically to gather and catalog information. It is important to differentiate between the information placed on the grievance fact sheet and that placed on the grievance form that is formally filed with management. The latter should contain only the information that states the grievance and not the arguments of the union in support of its position that will be made during the face-to-face meetings with management.

A steward must give careful thought to the settlement request of the grievance. The adjustment requested should make the grievant whole again. What this consists of is determined by the losses the grievant suffered as a result of management's actions.

Each union representative involved in the grievance procedure must have a filing system that contains both the grievance fact sheets and the grievance forms. These files can play an important role in determining how previous complaints of a similar nature were handled and provide clues to the union as to where the contract language needs to be improved.

The steward has workplace rights over and above those of the member—to leave the job or the department when required and to present and defend vigorously the union's position at meetings with management. In many cases the steward is also protected by superseniority during periods of layoff.

As the industrial relations picture becomes more complex, it becomes more important for the union to establish regular steward council meetings. There is no other alternative for providing the steward with an opportunity to receive information and counsel concerning the grievance process, as well as becoming informed in other areas in which the steward must act as communicator to the membership.

Key Words and Phrases

access to workplace	individual grievance
contract language	opinions
dual power structure	oral step
fractionalized bargaining	policy grievance
free speech rights	right to individual
grievance fact sheet	representation
grievance file	right to union representation
grievance form	steward council
group grievance	time limits
hearsay	time off for steward
horse trading	written grievance

Review and Discussion Questions

1. What are some of the major areas or subjects about which grievances are filed?

2. Who may process a grievance at the first step?

3. Explain the "five W's" involved in writing a grievance.

4. Where can a steward obtain information for processing a grievance?

5. Who should receive copies of the grievance form? Why?

6. What are some of the different seniority formulas that may apply to promotions?

7. What responsibility does a steward have to caution the workers he or she represents about their actions that may result in disciplinary action?

8. When does superseniority for stewards become controversial? Is this form of fictitious seniority desirable?

9. Why are regular steward council meetings desirable?

6

Grievance Procedures
in Public Employment

Collective bargaining has had phenomenal growth in the area of public employment among white-collar and professional employees (principally teachers) as well as among blue-collar employees during the past 20 years. To understand this development it is necessary to examine the obstacles that impeded the growth of public sector unions.

Workers in the public sector were excluded from coverage under the Wagner Act and its successor, the Taft-Hartley Act. Furthermore, for many years these workers were not covered by social security, unemployment insurance, and similar legislation. The justification for such treatment was that public employees were somehow different from those in the private sector. The efforts to develop a public collective bargaining system different from that in private industry (usually called "the industrial model") has resulted, however, in a system that largely parallels that of the private sector, except for the federal government where the scope of bargaining is severely limited.

History

The public workers who organized earliest in this country were skilled craftsmen employed in federal shipyards. During the 1830s they conducted strikes that won the 10-hour day. Although these unions continued to exist, little in the way of a formal relationship developed between them and the federal employer for over a century.

Postal unions also organized on a craft basis. The first to do so were the letter carriers shortly after the establishment of daily mail

126

delivery in 1863. Other postal unions did likewise soon after the turn of the century. They, too, continued to exist without formal collective bargaining procedures until the issuance of an executive order by President John F. Kennedy in 1962. The major activity of these unions up until that time had been to lobby in the halls of Congress rather than to engage in collective bargaining. Similarly, a number of unions and associations existed at the state and local government level, but it was not until 1959 that the first state, Wisconsin, passed legislation giving local government workers collective bargaining rights.

Aside from the lack of legislative sanction, there were other obstacles to collective bargaining in the public sector. An important one was the belief that civil service provided protection and made unions unnecessary. In the early years of public sector bargaining, the sovereignty theory of government was frequently raised by opponents of unionism. It held that the government, as sovereign, could not compromise its omnipotence by contracting with unions representing public employees. It was also difficult to locate managerial authority, divided as it was among legislative and executive bodies and, in many cases, civil service commissions. There existed the myth of superior working conditions for public employees, the fear that collective bargaining meant strikes, and the belief that unionization would jeopardize impartial performance of duty. Many of the notions that served as obstacles have been revised or discarded over the years as bargaining has proceeded with relative smoothness.

In 1962 President Kennedy's Executive Order 10988 provided a modified form of collective bargaining for federal employees. Despite many shortcomings in this executive order and its successor, Executive Order 11491, a phenomenal increase in union membership occurred in federal employment. Today over 60 percent of all federal employees, or about 1.5 million workers, are represented in units of exclusive recognition.

Even more important, the issuance of these federal executive orders encouraged employees of state and local governments to strike for, or to lobby for, state laws providing for collective bargaining rights. A number of states passed legislation which ranged in its coverage from comprehensive to mere lip service. Currently, some states provide collective bargaining rights only to specialized groups, such as nurses, fire fighters, or police, and restrict the scope of bargainable issues. State courts usually have ruled that in the absence of legislation requiring the public employer to bargain, it need not do so. Without federal legislation requiring public employers to bargain, 50 state laws would have to exist for all public employees to have the legal right to engage in collective bargaining. Today comprehensive laws governing collective bargaining rights for public employees exist in fewer than half of all states.

The fear of strikes has been a rallying point for opponents of public employee unionism. In point of fact, many public employee job classifications have counterparts in private industry where strikes are permitted without noticeable damage to the country. (See Table 5.) Furthermore, public sector strikes occur in states having no collective bargaining legislation as well as in those that do.

For example, in 1977 there were 62 public employment strikes in Ohio, a state with no collective bargaining law but one with a law making it illegal to strike. Ohio led the country that year in the category of public sector strikes. On the other hand, Pennsylvania, a state with a collective bargaining statute, followed with 59 strikes. In 1980 Pennsylvania took the lead with 82 strikes, while Ohio had 60. In 1983 Ohio enacted a public employment statute that legalizes the right to strike.

This indicates that strikes cannot be eliminated simply by passing laws making them illegal. If a sizable number of public employees strike, they are no more likely to be discharged than strikers in the private sector. As a result, nine states now have passed legislation legalizing strikes for many public employees under various circumstances.

There have also been significant developments in resolving conflicts between public sector bargaining and civil service commissions. The latter's original functions were twofold: to protect the public employee from political reprisals and to ensure that hiring and promotions were based on merit. These functions were ex-

---

Table 5. Public and Private Sector Job Classifications

Private Employment (Right to Strike)	Public Employment (Illegal to Strike)
Janitor, bank building	Janitor, public library
Highway construction crew	State or county highway maintenance crew
Nurse, nonprofit hospital	Nurse, city or county hospital
Electrician, privately owned power plant	Electrician, municipally owned power plant
Truck driver, fuel oil company	Truck driver, city recreation department
Parochial school teacher	Public school teacher

panded to make the civil service system, in effect, the personnel department of the public employee, placing it in the dubious position of settling disputes over its own policies. The conflicts inherent in this dual role stimulated interest in reevaluating the civil service system. As a result, efforts have been made both at the federal and state levels to separate the labor relations functions concerning wages, hours, and other conditions of employment from the personnel functions of employment testing, promotion standards, and classification systems. The Civil Service Reform Act of 1978, for example, abolished the U.S. Civil Service Commission and replaced it with two new agencies, the Office of Personnel Management and the Merit Systems Protection Board. That law also provided a statutory basis for federal labor relations, which previously had been sanctioned only by executive order.

The Multiplicity of Unions in Public Employment

Unlike the auto or basic steel industry, each of which has one union, public employment has been characterized by a multiplicity of unions. In federal employment almost 100 different unions have established units of exclusive recognition. In addition to those AFL-CIO affiliates that organize federal employees exclusively, the craft unions, often in the form of a metal trades council, are involved. Numerous independents are also involved. At the state and local government level, much the same situation prevails.

Unionism in public employment is further complicated by the existence of associations which historically opposed the idea of collective bargaining. The main recruitment appeals of these associations were recreational and social opportunities; a low dues structure; representation before state legislatures of all public employees, regardless of the level at which they are employed; and a philosophy that salary increases would be provided if the organization could convince the public and management that its members had engaged in professional development.

Under the pressure of militant unionism, however, a number of associations have adopted collective bargaining and in practice function like a union. A notable example is the National Education Association (NEA), which denounced the idea of collective bargaining in 1960, but in 1967 endorsed the use of the strike weapon. Whenever a strong union appears on the scene, it is likely that an association will adopt the "new" tactic of collective bargaining in order to stay in business.

The enormous membership growth of unions organizing exclusively in the public sector is shown by some of the figures for the period 1959–1981 set out in Table 6. In addition a number of unions based in the private sector, such as the Teamsters, Service Employees, Laborers, and numerous independents, have organized substantial numbers of public employees.

Militant union action, executive orders at the federal level, and state laws granting collective bargaining rights to state and local government employees have all contributed to this development.

Table 6. Growth of Public Sector Unions, 1959–1981

	1959	1981
International Association of Fire Fighters	93,000	178,000
American Federation of Government Employees	60,000	255,000
American Federation of State, County, and Municipal Employees	200,000	1,098,000
American Federation of Teachers	50,000	551,000

Source: U.S. Department of Labor, *Directory of National Unions and Employer Associations* (Washington, D.C.: Government Printing Office, 1961); Courtney D. Gifford, ed., *Directory of U.S. Labor Organizations* (Washington, D.C.: The Bureau of National Affairs, Inc., 1982).

Unique Characteristics of Public Sector Bargaining

The successful negotiation of thousands of contracts in this new arena meant that attention would be devoted to contract administration. Although the First Amendment of the U.S. Constitution gives public employees the right to petition their government on grievances, it should be remembered that the U.S. Supreme Court has ruled that, in the absence of collective bargaining legislation, a governmental employer has no duty to bargain with any union representing an employee.

Of major importance in enforcing any contract is the quality of the grievance procedure. On this score, contracts in the public sector fall short of those in private employment. The public employer is not anxious to concede that those governed by workplace rules should help make those rules. Rather than negotiate one grievance procedure, the public employer often proposes to handle workplace complaints in a variety of ways. Working conditions may be appealed through a departmental grievance procedure, wherein the final decision is made by a management representative; disciplinary actions may be appealed to a civil service commission; and disputes over pension eligibility may be referred to a special commission. As a result disputes develop as to which is the appropriate appeal procedure.

Furthermore, limitations exist on the scope and authority of an arbitrator. Only in 1959 did a state supreme court, i.e., Wisconsin, uphold the constitutionality of binding arbitration in public employment when used as the last step in a grievance procedure.[1] Some state courts, however, still take the position that in the absence of a statute authorizing it, binding arbitration in public employment remains illegal. Consequently, courts are less likely to uphold an arbitrator's decision in the public sector.

The public employer, unlike its counterpart in the private sector, often opposes arbitration as part of the grievance procedure. The employer believes that the union cannot resort to the strike alternative without incurring severe penalties for the participants, because public sector strikes are illegal in most states.

Other unique features characterize public employment grievance procedures. Sometimes mediation is used as the last step, or as the step preceding arbitration. This arrangement is open to question because the purpose of a mediator is to seek compromise, while the purpose of the grievance procedure is to enable a worker to obtain rights outlined in the contract. Union members should not be expected to compromise their rights; they are entitled to have their grievances heard on their merits. More common in public employment than in the private sector is the use of an arbitration board consisting of one representative of labor, one of management, and a neutral chairman. Once used widely in the private sector, arbitration boards no longer have much support. Experience has shown that the labor representative supports the worker, the employer representative supports management, and the impartial chairman plays a dual role, either casting the deciding vote in favor of the labor or management position or proposing a middle-of-the-road approach in order to obtain a majority decision. Most unions in public employment today try to negotiate a single arbitrator system to avoid these problems; faster action may result when only one person is involved in the decision-making process.

Politics also may be involved in a public employment grievance procedure. For example, prior to the passage of Hawaii's public em-

---

[1]*Rhinelander City Employees, Local 1226, State, County & Municipal Employees v. City of Rhinelander*, 151 N.W.2d 30, 65 LRRM 2793 (Wis. SupCt, 1967).

ployment act in 1970, the governor was the final step in the griev-ance procedure for state employees.

In the public sector, grievances tend to be regarded as the pri-vate property of the individual. The method of filing grievances, therefore, tends to differ from that in the private sector. In the pub-lic sector, often under the terms of the contract, the individual is required to sign the grievance form before the complaint can be pro-cessed. This policy may be pushed by management to emphasize the individual ownership of the complaint and to forestall the union from filing a complaint in its own name. The steward should be aware that, by requiring the worker to sign the grievance form, management may intimidate the individual who is concerned about the signed statement being placed in his or her file. Therefore, even if the individual wishes to drop the complaint, the union should pro-cess it provided the testimony of the worker is not required. For ex-ample, consider the case of a suspension involving an altercation with a supervisor. In the absence of witnesses, the hands of the union are tied if the worker, who may fear punitive action, refuses to testify against the supervisor.

The attitude towards publicizing a grievance also differs in the public and private sectors. Where the concept of individual owner-ship prevails in the public sector, much less emphasis is placed on advertising grievance successes; as a result the union loses an oppor-tunity to publicize its accomplishments.

Development of Contract Administration in the Federal Sector

A look at the development of contract administration in the federal sector illustrates the types of problems that arise in all levels of public employment. Most of the grievance and appeal procedures existing before the 1962 Executive Order were unilaterally estab-lished. (Exceptions were in the Government Printing Office, St. Law-rence Seaway, Tennessee Valley Authority, Bureau of Mines, Pan-ama Canal Zone, Alaska Railroad, and Bonneville Power.)

Three major actions governed the development of collective bargaining in the federal sector: the issuance of Executive Order 10988 by President Kennedy in 1962, the issuance of Executive Or-der 11491 by President Nixon in 1969, and the passage of the Civil Service Reform Act by Congress in 1978.

Executive Order 10988

Executive Order 10988 created the form but not the substance of collective bargaining. The scope of negotiations was restricted primarily to personnel policies and working conditions; the agency head made the final decision on such matters as the negotiability of a bargaining demand and the determination of unfair labor practice charges; this person also settled complaints concerning representation elections. The result was the charge by the unions that the system lacked impartiality—management wound up judging its own actions and it came as no surprise when it upheld them.

Even though the scope of negotiations was narrow, contract administration was difficult. The order specifically prohibited binding arbitration as the last step in the grievance procedure. The sovereignty theory was used to justify the outlawing of binding arbitration on the ground that government could not permit an outside third party, an arbitrator, to issue a decision overruling one the government itself had made. Instead, the order permitted something called advisory arbitration—in reality, fact-finding with a recommendation. Arbitration costs were shared by both parties, but unions were reluctant to negotiate advisory arbitration because management was free to reject an arbitrator's recommendation while the union had to accept it.

Executive Order 11491

Based on the report of a study committee, President Nixon in 1969 issued Executive Order 11491. It created a Federal Labor Relations Council (FLRC) composed of the Chairman of the U.S. Civil Service Commission, the Secretary of Labor, and the Director of the Office of Management and Budget. The FLRC had the authority to administer and interpret the new order, decide major policy issues, and consider appeals from decisions made by the Assistant Secretary of Labor for Labor-Management Relations.

In an effort to establish standardized administrative procedures, the Assistant Secretary of Labor for Labor-Management Relations was to: decide questions relating to the composition of the bargaining unit; supervise and certify representation elections; and decide complaints charging unfair labor practices.

The creation of the FLRC was a partial answer to only one of the major criticisms of unions: Final decision-making authority in many areas still remained in management's hands in the form of the agency head, because the FLRC was composed of three top management representatives. A comparable situation would exist if the UAW were forced to submit complaints against the Chrysler Corporation to a panel consisting of the heads of General Motors, Ford, and American Motors.

Executive Order 11491 and other amendments by Presidents Nixon and Ford continued to govern labor relations in the federal sector until the passage of the Civil Service Reform Act of 1978.

Civil Service Reform Act of 1978

This act, one of the major legislative accomplishments of the Carter administration, did the following:

(1) Split the U.S. Civil Service Commission into the Office of Personnel Management and the Merit Systems Protection Board;
(2) Created a Senior Executive Service; and
(3) Established statutory authority for federal labor relations in lieu of the executive order.

The administrative structure itself under law does not differ substantially from that under Executive Order 11491. However, its authority has been increased significantly. The FLRC has been replaced by the Federal Labor Relations Authority (FLRA). Instead of being composed of heads of three major federal departments as was the FLRC, the FLRA consists of three presidential appointees who do not hold any other federal government position. The act, thereby, insitutionalized a degree of impartiality into the bargaining process that had been lacking under the two previous executive orders. This was one of the reasons the labor movement had wanted federal labor relations transferred from executive order to statute.

The other major changes in labor relations made by the act apply to the grievance process. Grievance and appeal procedures tend to overlap or duplicate each other in the public sector. Nowhere was this more true than in federal employment. Sometimes a statute itself spelled out a separate appeal procedure, such as in complaints involving prohibited political practices. In other matters such as "adverse actions" (discipline and discharge being the major actions), the U.S. Civil Service Commission was authorized to set up its own appeal procedures. In addition the agency or department usually was responsible for establishing a separate appeal procedure as an alternative to that provided by the U.S. Civil Service Commission.

The issuance of the Kennedy and Nixon executive orders raised the question of which issues were subject to the negotiated grievance procedure and which required treatment under a separate grievance and appeal procedure. More than twenty different subjects were specifically excluded from the negotiated grievance procedure.

The steward's first job, therefore, was to decide whether a complaint raised by a worker was eligible for the negotiated grievance procedure. If not, the next problem was to determine which grievance procedure was the correct one to follow. Becoming familiar with the many different appeal procedures was the single most difficult job faced by stewards during that period. One union representative, commenting on the pre-1978 system, remarked that "The multiplicity and hodge-podge of statutory appeal procedures is incomprehensible to the average Federal employee and in fact to almost anyone who tries to make sense out of them."[2]

With this background it is now necessary to compare the status of contract administration under the amended Executive Order 11491 with that of Section 7 of the Civil Service Reform Act of 1978. Unless negotiated away by the union, the scope of the grievance is broadly defined to include any matter relating to the agency's employment process and any claimed violation, misinterpretation, or misapplication of any law, rule, or regulation affecting conditions of employment. The only issues excluded from the negotiated grievance procedure are grievances about classifications that do not result in a reduction in grade or pay; prohibited political activities; retirement and life and health insurance disputes; suspensions and discharges for national security reasons; and complaints related to examination, certification, and appointments. Thus more than a dozen different appeals procedures are eliminated. The negotiated grievance procedure is now the exclusive channel for all members of the bargaining unit, except in adverse action and discrimination cases where the worker may choose the negotiated or the statutory procedure but not both. "Adverse actions" are now defined as discharges, suspensions for more than 14 days, grade and pay reductions, and layoffs of 30 days or less.

---

[2]Edward H. Passman, "Federal Employees Statutory Appeals Procedures—Status Quo or Change" (Paper delivered to a meeting of the Society of Federal Labor Relations Professionals, Washington, D.C., February 19, 1976), p. 2.

All contracts are required to provide for the binding arbitration of grievances. The FLRA has the right to review decisions if they are contrary to law, rule, regulation, or on other grounds similar to those applied by federal courts in the private sector. These include charges that an arbitrator has exceeded his or her authority or has engaged in an illegal or fradulent practice. An employee may request that an arbitrator's decision dealing with discriminatory treatment based on race, color, religion, sex, national origin, age, handicap, marital status, or political affiliation be reviewed by the Merit Systems Protection Board or the Equal Employment Opportunity Commission. The decision on this type of grievance may be subject to judicial review.

The Civil Service Reform Act specifically states that employees are entitled to backpay when they are deprived of pay or allowances as a result of an unjustified personnel action. Federal employees' entitlement to backpay is now based on statute rather than the whim of the Comptroller General.

Workers have the right to union representation at each step of the grievance procedure, as well as at any examination in connection with an investigation if it is believed that disciplinary action may result. The law requires that workers be informed of this right annually. Individuals have the right to process their own grievances, but the union has the right to be present during discussions with management in order to ensure that any settlement does not violate the contract.

Despite the considerable experience of contract administration in the private sector, it has taken 20 years of "two steps forward and one step backward" for contract administration in the federal sector to reach a similar stage. Although the development of contract administration in federal employment has been slow, confusing, and complicated, most of the elements responsible for such foot dragging also exist to some degree in other levels of public employment.

Grievances of Professional Employees

The organization of professional employees over the past 20 years has added a new dimension to contract administration. Since professional employees are expected to exercise independent judgment, these workers assume that they have the right to participate in decision making in such matters as professional standards.

Nurses, teachers, university faculty, social workers, interns, doctors, and police officers file grievances in areas not normally grieved by blue-collar workers. Many of their grievances deal with issues which in other workplaces would be viewed as a management right, relating to the type and quality of the product or service produced as well as its price.

Reorganization of assignments in health care units often provoke grievances if the quality of health care is involved. For example, what is the proper staffing mix between licensed practical nurses (LPNs) and registered nurses (RNs), who have different educational backgrounds yet may perform the same duties? Should LPNs be permitted to give shots or should that assignment be reserved exclusively to the more highly paid RNs? Grievances of nurses relating to quality of care also may involve the degree to which a reduction of staff on the night shift can be implemented without jeopardizing patient care.

Social workers may file workload grievances involving the issue of quality, arguing that a professional performance cannot be maintained if only a few minutes can be devoted to each client. For example, can a probation officer with a case load of 50 or more parolees ensure that the parolees receive proper supervision and at the same time appear in court or conduct background investigations required by the judicial system? A strong case can be made that fewer clients may result in better quality service, although the direct financial cost may increase. This increased expense must be balanced against the higher indirect costs resulting from lower quality care. Poor supervision of parolees may result in a higher percentage of parole violations and the consequent return to prison of parole violators may very well involve more expense than hiring more probation officers. Similarly, more complete investigation of a prisoner's background before sentencing may result in penalties better suited to the crime.

Similar quality considerations arise in other areas: for teachers, classroom size; for police, the number of police officers in the patrol car, the geographic area covered, or the use of foot patrols; for doctors, the maintenance of quality care in emergency rooms when staffing is reduced to such a degree that patients are treated on an assembly-line basis.

Professionals tend to be highly individualistic and therefore often react negatively to uniform requirements of employment. This may mean that an administrator must judge the individual's performance on its own merits rather than against a set of fixed rules. For example, school board requirements for the use of uniform lesson plans are difficult to enforce, because the teacher claims the right to make the determination of what and how to teach. The teacher feels justified in so doing because of professional training and background which presumably makes the teacher an expert in the field. The problem is further complicated, however, because lay members of elected school boards determine educational policy and because the public has the right to have an input into educational decisions. As a result, the school board or community may seek to dictate what should be taught and the textbooks to be used.

Professional employees may get into trouble when they make recommendations or produce findings on policy matters that conflict with those already in existence. What often happens is that a management body which feels threatened by such employee encroachment will draw up new uniform policies to deal with every conceivable situation. The net result may further frustrate the professional, who will then file a grievance over the matter at issue. The employer's attorney then explains to the professional the management residual rights theory, according to which anything not negotiated into the contract remains in the hands of management. The professional soon discovers that in this environment an individual has little clout and as a result will turn to collective bargaining in an effort to become a part of the decision-making process.

Contract Administration in Elementary and High Schools

In order to get a better understanding of contract administration among professionals, we will examine its development in the field of education, first at kindergarten through grade 12 (K-12) and, then, in higher education.

Two very different organizations have been active at the K-12 level: The National Education Association (NEA) and the American Federation of Teachers (AFT). The NEA was founded in 1857 for the purpose of improving standards for the education profession. Participating in this organization from the beginning were various groups in education such as classroom teachers, principals, school superintendents, and school board members. Historically, NEA opposed collective bargaining and shunned any formal relationship with the labor movement.

Its opponent, the AFT, was founded in 1916 as an affiliate of the American Federation of Labor (AFL). Although from its inception it concerned itself with salaries and working conditions, not until 1935 did it formally endorse collective bargaining—a goal not to be obtained in any significant manner for another 30 years.

The first breakthrough took place in New York City. The United Federation of Teachers, composed of a number of local teacher groups, struck in 1960 in an effort to force the city's board of education to hold a representation election. This strike, supported by about 4,500 teachers, and pressure exerted by the New York central labor body and its affiliates convinced the school board to hold an election. In 1961 the AFT defeated its NEA-supported opponent by an overwhelming vote in the country's largest professional representation election. Collective bargaining had arrived in the teaching profession. In short order, the AFT obtained recognition in Baltimore, Boston, Chicago, Cleveland, Philadelphia, Detroit, and Washington, D.C.

At the same time the AFT was winning bargaining rights in New York, the NEA continued to argue that teachers and school boards had common goals and that collective bargaining and the use of the strike was therefore unprofessional. Under pressure produced by AFT successes, however, the NEA began to talk about professional negotiations and the use of sanctions. As these terms were translated into action, they became synonymous with collective bargaining and the use of the strike. Changing the American Association of School Administrators and the Department of Secondary School Principals from NEA departments to associate organizations reduced the influence of administrators in the NEA and made the shift to collective bargaining easier. Today, in many instances, the contracts of the AFT and NEA are indistinguishable. The major difference between the two organizations is the NEA's refusal to consider affiliation with the rest of the labor movement.

Because the governmental structure of most school boards differs from that of other levels of government, collective bargaining has raised unique problems. In contrast to federal, state, and most levels of local government, a school board has no executive officer. The chairman of the school board holds what is primarily an honorary position that conveys no powers or duties beyond those held by any other board member. Legislative and executive authority are therefore in the hands of the same group, making it unclear who really holds power. This dilemma affects bargaining because a decision must be made as to management representation at the bargaining table. Should the board involve itself directly in negotiations? This raises the question of their qualifications for this assignment. A typical board may comprise a homemaker, an accountant, a local contractor, a barber, a real estate agent, and the butcher, the baker, and the candlestick maker, none of whom have had previous bargaining experience.

Sometimes the school superintendent conducts negotiations. For years a debate raged over whether the superintendent was the teachers' representative to the board or the board's representative responsible for enacting its policy. Today, it is generally recognized that the superintendent is the representative of management. Whether the superintendent should conduct negotiations depends on the size of the school district and that person's background. In larger school districts a specialist, such as an assistant superintendent in charge of personnel matters and labor relations, may have the responsibility for bargaining and overseeing the handling of grievances.

Occasionally, attorneys are hired by school boards. This practice may be based on the assumption that a law degree conveys all knowledge. Instead the board may discover it is paying an apprentice to learn about the collective bargaining process. The attorney may give away the rights of the school district out of ignorance or carelessness or may provoke an unnecessary strike by being especially hard-nosed to please the client.

In some states the school board association hires a staff of negotiators who bargain for smaller school districts on a contract basis. This policy has been beneficial, because boards have some assurance of obtaining experienced personnel without having to add additional staff.

Another peculiarity of school districts is that in most cases operating millage increases and construction bond issues must be submitted to public referendum. Often the community, frustrated by actions of other governmental units not requiring public approval, vents its unhappiness by voting down the school proposals.

Teacher Grievances

A typical K-12 contract includes salary schedules based on educational attainment and seniority and usually consists of 10 or 12 steps. Each year the teacher progresses a step up the scale until the maximum is reached. Working conditions and professional standards are covered. Grievances tend to fall into five major areas:

(1) Salaries
(2) Working conditions
(3) Tenure and reappointments

(4) Personal conduct

(5) Professional standards

Salaries. Salary schedules for K-12 teachers provide for increases if the teacher earns additional university course credits. Disputes arise over whether or not a given course is educationally related to the teacher's job and therefore to be counted toward a salary increase. If such a dispute arises who should make the determination and what are the guidelines? Other salary disputes may involve the number of years of past credit a new teacher in the district receives for teaching experience elsewhere. Grievances involving extra pay also arise. Should the coaches of the football, basketball, track, tennis, and baseball teams all receive the same extra pay? In those sports with female teams, should their coaches receive the same pay as those for males? Should coaches of winning teams who participate in postseason tournaments receive extra pay since their seasons are extended?

Working Conditions. Grievances over working conditions may cover a wide range of subjects. Should a teacher with a major in mathematics and a minor in English literature be required to teach history if a vacancy exists in the field? How many consecutive hours should a teacher be required to teach without a break? The subject of support services may generate grievances. How much, if any, secretarial help is available? Are laboratory facilities adequate? Who is responsible for their supplies? Which teachers should receive teaching aides and for how long?

A major source of grievances involves student discipline. Under what circumstances can a teacher have a student removed from the classroom? Who determines the disciplinary punishment as well as whether the student is to return to the classroom and when? With the increase of physical assaults on both students and teachers this has become an increasingly important issue. Other grievances relating to working conditions involve the availability of lounges and lockers for teachers, duty-free lunch periods, and a freedom from, or limitation on, hall and playground supervision assignments.

Certain working conditions may be governed by law as well as by the contract and sometimes it is difficult to determine which applies. Class size is one of these conditions. Teachers argue that it is properly a working condition—it takes more time to correct and grade 40 essays than it does 20—and therefore class size should be a negotiable item and properly grievable. Some school boards have responded by saying that it is an educational policy since a reduction in class size may require additional classrooms, additional teachers, and a vote on increased expenditures. Under Michigan's public employment law and its subsequent interpretation, class size is considered a working condition; under New York's it is judged to be an educational policy and therefore neither negotiable nor grievable.

The right of a teacher to transfer to another school also involves law, this time federal law in the form of equal opportunity legislation. Teacher unions historically have fought for transfer rights based on seniority. Usually teachers want to transfer to the newer schools, because they have separate teacher lounges and lunch rooms, individual lockers, adequate parking facilities, and better lit and designed classrooms. Most of these schools are located in the newer areas with few if any minority children. As a result the most experienced teachers wind up in the newer schools while the young inexperienced teacher faces the more difficult teaching assignment. Legal challenges mounted against this practice argue that minority children are deprived of the same teacher quality because of contractual language. School districts under affirmative action orders have been required to work out policies providing experienced teachers for inner city schools.

Tenure and Reappointments. Tenure and reappointments represent working conditions most involved with the legal process. The purpose of tenure is to grant qualified teachers employment that is free of political interference. Tenure protects teachers from discharge based on the personal bias of administrators or the community. Tenure has been more difficult to obtain for K-12 teachers than for university faculty because the insistence on local control has meant that school boards often seek to mandate how and what should be taught.

Contrary to public belief, tenure does not guarantee a lifetime job. Tenure can be revoked for cause. At the K-12 level, a school system's grave financial emergency has been considered "cause," as has the incompetence or gross misconduct of individual teachers.

Whether tenure is negotiable depends on the scope of negotiations under a state law. In most cases it is not. Therefore, an arbitrator ruling on a refusal to grant tenure could not grant it to someone discharged at the end of the probationary period. The arbitrator would be restricted to examining the evaluative process and, if it was faulty, to granting another year of probation. School boards vigorously oppose the arbitration of reemployment and tenure grievances, arguing that such action represents the unlawful delegation of their power to a third party.

Nontenured teachers also have some rights. If they are covered by the scope of the law, they may be protected against the arbitrary nonrenewal of the contract during their probationary period. This same protection, however, does not extend to decisions made at the end of their probationary period. Unions have negotiated limited protections for nontenured teachers. Some contracts provide that teachers must be shown their performance evaluations, while others contain time limits for improving deficiencies and the right to refute any adverse reviews. We shall see in our discussion of higher education that the tenure issue is somewhat more complex at that level.

Personal Conduct. Another area of teacher grievances involves personal conduct. In the past drinking and smoking in public were often taboo, particularly for female teachers in smaller school districts. During the 1960s, a period of changing social customs when teachers strove to be treated as adults, grievances centered around the length of the male teacher's beard or the female miniskirt. Personal conduct grievances today may deal with the single teacher who is pregnant or those following an unorthodox life style. Do any of these unconventional actions affect the quality of teaching so that discharge or other penalties are justified?

Professional Standards. One of the major arguments made by the opponents of teacher unionism was that professional standards would be ignored and that emphasis would be placed on economic matters to the exclusion of all other issues. A reading of the teacher union press indicates otherwise. The papers print lengthy bibliographies, summarize special studies of educational research, and discuss useful educational techniques covering a wide variety of subjects, such as the Holocaust, labor unions, and other matters. Much of this material made its way into the classroom through the collective bargaining process.

In contrast to many four year institutions of higher learning where faculty members are involved in curriculum decisions, K-12 teachers became involved in this subject for the first time at the bargaining table. Sabbatical and other arrangements for time off were negotiated in order to provide for professional improvement.

Teacher unions have been instrumental in making tenure a reality by providing a mechanism to defend academic freedom. The power elite in many communities tends to regard a certain number of "kooks" or "radicals" as a normal part of a major university campus. This same tolerance has never been accorded to the K-12 social studies teacher who is expected to conform to the community standards. The support of academic freedom by teacher unions, which are now major institutions, helps the classroom teacher to stand up to such pressures.

Grievance Procedures. Grievance procedures in K-12 school districts tend to be relatively simple and follow the industrial model. (See Table 7 below.) The number of steps is usually determined by school enrollment. A small school district may have only three steps including arbitration, while a large one may include as many as six. Time limits exist both as to when the grievance must be filed and when the parties must respond at each step in the procedure.

Table 7. Typical K-12 Grievance Procedure

Grievance Step	Union Representative	Management Representative
1	Area or building representative	School principal
2	Grievance committee	Assistant superintendent
3	Grievance committee & outside union representative	Board of education
4	Arbitration*	

*Each party decides who will present its case to the arbitrator.

Initially school boards bitterly opposed arbitration as the last step in the grievance procedure, arguing that it was an infringement on their sovereignty. When the courts in 1959 began to uphold the constitutionality of arbitration, the school boards shifted their objection, charging that no outsider could possibly understand the intricacies of the school environment. After the AFT successfully negotiated arbitration in the large cities with no ill effects, opposition gradually lessened in those states with fairly comprehensive collective bargaining laws.

Community and junior colleges organized closely on the heels of the K-12 districts. Faculty opposing such action argued that unions were acceptable for K-12 teachers but were not needed by professionals at their level, an argument reminiscent of that made earlier by K-12 teachers who felt unions were suitable only for blue-collar workers.

The community college union model closely parallels that of the K-12 districts. Many community colleges were originally part of those same districts and faced the same problems. Their faculty had limited input into determining professional standards. Likewise salaries in both systems were based on several grids combining educational attainment with seniority. The grievance procedures are also based on the K-12 model, with a limited number of steps ending in binding arbitration.

Contract Administration at Four Year Colleges and Universities

Today about one-third of all faculty in higher education are organized, with about two-thirds of that number employed at four year institutions. Table 8 provides a breakdown of the total figure, giving the distribution of bargaining units among unions by type of institution.

Table 8. Faculty Bargaining Units, 1982

	Four Year & Professional		Two Year Campuses		
	Public	Private	Public	Private	Total
AAUP	21	22	5	1	49
AFT	15	25	75	6	121
NEA	18	16	169	4	207
AAUP/AFT	2	0	1	0	3
AAUP/NEA	2	0	0	0	2
Independent & Other	10	6	23	2	41
TOTAL	68	69	273	13	423

Source: Directory of Faculty Contracts and Bargaining Agents in Institutions of Higher Education, vol. 9, eds. Joel M. Douglas and Carol Rosenberg (New York: Bernard Baruch College, CUNY, 1983).

Three major organizations dominate collective bargaining in higher education. Two are the AFT and the NEA, the same organizations that first clashed in efforts to organize K-12 school districts. The third rival is the American Association of University Professors (AAUP), which seeks to organize solely in higher education and primarily at the level of four year colleges and universities. Founded in 1915, the AAUP concentrated on establishing standards to safeguard academic freedom—that is, the right of faculty members to teach, speak, and write their views free from fear of political reprisals by either the institution, the legislature, or the community at large.

One of the strengths of the AAUP, as well as its weakness, is its policy of including administrators among its members, as well as faculty. The inclusion of administrators (management) in the organization makes it easier to get agreement on standards to which the institutions would adhere. AAUP principles adopted by colleges and institutions in most cases, however, represent minimum rather than ideal standards. But membership for administrators creates the same problem for the AAUP that plagued the NEA at the K-12 level. When the AAUP, which historically opposed collective bargaining in higher education, saw the handwriting on the wall and decided to shift its position, it ran into strong opposition, much of it from those members who were administrators or former administrators. As a result the AAUP makes attainment of collective bargaining an optional item for each chapter. This position is in sharp contrast to the strong endorsements of collective bargaining made by the AFT and the NEA.

Because of this substantial internal opposition to collective bargaining, the AAUP finds it difficult to devote the necessary resources to this activity. Furthermore, it has suffered a significant decline in membership since the new policy was adopted in 1972. From a high of about 90,000 in that year, membership has fallen to about 70,000 despite the fact that it has won bargaining elections in the interim.

Probably the best explanation for the development of unions at four year colleges is that collective bargaining is contagious. The bargaining units at both the K-12 districts and the community colleges surround the four year institutions and have a spillover effect on them. Despite the often heard complaint that a bargaining relationship is not for true professionals, university faculties have found an institutional arrangement that gives them specific powers as a matter of right rather than privilege hard to resist.

Prior to 1969 only two union contracts existed at four year institutions, one at the Bryant College of Business Administration in Rhode Island and the other at the U.S. Merchant Marine Academy in King's Point, New York.[3] Just as the strike by AFT teachers in New York City in 1960 led to unionization in K-12 districts across the country, so did the formal recognition of two bargaining units at the City University of New York (CUNY) in 1969 lead to organizing

---

[3]June Weisberger, *Faculty Grievance Arbitration in Higher Education*, IPE Monograph No. 5 (Ithaca: Cornell University, Institute of Public Employment, 1976).

at other four year institutions. These two contracts covered 20 campuses with a total employment of about 15,000 faculty. The Legislative Conference, an independent union, held bargaining rights for
regular faculty while part-time faculty were covered by an AFT contract. In 1972 the two units merged, with the AFT obtaining sole
bargaining rights. In 1970 Rutgers University was organized by the
AAUP, and in early 1971 the State University of New York (SUNY),
consisting of 26 campuses and about 15,000 faculty, organized an
independent union, then joined the NEA, and ultimately affiliated
with AFT.

Shared Authority. Contract administration in higher education must deal with the problems presented by a system of shared
authority and peer review. Most faculty unions seek to limit the
scope of shared authority, rather than to destroy it, through collective bargaining. As a result two different systems manage to coexist,
with collective bargaining eventually becoming the more important
of the two. Even when joint committees are permitted to deal with
issues, the union will insist on appointing the faculty members.

The shared authority system presents major problems in the
grievance procedure. Recommendations on appointments, reappointments, promotions, and tenure are typically made by a faculty
body. The matter is then forwarded to a department head, who approves or disapproves the recommendation and in turn sends it to a
dean. If the dean approves the actions of the department head, it is
forwarded upward to another official, such as a provost, president,
or chancellor. Eventually it comes before the governing board of the
college. If the faculty disapproves, and the department head supports that decision, against whom is the grievance filed—the faculty, the department head, or both?

Closely associated with this problem is the question of who
should hear the grievance. Some grievance procedures follow the
common pattern prevailing elsewhere, where representatives of various levels of management, or a designee, such as the chairman,
dean, provost, or president, meet with representatives of the union.
These procedures take less time to reach a decision than those requiring a hearing board.

The scope of the grievance procedure in higher education is a
matter of debate just as it is in other newly organized workplaces.
The administration seeks to restrict its scope to disputes over the
violation or interpretation of the contract while the union aims at
expanding the definition to include violation of policies, rules, and

established practices. Sometimes the union will agree to exempt from the grievance procedure decisions about academic judgments on appointments, promotions, and tenure. The union, however, will always seek to challenge procedural violations involved in these areas.

No consensus has been reached regarding the final step in the grievance procedure. Management still seeks to retain the traditional role of the university president, while the union pushes for arbitration. Even when the principle of arbitration is agreed upon, differences of opinion exist over what should be submitted to arbitration and who should be the arbitrators. Management wants arbitrators to be drawn from the academic community, but at the same time seeks to prevent grievances involving academic judgment from being arbitrated. These positions appear to be contradictory. Presumably the reason for requiring an arbitrator to have an academic background is to ensure that a qualified person is chosen who can deal with areas unique to higher education. If these issues are not arbitrable, however, it is hard to understand why an arbitrator needs an academic background to determine whether a faculty member's teaching schedule is unfair. Because of the intertwining of faculty rights with what are normally considered to be management prerogatives, it is sometimes difficult for the arbitrator to determine against whom the individual is grieving—the peers within the teacher's own department or management outside of the unit—particularly when no one wishes to assume responsibility.

The status of the arbitrator's decision in the eyes of the courts follows the precedent in the private sector. Judges uphold the arbitrator unless the decisions are contrary to the contract or public policy.

The shared authority concept, which emphasizes decision making on the basis of confidential deliberations, complicates the arbitration process. Successful prosecution of grievances requires access to personnel records and related information. But if this information is given in confidence, can it be released in a grievance hearing which challenges the promotion itself rather than the procedures used? Unions must and will continue to demand this information. It is hoped that arbitrators who are steeped in the tradition of academic secrecy will understand the necessity for changes in this area.

Higher Education Grievances. When a grievance is under consideration the faculty member or the nominal union representative in the department calls upon the full-time union representative or one of a handful of union activists who process the grievance. Often the same union representative may appear at several steps in the procedure.

Most grievances deal with hiring, reappointments, promotions, tenure, salaries, and working conditions. Working conditions cover a wide range of subjects that ordinarily do not involve academic judgments: availability of secretarial help, access to computers, adequate laboratory supplies, teaching timetables, course assignments, classroom facilities, access to audio-visual equipment, parking facilities, workload, temporary versus permanent appointment status, the determination of whether time spent on a temporary appointment counts towards tenure, and the temporary layoff of tenured faculty to save money. Many of these grievances, particularly those involving working conditions, are settled informally.

Administrators have also received benefits from the collective bargaining process. A whole range of items is now discussed with the union, and agreement is reached on an integrated package rather than on isolated items. Multiple committees with changing memberships are avoided. This can be of particular value in processing grievances if the use of ad hoc committees is abolished. Gradually rules of the workplace develop because the union strives for uniformity of decisions, while arbitration makes its own contribution to this development. Both parties benefit from the development of clear-cut guidelines.

A union, under pressure from its membership, will strive for early settlement of grievances in its own self-interest and to reduce the delays experienced in the nonunion sector of higher education. The union will assume the responsibility of settling the competing claims of faculty members, and its success will depend on the political skills of its leadership.

The benefits to be derived from the grievance procedure in higher education are illustrated in the Rutgers case. To date those benefits include:

(1) The grievance procedure was streamlined and improvements were made in due process.

(2) Peer review was maintained, and the quality of peer review was not lowered.

(3) Authority was redistributed between faculty and administration.

(4) Grievants gained better access to expert representation.
(5) Departments not following university policies were discovered.
(6) The problems to be dealt with through collective bargaining were identified.[4]

Summary

The last two decades have seen the growth of unions in the public sector to a degree never anticipated. Executive Order 10988 issued by President Kennedy deserves much of the credit. Although it provided federal employees with only the form and not the substance of collective bargaining, it had significant impact on the sovereignty theory, historically the major obstacle to public sector collective bargaining. The concession by the federal government that it has not only the right but the duty to engage in collective bargaining made it impossible for other branches of government to continue to argue that they were prohibited from doing the same.

Public employees and industrial relations experts have searched far and wide for an alternative to the private sector collective bargaining model, with little success. The search took place because public employers proclaimed that government services were unique and required a different set of rules to handle their labor-management problems. Upon reflection this position does not differ greatly from the positions taken in the past by automobile manufacturers, building contractors, garment shop operators, or the heads of steel mills, each of whom argued that the conditions of employment at its workplace were unique and could not possibly be handled through the same set of rules. Although no one law governs labor relations in the public sector, as the Taft-Hartley Act does in private employment, most state laws are based on common principles adopted from the private sector.

Several basic issues still need to be resolved in public employment. At the federal level the scope of negotiations needs to be expanded to include wages and fringe benefits. Only employees of the postal service, TVA, and a few other units, primarily in the Department of the Interior, negotiate wages and, in some cases, fringe benefits. The need for this change is shown by the fact that postal employees, who were placed under the Taft-Hartley Act in 1970,

---

[4]James P. Begin, "Grievance Mechanisms and Faculty Collegiality: The Rutgers Case," *Industrial and Labor Relations Review* 31, no. 3 (April 1978), pp. 295–309.

have doubled their wage increases over those received by other federal employees at a comparable classification.

Grievance and appeal procedures still need to be simplified. Although this was partly rectified by the passage of the Civil Service Reform Act, a multiplicity of appeal procedures still exist at the federal level which proves confusing to both the individual worker and the union representative.

Resistance to outside binding arbitration as the final step in the grievance procedure is still strong. The executive branch of government maintains that it does not want to meddle in administrative matters, yet it is the rare school board head or university president who is willing to be written out of the grievance procedure. Even when agreeing to incorporate arbitration, they still prefer to retain a slot for themselves in the grievance procedure.

In general, grievance procedures in the public sector are not as streamlined as those in the private sector. Often they require tedious committee hearings and the shuffling of much written material between the parties. Nowhere is this more true then at the university level. A large share of the difficulty stems from the system of academic governance and peer review in existence at most universities. Under this system faculty members make recommendations on hiring, promotions, and the granting of tenure and salaries, a function in other workplaces reserved for management. Therefore, it is argued that these matters should not be subject to the grievance procedure, or at least not eligible for arbitration because these academic decisions can be made only by other faculty members who possess the necessary technical knowledge. Gradually the idea is spreading that faculty members may be subject to their own form of prejudice and may upon occasion violate due process procedures or even arrive at the wrong decision. The fact that the average citizen may be called upon as a juror to reach a verdict on a complicated antitrust case supports the argument that impartial third parties in the form of arbitrators can be utilized at the faculty level.

Review and Discussion Questions

1. Why is it more difficult to negotiate an adequate grievance procedure with a public than a private employer?

2. How has the scope of the grievance procedure in federal employment changed over the years? Is this good or bad?

3. What are some of the traditional rights of management about which professional employees seek to negotiate and grieve? Why?

4. Why was it difficult in public employment to negotiate arbitration as the last step in the grievance procedure?

5. What problems does academic governance pose at four year colleges and universities in the handling of grievances?

6. What relationship should tenure have to layoffs if they become necessary at a university?

7. What steps can be taken in public employment to streamline grievance procedures?

Key Words and Phrases

advisory arbitration
American Association of
  University Professors
American Federation of
  Teachers
Civil Service Reform Act
civil service system
Executive Order 10988
Executive Order 11491

Federal Labor Relations
  Authority
industrial model
Merit Systems Protection Board
National Education Association
Office of Personnel
  Management
professional standards
sovereignty theory

7

The Duty of Fair Representation

The so-called "duty of fair representation" is a doctrine that was developed by the federal courts and the National Labor Relations Board (NLRB) to interpret the Railway Labor Act and the National Labor Relations Act (NLRA). The doctrine states that the union holding exclusive recognition must represent all workers in the unit, members and nonmembers alike, in an impartial manner.

The first court case arose in 1944 under the Railway Labor Act when black workers sued charging their union with racial discrimination, because it negotiated a contract designed to eliminate all blacks from firemen jobs.[1] The U.S. Supreme Court ruled that the union had the duty to represent all workers in a craft without discrimination based on race and that the court had a right to protect minorities when treated unfairly.

Duty of fair representation cases today, however, usually involve the manner in which the union handles grievances rather than complaints relating to the negotiating process.

Current duty of fair representation cases have evolved from the union's refusal to file a grievance or the quality of its performance in processing grievances, and in most cases these involve individual rather than group complaints. The union is required to investigate the grievance with a degree of care and then it must decide whether to pursue it, including taking it to arbitration.

A union has greater leeway in negotiating the terms of the contract than it does in processing a grievance. Grievances involve rights for the individual that presumably are guaranteed by the contract. However, in negotiating the contract the union may agree to different benefits for the membership. For example, the union may

---

[1] *Steele v. Louisville Railroad*, 323 US 192, 15 LRRM 708 (1944).

153

negotiate separate pay rates or increases for people in the bargaining unit providing it is done on a nondiscriminatory basis; provision may be made for all members to receive a 10 percent increase, with the skilled trades allotted an additional 50 cents per hour. Failure to submit the contract to the membership for ratification is not a breach of the duty of fair representation, because a majority vote does not automatically guarantee fair treatment.

There are two routes through which a breach of a duty of fair representation charge can be processed: through the NLRB as an unfair labor practice or through the court system as a violation of Section 301 of the Taft-Hartley Act. If the latter route is used the worker must jointly sue the employer and the union—the employer because it violated the contract and the union because it breached its duty of fair representation.

The question of whether the union is required to take a grievance to arbitration has spawned a number of complaints charging a breach of the duty of fair representation. A union, however, is not required to go to arbitration. It has more discretion in reaching that decision than it has in either refusing to process the grievance initially or appealing it to the next step in the grievance procedure, providing the decision is reached free of arbitrary or discriminatory treatment. A union may refuse to go to arbitration because:

(1) It does not have a good case under the terms of the contract. Even though proven wrong at a later date, it will not be found liable if its judgment was made in good faith.
(2) It does not have the money to do so.
(3) The cost of arbitration does not equal the benefits received. (For example, a grievance involving management's refusal to pay $50 for overtime work may cost the union $2,000 to arbitrate.)
(4) It feels the grievance is minor or of a frivolous nature that will divert time and money from more important cases.

The union, however, may not refuse to arbitrate because the member is not in the good graces of the organization, nor may it refuse if it has arbitrated similar cases.

A union may develop any procedure it desires for deciding whether a grievance is to be arbitrated, providing it is fair and applied consistently. If the union refuses to arbitrate, the individual has no right to take the case to arbitration on his or her own unless the contract specifically permits such action, and very few do. Nor does the individual have the right to process his or her own grievance at the arbitration hearing or to have an attorney present without the permission of the union.

The manner in which the union prepares and presents the case in arbitration may also be the basis for a charge of a breach of the duty of fair representation. For example, there may be a breach if the union representative never interviewed the grievant or key witnesses before the hearing. Merely presenting the grievant's case in an ineffective manner does not justify a charge of the breach of the duty of fair representation.

General Counsel's Guidelines

In 1967 the U.S. Supreme Court ruled that a union breached its duty of fair representation if its actions were "arbitrary, discriminatory or based on bad faith."[2] The NLRB's General Counsel has expressed alarm over the wide range of conflicting standards used by the lower federal courts in applying the Supreme Court's ruling. The list of standards compiled includes: "Without hostile discrimination, fairly, impartially, and in good faith"; "honest of purpose"; "substantial evidence of fraud, deceitful action, or dishonest conduct"; "arbitrarily ignored a meritorious grievance or processed it in a perfunctory manner."[3]

The General Counsel found that the absence of clear standards resulted in the processing of unmerited grievances to arbitration, which clogged the arbitration process; in the filing of a large number of unfair labor practice charges; and in time-consuming searches by local unions to find stewards who had the legal know-how to deal with these standards.[4]

As a result of the lack of clear standards, the General Counsel announced four guidelines to be used in determining whether to prosecute an unfair labor practice charging a breach of the duty of fair representation:[5]

(1) A union breaches its duty when its actions are attributable to improper motives such as discrimination or fraud.

The examples of discrimination cited by the General Counsel include the failure to properly process grievances

---

[2]*Vaca v. Sipes*, 386 U.S. 171, 64 LRRM 2369 (1967).

[3]NLRB General Counsel Memorandum 79-55, reprinted as "NLRB Policy on Union's Duty of Fair Representation," *Labor Relations Yearbook, 1979* (Washington, D.C.: The Bureau of National Affairs, Inc., 1979), pp. 341–345.

[4]*Ibid.*, p. 342.

[5]*Ibid.*, p. 343–345.

for any of the following reasons: the grievant attempted to bring in another union; the grievants were in another political caucus; the grievants were nonmembers; personal animosity; the grievants' race, color, or sex.

(2) A union breaches its duty when its conduct is arbitrary.

Examples of such conduct include: refusal to process a grievance without making any inquiry, or refusal to support the grievant when the contract clearly supports his or her position. The union's inquiry, however, need not be equivalent to that made by a trained investigator. The General Counsel explained "So long as the union makes some inquiry into the facts and/or so long as the union's contract interpretation has some basis in reason, the union's refusal to process the grievance will not be considered arbitrary."[6]

(3) A union breaches its duty of fair representation if its conduct consists of gross negligence.

This standard has also been adopted by the Sixth, Ninth and Tenth U.S. Circuit Courts of Appeals. As an example of the standard, the General Counsel cited a case where the union neglected to inform a worker that her grievance would not be taken to arbitration. As a result she rejected a settlement she would otherwise have accepted.

(4) A union breaches its duty if it undercuts a worker's grievance without some reasonable explanation.

An example of this conduct occurs when a union drops a grievance at some point in the grievance process without an explanation as to why the grievance lacks merit.

If the unfair labor practice charge does not fall within these guidelines then the complaint will be dismissed. About 80 percent of all complaints charging a breach of the duty of fair representation are not prosecuted.

The union's defense against a charge of failure to provide fair representation may fall into three major categories:

(1) The statute of limitations may have been exhausted. The time limit for Section 301 suits, as well as for duty of fair representation charges filed with the NLRB, is six months.

---

[6]*Ibid.*, p. 344.

(2) The worker failed to exhaust either the remedies under the grievance procedure or the internal remedies found in the union's constitution and bylaws; or

(3) The worker failed to cite the injury for which relief can be granted.

The best advice for a union to insure that it will not face a charge of breaching its duty of fair representation is to use common sense. Although a union is not required to process every complaint brought to it, it must have a reason for not doing so. It has the right to make a value judgment concerning the validity of a complaint, but that decision must be made free from arbitrary or discriminatory intent. Even if the decision is later proven wrong, the union probably will not be liable for damages if it follows these procedures:

(1) Every complaint, no matter how far-fetched it appears on the surface, should be investigated.

(2) The union must be able to show that it did investigate the complaint.

   The union's grievance file should contain a grievance fact sheet and a grievance form (see Chapter 6), which show how the complaint was investigated and its final disposition.

(3) Every effort should be made to convince the grievant that the complaint is not legitimate when that is the case.

   If the union representative is unable to do so, the worker should be informed of internal appeal rights. It is imperative that every union establish such a procedure in writing and that the membership be informed of its existence.

(4) Some unions now recommend that discharges of long-term seniority workers should automatically be arbitrated.

(5) A grievant should be given in writing the terms of the settlement or the reasons for withdrawing the grievance.

The types of complaints which may lead to a charge of breach of duty include long-term suspensions, discharges, loss of seniority, and loss of pension rights and other tangible benefits. It is unlikely that a union would be charged with a breach of its duty of fair representation if it failed to grieve minor complaints.

If the guidelines of the NLRB cited earlier are observed, the union has little to fear from unfounded complaints charging a breach of its duty of fair representation. One cannot, however, be as sure of the position of the courts.

Despite the fears expressed by some unions, it is hard to fault the standard of gross negligence which some courts have adopted as a test to determine if a breach of the duty of fair representation has taken place. The ticklish issue this standard poses is how to distinguish between gross and simple negligence. For example, it is hard to argue that a union is not guilty of gross negligence and should not be held liable when it fails to arbitrate the discharge of a long-term seniority employee because it missed the time limits in the contract after receiving several extensions in writing. Should a union also be held liable if the same mistake occurs in respect to a 6-month suspension, a 30-day suspension, a 5-day suspension, or a written reprimand? Where should the line be drawn separating gross negligence from simple negligence?

The inclusion of gross negligence as a standard for determining a breach of the duty of fair representation should encourage every union to develop a training program for its stewards and other union representatives involved in processing grievances. In the long run it will save the union money, insure fair treatment for the membership, and avoid the possibility of lengthy legal hassles. Unions without resources necessary to conduct their own training programs should contact their nearest state university to see if it has a department offering programs and resource materials to union members. The American Civil Liberties Union has produced an excellent book of questions and answers for union members who want to know their rights as well as unions which want to know their responsibilities. It has a good chapter on the duty of fair representation as well as chapters covering the main provisions of the Landrum-Griffin Act.[7]

Again it must be noted that the duty of fair representation does not require an investigation on the level of a professional investigator nor does it require a grievance to be processed with the skill of a trained defense attorney. It does, however, require that a worker's grievance be handled free from discriminatory or arbitrary treatment.

---

[7]Clyde W. Summers and Robert J. Rabin, *The Rights of Union Members* (New York: Avon Books, 1979).

Key Words and Phrases	
discriminatory or arbitrary treatment	gross negligence
General Counsel's Guidelines	Section 301 of the Taft-Hartley Act
	unfair labor practice

Review and Discussion Questions

1. How did the concept of the duty of fair representation develop?

2. What are the two routes through which a breach of the duty of fair representation may be pursued?

3. Should gross negligence be a basis for charging a breach of the duty of fair representation?

4. What are some of the issues that may be the basis for charging a breach of the duty of fair representation?

5. What are the guidelines drawn up by the NLRB's General Counsel to determine whether a breach of the duty of fair representation occurred?

6. What are some of the safeguards that unions can implement to protect themselves from suits charging a breach of the duty of fair representation?

8

The Arbitration Process

Impartial third parties are used to settle disputes arising out of negotiating the terms of a contract and, more frequently, those charging a violation of the terms of an already negotiated agreement. The techniques commonly used are mediation, fact-finding, and arbitration. In their pure form these techniques are separate and distinct, but in practice they may overlap.

Although arbitration may serve more than one purpose in industrial relations, this chapter will explore this third party process only in respect to the settlement of grievances arising out of an already agreed-upon contract (rights arbitration) rather than impasses arising out of negotiating the terms of the agreement itself (interest arbitration). Among the subjects discussed are the development of arbitration, the types of arbitration, the sources of arbitrators, choice of arbitrator, the issues arbitrated, the arbitration hearing, the costs of arbitration, expedited arbitration, the legal status of arbitration, and the guidelines evolving out of arbitration.

Arbitration can be a relatively formal procedure in which both parties present evidence and have the right to cross-examine witnesses. In practice an arbitrator sometimes engages first in mediation, seeking to get labor and management to agree without imposing a settlement. This practice was utilized in the hosiery and garment industries for many years. Individual arbitrators like the late Harry Shulman, the umpire under the Ford Motor Company contract, operated in this fashion. Today, however, most arbitrators will not mediate unless they are requested to do so by both parties.

Virtually all grievance procedures in the private sector, including many in construction, now provide for arbitration as the terminal point of the grievance process. Most public employee grievance procedures in states covered by collective bargaining legislation also

160

end in binding arbitration. It appears that in the foreseeable future no significant difference will exist between public and private sector contracts in respect to the use of arbitration.

The Development of Arbitration

Arbitration was first employed in industrial relations at the beginning of this century when it was proposed as a substitute for the strike in the settlement of wage disputes. The early unions in the clothing, hosiery, printing, and mining industries, after negotiating contracts, used arbitration for settling disputes arising out of their agreements. In 1913 the federal government created the U.S. Conciliation Service within the Department of Labor. The primary function of the Service was to provide mediation, but it also had the authority to suggest arbitration to the parties and could name and select the arbitrator.[1] But it was not until the organization of industrial unions in the mines, mills, and factories that arbitration began its large-scale penetration of American industrial life.

Arbitration received support in 1937 when General Motors agreed to an umpire system in its contract with the United Auto Workers. The umpire was restricted to hearing those cases which the two parties jointly agreed to refer to him. Upon the insistence of Walter Reuther, then head of the union's General Motors department, a permanent umpire system was installed in 1940 under which *either* party could request arbitration, a program still in existence. General Motors' acceptance of arbitration made it more palatable to other major corporations.

Prior to 1940, estimates indicate that fewer than 10 percent of all contracts provided arbitration as the terminal point in the grievance procedure. By 1944 the figure rose to 73 percent and by 1949 to 83 percent.[2] This phenomenal growth was due in large part to the actions of the War Labor Board (WLB).

Created in 1942 by a presidential order, the WLB established jurisdiction over labor disputes that might lead to strikes.[3] The board's membership was tripartite, consisting of four public members, four labor representatives, and an equal number from management. Although many of its rulings in respect to arbitration were

---

[1]R. W. Fleming, *The Labor Arbitration Process* (Urbana: University of Illinois Press, 1965), p. 11. See Chapter 1 which summarizes the development of arbitration in the United States.

[2]*Ibid.*, p. 18.

[3]"Arbitration and the National War Labor Board," 58 HARV. L. REV. 309 (1945).

made almost 40 years ago, they are still in effect, in large part because labor and management, the NLRB, and the courts have found they withstood the test of time.

The WLB institutionalized arbitration when it ruled that it would not permit either of the parties or itself to interfere with the finality of the arbitrator's award. The WLB proceeded to promote the inclusion of arbitration into contracts by requiring its incorportation when one of the parties failed to accept it during negotiations. Its insistence on the acceptance of arbitration was based on the success of arbitration in preventing strikes over grievances before World War II. Since labor had voluntarily given a no-strike pledge for the duration of the war, it was essential to devise a formula for settling disputes. A number of unions which were unable to negotiate the right of arbitration obtained it by order of the WLB.

Types of Arbitration

Arbitration related to grievances takes the forms of *ad hoc arbitration* or an *umpire system*. Whether called arbitrator or umpire, the individual operates in the same manner and renders a final, binding decision.

Ad hoc arbitration may use either one person or a panel of three members, selected for each separate grievance or group of grievances. A panel may be of two kinds. The first type of panel is one wherein labor and management appoint their own representatives to the panel, and they in turn select an impartial chairman. If they are unable to agree on a chairman, assistance from an outside source may then be requested. In a few cases, as with the steel and postal workers, an ad hoc arbitrator is obtained on a rotation basis from a panel agreed to by the parties. While less frequent there are still a few contracts that require the second type of panel, one consisting solely of neutrals. Today, however, a single arbitrator is the most common form of ad hoc arbitration.

Under an umpire system the same person hears all grievances for the duration of the contract provided that person remains acceptable to both parties. An umpire system is used primarily when a multiplant company has an agreement with a single union. This situation exists in many industries, including auto, steel, aircraft, meat packing, rubber, and clothing.

A variation of the umpire system governs railroad disputes. The Railway Labor Act requires grievances of railroad workers to be settled by arbitration. The 1934 amendments to this act created a National Railroad Adjustment Board (NRAB).

Under the 1966 amendments to the act, the NRAB was divided into four separate boards, each with jurisdiction over a different division within the industry. Division one covers all operating employees; division two covers shop employees; division three covers nonoperating employees; and division four, waterborne employees and supervisors. Each division set up its own procedures, which closely follow those governing the NRAB. If the labor and management representatives within a division are unable to reach a settlement, a neutral chairman is appointed. The chairman's fees as well as the administrative costs of hearings are borne by the federal government.

The law was amended because the NRAB was unable to handle the vast number of cases submitted to arbitration. Some critics argue that this backlog resulted from the unions' failure to screen cases because the process is free. The unions argue that the backlog was caused by management's insistence on changing work rules.

Both ad hoc arbitration and the umpire system have their advocates. The ad hoc system often is preferred when labor and management first enter a collective bargaining relationship because it is easy to change arbitrators if the arbitrator dissatisfies one or both parties. Of course, they may request the same arbitrator as often as they wish. The use of ad hoc arbitration tends to eliminate the frequently expressed fear of both labor and management that arbitrators will split their decisions, awarding some to the union and some to management, in an effort to retain clients. Because there is no guarantee under ad hoc arbitration that the arbitrator will be reemployed by the parties, such action is less probable. In addition, ad hoc arbitration permits an easier access to a specialist if the nature of the grievance involves technical knowledge, as in a dispute over an incentive system or a job evaluation plan.

Ad hoc arbitration also has certain disadvantages. The time wasted in the selection process may affect worker morale and, therefore, create dissatisfaction with the entire grievance process. Using different arbitrators sometimes results in conflicting decisions on similar grievances, in part because the arbitrators may not know the background of the dispute or may be unfamiliar with the practices of labor and management. More often than not the losing party will want a different arbitrator next time, which means that a new person must be educated in the practices of the workplace.

The umpire system also has certain advantages and disadvantages. Careful consideration can be given to the selection of the umpire and once this is accomplished, the process need not be repeated each time a grievance is arbitrated. An umpire who initially is unfamiliar with the contract will become knowledgeable, and consequently decisions will be more consistent than those rendered by ad hoc arbitrators. An umpire must exert more care in reaching a decision than an ad hoc arbitrator, because the umpire usually retains the position for the duration of the contract and therefore must live with a poor verdict. Furthermore, the umpire's decision will have greater precedent value since he or she will be bound by them, whereas individual arbitrators may not feel limited by a ruling of a predecessor. In the long run an umpire system may be cheaper because of time saved in the selection process and the greater consistency in interpretation of the contract.

Other advantages: The umpire will be familiar with the personalities on both sides as well as workplace practices and therefore should require less time to reach a decision; the union may be less likely to take weak cases to arbitration knowing that the umpire is familiar with the agreement and the history of the negotiations; an umpire may exert more care in reaching a decision, because as the incumbent arbitrator, he or she must retain any stance taken for the duration of the contract and will have to live with a poor verdict.

Usually an umpire serves for the duration of the contract, with the term automatically renewed unless one party objects. The party who discharges the umpire during the contract term must pay the remainder of the umpire's retainer, which otherwise is split between the two parties.

Just as with the ad hoc system, the umpire arrangement has certain disadvantages. Well-known persons sought by both labor and management are in short supply. This shortage has become more acute as the veterans of the War Labor Board, the respected names in the arbitration field, have retired or died. Both the American Arbitration Association (AAA), a private organization, and the Federal Mediation and Conciliation Service (FMCS), a government agency, have in recent years conducted training programs in an effort to increase the supply of arbitrators, as requests for them increase yearly.

Other criticisms of the umpire system are:

(1) The grievance process is too easily available.
(2) It relieves labor and management of the responsibility of settling their differences; the parties, therefore, fail to exhaust other means of settlement.

(3)   The union may fail to arbitrate some cases with merit because it feels it made a poor choice in its selection of the umpire.

(4)   Cost is involved even if the umpire is not used, because the two parties must still pay the retainer fee, even though the umpire may hear no cases.

In adopting an umpire system, labor and management should decide whether they want the umpire to mediate as well as arbitrate. The argument favoring such a policy contends that conflict can be eliminated if a knowledgeable person is permitted to reconcile differences between the inexperienced representatives of labor and management. Today, most umpires do not engage in mediation. Ad hoc arbitrators will not mediate either unless specifically requested to do so by both parties, on the ground that they have no special background concerning the history of negotiations and therefore feel they are properly restricted to the terms of the agreement.

Sources of Arbitrators

The dominant form of ad hoc arbitration today is the single arbitrator rather than the tripartite board. Most contracts call for the union and management jointly to select the ad hoc arbitrator. The contract usually provides that if they are unable to agree, a list of names is requested from either the FMCS or the AAA. Here is a typical clause outlining the selection process.

> Within ten (10) days after a receipt of a demand to arbitrate, the parties shall confer in an attempt to select an impartial arbitrator. If, within such ten (10) day period, the parties are unable to agree, either party may request the Federal Mediation and Conciliation Service to furnish a list of available arbitrators. After receipt of such a list the parties shall alternate in striking names until one remains. The parties shall have the right to reject a panel in its entirety and to request another.

Fees and expenses for arbitrators obtained through the FMCS are paid by the union and management and not by the government. They are not FMCS employees. The Mediation Service compiles a roster of qualified persons who set their own fees. This agency then supplies a list of names and biographic sketches when requested by the interested parties.

The AAA, founded in 1926, supplies arbitrators for business and commercial disputes, as well as for those involving industrial relations. Its roster of arbitrators contains many of the same names listed with the FMCS. Like the FMCS, the AAA supplies a list of arbitrators to interested parties upon request. It charges both the union and management a $50 administrative fee for which it assumes the responsibility of arranging the time and place of the hearing. The FMCS makes no charge for its services, but the arbitrator and the two parties must themselves determine the time and place of the hearing.

The method of selecting an arbitrator from the list varies with different contracts. Usually a coin is flipped to determine who first strikes a name from the list. Alternate striking takes place between the union and management until one name remains. The parties by agreement may reject the entire list and request the appropriate agency to send a new one. The union, if it has the choice, should permit management to strike first. It then will be in position to make the final decision of who will arbitrate.

Choosing the Arbitrator

Under most contracts either the AAA or the FMCS is requested to supply a list of names when the union and management fail to agree upon an arbitrator. Both organizations use similar procedures in compiling their rosters. Most arbitrators are professional people—many from the academic community—and usually have a background in law, industrial relations, economics, or industrial engineering. Occasionally, a member of the clergy may be employed. Persons with specific backgrounds may be used in grievances involving their specialties. For example, when the arbitrability of the grievance is at issue, a person with a legal background may be preferred; in a dispute involving contract interpretation a person with an industrial relations background may be sought. Likewise when a grievance concerns a wage incentive problem or a job evaluation plan, an industrial engineer may be desired. It is in this area that a union may have great difficulty in selecting an arbitrator it considers impartial, because most industrial engineers have a management orientation.

Although the AAA lists 2,800 persons on its roster, fewer than 600 persons handle most of its cases. In order to be placed on its roster, the applicant submits to the AAA his or her present and past work experience with the names of 15 references: five each from labor, management, and the public.

The FMCS has a similar procedure. In addition, applicants must submit their awards rendered in five previous arbitrations for review. An applicant who appears to have the necessary qualifications is listed on the organization's roster.

A person may be removed from either list for such reasons as illness, excessive charges, consistent lateness in issuing decisions, failure to be selected, or a change in occupation that may pose a conflict of interest. For example, an attorney in private practice may become a member of a company's industrial relations department, and therefore is no longer regarded as neutral.

In selecting an arbitrator most unions use one of two methods. They may read the available published cases of the arbitrator or they may ask the opinion of someone who has had experience with the individual. Both methods require that caution be exercised.

The first alternative poses a problem because only a small minority of awards are published. Sometimes the arbitrator, the union, or management may refuse permission to publish. Or the case may be so similar to others that its publication would represent duplication. Therefore, the union, by using the scoreboard approach of totaling the printed awards rendered for or against unions, may receive a highly selective version of the arbitrator's views. This is especially true because some arbitrators grant permission to publish a selection of their cases to demonstrate an equal number of decisions for each party. Examining a published award may prove more profitable when the process by which the arbitrator reached the decision is studied rather than the decision itself.

Where can the union find published decisions? One source is the AAA, which produces a variety of services: three monthly arbitration award reporting services, a quarterly journal, a quarterly arbitration law reporting service, and numerous other specialized materials, including arbitration films widely used in labor education programs conducted both by universities and unions.[4]

In addition, several private companies publish information related to labor law, collective bargaining, and arbitration. Two are The Bureau of National Affairs and Commerce Clearing House. Both periodically publish arbitrators' awards, and from time to time print biographic sketches of those persons whose decisions they have published. If a union is interested in an individual's back-

---

[4]Robert Coulson, *Labor Arbitration—What You Need to Know* (New York: American Arbitration Association, 1978), p. 5.

ground, it should check as many of these sources as possible, because an arbitrator may be listed in one publication but not in another. This reference material can be purchased on a subscription basis, though this may be too expensive for a local union. The international union headquarters or a regional office of a number of unions have some of these services. A large municipal library may also prove helpful. A few libraries have a separate "labor" section, but more often this material is located in its "business and industry" section. Some state universities have many or all of these publications, sometimes located in a special labor and industrial relations library. The Appendix, "Arbitration Resource Material," lists and summarizes the basic arbitration material found in the labor and industrial relations library of one large midwestern state university.[5] Public employee unions should be aware that several services deal solely with arbitration cases in the public sector.

Any advice on whom to select as an arbitrator should be evaluated carefully. A person with a limited background in arbitration may not possess the experience necessary to make a meaningful recommendation. The objectivity of the recommender needs to be determined. It is not enough to be told that the individual under consideration awarded his or her last case to the union. The recommendation of an arbitrator by a union representative who lost the case is important, because it indicates that the organization felt it was treated fairly and that it understood the award while not necessarily agreeing with it. Again, it must be emphasized that the arbitrator's decision may not be as important as the process and the arguments developed in reaching the conclusion, because no two cases are identical and a slight variation in facts may lead to a different result.

In selecting an arbitrator the assumption, of course, is that the individual is both competent and impartial. At the same time, however, it should be realized that every person approaches a number of problems with fixed views as to what is right or wrong. Therefore, the union should try to find out the arbitrator's views regarding

---

[5]Three books dealing with arbitration that a union should have in its library are: Frank Elkouri and Edna Asper Elkouri, *How Arbitration Works*, 3rd ed. (Washington, D.C.: The Bureau of National Affairs, Inc., 1973); Duane Beeler, *Arbitration for the Local Union* (Chicago: Duane Beeler, 1977); and Allan J. Harrison, *Preparing and Presenting Your Arbitration Case* (Washington, D.C.: The Bureau of National Affairs, Inc., 1979). The Elkouri book is the most comprehensive book available on arbitration. The book summarizes the legal status of arbitration, the hearing process, and the standards applied by most arbitrators. The Beeler and Harrison books are valuable because they make practical suggestions as to how a union can best present its case.

some of the issues that commonly arise in a given type of grievance. For example, does the arbitrator concentrate on technicalities rather than on the basic arguments being presented? Does he or she persist in trying to mediate and seek to instill personal views into the hearing rather than resolve the issues presented?

An effort should be made to determine whether the arbitrator is strict or lax in enforcing the rules of evidence. An arbitrator is not required to follow the legal rules of evidence. The union is probably better off when these rules are not followed, because often the union presentation is made by a person without legal training. The union may be at a disadvantage if the arbitrator permits legal technicalities to dominate the hearing. Since labor, management, and the arbitrator usually do not have subpoena powers, a certain amount of hearsay and irrelevant testimony may be necessary to get at the truth. On the other hand, an arbitrator must ensure that the hearing does not degenerate into chaos.

The arbitrator's attitude toward management and union rights may also be important. If the arbitrator takes the position that management retains all rights not specifically modified by the contract, the union will have a hard time winning a grievance based on past practice. Most arbitrators take the position that a grievance charging a violation of past practice is valid only when it involves an issue about which the contract is silent or unclear. A few arbitrators, however, argue that a past-practice grievance may have validity even when it conflicts with contract language, particularly when the practice bridges more than one agreement. This information would be important to the union when arbitrating such a grievance.

An arbitrator's attitude on other issues is useful to know—for example, the arbitrator's views on discharge of long-term seniority employees, the relative merits of seniority and ability, or on alcoholism as a basis for discharge. An arbitrator who views alcoholism as an illness rather than as an indicator of a faulty personal behavior pattern may, in a disciplinary case involving alcoholism, order remedial treatment rather than punitive action. Arbitrators who view discharge as a form of capital punishment in the workplace are reluctant to sustain the dismissals of older workers with high seniority even when they have been found guilty as charged. Often these arbitrators will modify the discharge either by reinstatement without backpay or by some form of suspension. Likewise an arbitrator who feels that limited promotional opportunities exist for many blue-collar and clerical workers may be receptive to placing the burden of proof on management to document why the senior employee was denied the better job opportunity.

How does one determine what an arbitrator's view is on these subjects? Many arbitrators, including the lesser known, write articles or give speeches that may give clues. Such articles appear in the annual proceedings of the Industrial Relations Research Association and the National Academy of Arbitrators or in such journals as the *Labor Law Journal, The Arbitration Journal, The Industrial and Labor Relations Review*, and *Industrial Relations*. A university or municipal librarian can help the union locate the material if it is available.

Although unions should exercise care in selecting an arbitrator, they should not neglect other aspects of the arbitration process. Sometimes excessive time is spent poring over the awards of an arbitrator in an attempt to determine his or her views. This time and effort might well be better spent in preparing the case for presentation.

The personal experience of the union with an arbitrator is probably the most important factor in determining the union's choice. Often the union prefers to postpone a hearing until an arbitrator used previously is available. The total amount of experience of the arbitrator is the next most important consideration. Unions usually prefer the old hand to the novice even when not personally acquainted with the old hand.

Sometimes the nature of the case dictates the choice of arbitrators. To get a speedy hearing on a discharge grievance, a union may be willing to accept an inexperienced arbitrator, rather than wait until the preferred individual is available, so that the grievant will know as soon as possible whether or not new employment must be sought. Management, too, may seek an early resolution of grievances involving monetary liability arising out of discharge and promotion cases, particularly when the contract places no time limits on the amount of backpay awards.

Unions complain, often long and loud, about the excessive fees charged by arbitrators. Yet little evidence exists to show costs play an important part for either labor or management in the selection of an arbitrator. Much more consideration is given to past experience and the perceived attitude of the arbitrator toward the issue under consideration.

Issues Arbitrated

The range of issues over which grievances are filed is virtually unlimited. But most grievances that are arbitrated cover relatively few subjects. Discharge and disciplinary cases traditionally constitute the largest single category. Table 9 shows that while the total number of hearings conducted by the FMCS between 1971 and 1980 increased by 162.6 percent, disciplinary cases rose at the much faster rate of 259.3 percent.

The sharp increase in disciplinary cases may result from high unemployment in the later year. During periods of recession management may seek to recapture its allegedly lost authority by requiring strict compliance with its work rules. At the same time, the union's power to resist is lessened because its members fear being laid off.

Arbitrations over subcontracting also increase during a period of high unemployment. When there is plenty of overtime, the union pays little attention to subcontracting. When work is slow and lay-

Table 9. Types of Grievances Resulting in 100 or More FMCS Arbitrations in 1971 and 1980

	1971	1980	Percentage Increase 1971–1980
Total Cases	3,230	8,482	162.6
Discharge and disciplinary issues	1,009	3,625	259.3
Work assignments	—	446	—
Arbitrability challenged on procedural grounds	—	395	—
Seniority: layoff, bumping and recall	208	286	37.5
Seniority: promotion and upgrading	169	268	58.6
Overtime pay	151	248	64.2
Fringe benefits	106	236	122.6
Distribution of overtime	178	223	25.3
Management rights	—	222	—
Arbitrability challenged on substantive grounds	—	203	—
Rates of pay	—	202	—
Job classification	—	172	—
Vacations and vacation pay	99	165	66.6
Scheduling of work	147	160	8.8
Holiday and holiday pay	85	160	88.2
Job posting and bidding	—	156	—
Subcontracting	66	149	125.8
Reporting, call in, and call-back pay	51	112	119.6
Arbitrability challenged on procedural and substantive grounds	—	107	—
Seniority: Transfer	73	106	45.2
Seniority: Other	92	104	13.0

Source: Federal Mediation and Conciliation Service, Thirty-Third Annual Report, Fiscal Year 1980 (Washington, D.C.: Government Printing Office, 1981) pp. 40–41.

offs occur, then unions make every effort to retain or to bring back work normally done by members of the bargaining unit.

The number of cases challenging the arbitrability of an issue either on procedural or substantive grounds is rising as well. This is not surprising in light of the strong hostility presently displayed by large segments of the management community toward the labor movement on both the political and collective bargaining fronts.

The Arbitration Hearing

A union wishing to arbitrate a grievance must first exhaust the prior steps in the grievance procedure, unless the agreement states otherwise. It is no defense for the union to argue that it would be futile to do so in light of management's past history in denying grievances.

The best way for a union to prepare a case for arbitration is to review the history of the grievance. The arguments made by both sides at each step of the grievance procedure should be examined. The contract itself should again be researched to determine if any contract language has been overlooked, including clauses in previous agreements whose alteration or elimination may have an impact on this case.

Next, an outline of the case should be prepared listing the arguments the union will make as well as those it expects from management. After outlining the arguments, the union must develop the proof needed to substantiate them. Proof in arbitration takes two forms: written records and oral testimony of witnesses. *Written records* include personnel records, medical records, wage data, minutes of negotiation sessions, and arbitrator's decisions. When written records are introduced at the hearing, the union should make copies available to both the arbitrator and management. As much evidence as possible should be submitted in writing so the arbitrator will be able to refer to it while preparing the award. The union should not hesitate to request from management all the written material it feels necessary for the preparation and presentation of its case; the law requires the employer to provide the relevant material needed to process grievances. Cases with no disputes over the facts are usually determined by the language of the contract.

The *oral testimony* of witnesses rather than written material is more commonly used to introduce evidence at an arbitration hearing. The use of witnesses requires special preparation. The presenter of the union's case should interview them so that they know the questions they will be asked at the hearing. In preparation, the union representative should also assume the role of management and cross-examine them with questions the other side is expected to raise. Thus the witness will know what to expect when called to testify. Cases involving disputes over facts, such as those involving discipline or promotions, are usually determined by the oral testimony of witnesses.

The union representative should advise the witness of the right to ask that a question be repeated if not heard the first time or if it is unclear. The witness might also ask that a question be repeated if he or she is unclear at the moment as to what answer should be given. It is important that the witness know that answers can be qualified so that he or she is not browbeaten into a "yes" or "no" response. The witness should also be instructed to answer all questions because a refusal to do so may prejudice the union's case. The witness should keep the answers brief, supplying only the information requested.

The union may find it useful to examine the decisions by the arbitrator as well as those of others that deal with the same subject. This may help a union to determine whether a general set of principles exists that arbitrators apply to the subject under consideration. As a result of its findings, the union may alter its line of argument to incorporate standards generally recognized by arbitrators.

Sometimes the physical surroundings where the grievance occurred are of importance. If so, the union should not hesitate to request a visit to them by the arbitrator. In a discharge case the ability of witnesses to see and hear who said what might well be determined by exactly where the event took place. The representatives of both parties should accompany the arbitrator on a visit to the workplace.

The parties to the grievance have the authority to determine the procedures governing the hearing. More often than not, however, they choose not to exercise this right and the arbitrator makes this decision.

Sometimes union and management can agree on a submission that is presented to the arbitrator either before or at the hearing. The submission is a written memorandum signed by both parties that states the exact issue or issues on which the arbitrator is to rule. If more than one question is involved, it may list the order in which the parties wish the questions to be heard. The purpose of the submission is to eliminate the delay resulting when the parties disagree at a hearing over the issues to be decided. Use of the submission can speed the hearing process and cut costs because it reduces the number of witnesses required by both sides. If the parties cannot agree, the arbitrator may adopt the statement found on the original grievance form. If the original grievance is poorly written and is unclear, the arbitrator may formulate the issue. Sometimes the arbitrator is unable to do so until late in the hearing, after a good deal of the testimony has been given by both sides.

Often the parties are unable to agree because the union wants the submission stated in broad terms while management prefers the questions to be drawn as narrowly as possible. In many cases the grievance deals with an issue where the contract is silent or unclear. Therefore, the union may attempt to base its case on evidence broader than the specific language of the contract.

Sometimes one of the parties may seek to introduce a new issue at the hearing. For example, management originally may have stated its reason for discharge to be excessive absenteeism. At the hearing it announces that the discharge was based on the grievant's poor quality work. If the union objects to this switch, it will probably be upheld by the arbitrator on the ground that no previous discussions took place on this subject, and the union is therefore in no position to judge the validity of this charge.

Each side determines who will present its case. The union's case may be handled by an international union representative, by the staff counsel of the union, an ad hoc attorney, or by any other designated representative. Management's case is usually handled by the industrial relations department, the company counsel, or an outside attorney. Neither side may restrict the choice of the other.

The arbitration hearing is not open to the public. Only persons with a direct interest may be present. Others may attend with the permission of the arbitrator. Sometimes college students studying industrial relations are invited to observe the process. Occasionally a controversy develops concerning when witnesses should be present. The rule of thumb is that they may not be in the room when others are testifying so that they are not unduly influenced.

The hearing begins with an oral opening statement made first by the party initiating the grievance—usually the union, except in discipline cases. Management then does likewise. In discharge and disciplinary grievances management is expect to go first. To do otherwise makes it difficult for the union to offer a defense because it has not received management's rationale for its actions. Sometimes the arbitrator will request management to make the initial presentation when an employee has been turned down for promotion because he or she was judged unequal in ability to a junior employee. Because blue-collar workers lack promotional opportunities within the bargaining unit, arbitrators may place the burden of proof on management to demonstrate clearly the alleged lack of ability.

Sometimes an expanded opening statement in writing, called the prehearing brief, is also presented to the arbitrator. Its purpose is to lay out the theory of the case for the arbitrator. The union should assume the arbitrator knows nothing about the grievance other than what is presented at the hearing. A good opening statement identifies the issue before the arbitrator, states what the union seeks to prove, and what evidence the union will provide as proof, and then specifies the relief sought and the authority for the arbitrator to grant it. The settlement request should be specific since the arbitrator may be unaware of all the remedies required to make the grievant whole again.

In most cases the testimony of witnesses is used to prove the union's case.[6] This should be done through the use of its own witnesses rather than by attempting to break down those of management during cross-examination. The identity and competency of the witness is established first. Then, with as few interruptions as possible, the witness should be permitted to give testimony in his or her own words, stating only that which is known, i.e., what was seen and heard. In contrast to the courts, arbitrators permit some irrelevant testimony because it is assumed that they are better qualified to sift fact from fiction than is a jury of peers. Whether or not arbitrators have the authority to subpoena witnesses or compel them to testify in arbitration cases is a matter of state law. But arbitrators will take into account the failure of a party to provide a witness or to cooperate.

Each witness is subject to cross-examination. The cross examination should disclose facts the witness may not have related during his or her testimony, correct inaccurate statements, reconcile apparent contradictions, and attack the reliability of management's witnesses. The union may reexamine any of its witnesses who were cross-examined by management in order to clarify any of the answers that were given.

Sometimes the union is tempted to prove its case through a vigorous cross-examination of a hostile witness. When doing so, the union should never ask a question to which it does not know the

---

[6]Boaz Siegal, *Proving Your Arbitration Case* (Washington, D.C.: The Bureau of National Affairs, Inc., 1961).

answer. The danger exists that the witness may provide answers with which the union is unprepared to deal or the witness may simply repeat previous testimony and as a result emphasize damaging points made earlier. The cross-examination should be kept short. In some cases where contradictory testimony is involved it may be best not to cross-examine at all. The arbitrator will resolve the conflict by determining which witness seemed the most credible.

Careful preparation of witnesses can help establish their credibility, which depends on a number of factors. When the facts are in dispute, arbitrators tend to accept the testimony of those having the least to gain. For example, the testimony of a worker with a long disciplinary record grieving a discharge for insubordination will be viewed as less believable than the word of the supervisor who was responsible for the action.

Other factors are also used to determine credibility.[7] Does the witness appear nervous? Make eye contact with the questioner? Recollect the details of the situation about which he or she is testifying and communicate them effectively? All these qualities can be developed if the witness is informed about what to expect on the stand. In addition the witness's reputation for honesty will be weighed together with any of his or her previous statements on the same subject that are inconsistent with the testimony.

Post-hearing briefs are often utilized in arbitration hearings. These are more common than prehearing briefs, as well as more voluminous, because they not only summarize the testimony, but also draw conclusions. No new evidence should be introduced into the post-hearing brief, but it is appropriate to discuss similar cases and to cite articles and other references. If management requests the right to submit a post-hearing brief, the union usually feels it must do likewise to provide balance.

Transcripts will sometimes be made of an arbitration hearing. The main material contained in the transcript is the opening statement, the testimony of witnesses, and the closing statement. If written material is introduced as evidence, the union should be sure to provide the recorder with a copy so it can be included in the transcript. The use of post-hearing briefs and transcripts will often delay an arbitrator's award.[8] It may take two or more weeks before the

---

[7]Beeler, *Arbitration for the Local Union*, pp. 55–56.

[8]In 1980, 27 percent of the cases employing FMCS arbitrators used transcripts. 33 FMCS ANN. REP. 38 (1980).

transcript is available. Then the arbitrator sets a deadline for receiving the briefs, which usually adds an additional two or three weeks. Upon receipt of the briefs the arbitrator has 30 days to render the award.

In order to limit the expenses of a transcript and post-hearing brief, a union can try to negotiate these two clauses as additions to the arbitration section of its contract:

> Written transcripts will be made of an arbitration hearing only with the mutual consent of the two parties.
>
> Post-hearing briefs will be permitted only when both parties agree to file such briefs.

Unless the grievance involves an important contract interpretation or is otherwise an extremely complicated case, the union may be better off seeking to restrict the use of transcripts and post-hearing briefs. Ordinarily the notes of the arbitrator provide adequate information to reach a decision.

An arbitrator is responsible for becoming fully informed about the issue. Therefore, the arbitrator has the right to ask questions of all parties at the hearing when the facts are in dispute or when additional information is required. The arbitrator may also examine the entire contract to determine if additional clauses have a bearing on the case.

The purpose of the arbitrator's award is to end the grievance with a final and binding decision. The award itself should be short and should deal with each of the issues raised. The opinion, which is the reasoning used to arrive at the award, varies in length depending on the complexity of the case. The award should deal only with the issues submitted and should not cover other questions regardless of how important the arbitrator may regard them.

An arbitrator's decision in an ad hoc case usually applies only to the employees at a single workplace; an umpire's decision, on the other hand, is binding on all of the employees at all of the plants of the company covered by the contract. In either case a decision remains in effect unless overturned in a later arbitration or altered by the mutual consent of the union and management.

Sometimes the award may be unclear and the parties will request a rehearing to clarify an issue. When jointly requested by the parties, the arbitrator will normally comply. When only one side makes the request, the arbitrator is reluctant to act unless there are important reasons to do so.

A number of practices of labor and management are harmful to the arbitration process.[9] These practices include the excessive use of arbitration for the purpose of increasing costs, thereby harassing the other side; concealment of the facts; distortion of the truth or falsification of records; refusal to provide the other party with relevant information; resort to legal technicalities; failure to prepare witnesses for testimony; failure to cooperate with the arbitrator; and name calling or argumentation with the other side.

Winning an arbitration case begins with the steward's collection of information when the grievance is first filed. Effective record keeping and careful interviewing of all parties involved are essential. Because of the substantial amount of money involved in arbitration, the union must screen its cases carefully to decide whether it wishes to invest not only the money but the necessary time.

The Costs of Arbitration

The rising costs of arbitration are a major concern of both labor and management. In part these increased costs are due to increasingly complex grievances which require longer hearings and more time spent studying and writing the awards. Problems which have given rise to more complex grievances in recent years have been bumping procedures governing layoffs, the subcontracting of work previously done by members of the bargaining unit, and changes in incentive systems. As a result, the fees of arbitrators have increased. In addition, charges associated with the hearing itself have risen.

The costs a union may face in a typical arbitration case are:

- Arbitrator's fee and expenses;
- Lost-time pay for the grievant and witnesses;
- Fee for the presenter of the union's case;
- Expenses for the preparation of exhibits;
- Cost of a prehearing brief;
- Cost of a post-hearing brief and written transcript of the hearing;
- Meeting room costs;
- The fee charged by the AAA if it supplies a panel of names.

Areas of Cost Control. A union has some control over the total cost of arbitration. To begin with, it can more carefully screen

---

[9]Elkouri and Elkouri, *How Arbitration Works*, p. 249.

cases, thereby eliminating weak cases from arbitration. If union and management can mutually agree on an arbitrator, the AAA's fee for supplying a list of arbitrators can be avoided.

Some contracts call for management to pay the lost time of all witnesses regardless of whether they appear on behalf of the union or management. If the union is unable to negotiate such a provision, it should restrict its witnesses to the number necessary to prove its cases. Quite frequently a union will engage in overkill by producing several witnesses who testify to the same set of facts.

If an attorney presents the union's case, his or her fee may be the single largest cost item, because an attorney's hourly or per diem rate is considerably higher than an arbitrator's. Most grievances do not involve legal issues; an attorney is not required unless a union is convinced that all of mankind's knowledge is embodied in a law degree. As an alternative the union can provide training for its own representatives to present arbitration cases. A number of unions, as a matter of policy, use this procedure. The AAA, the FMCS, and the labor programs at a number of state universities conduct such training programs.

Meeting room costs are involved when either one or both parties refuses to meet on the premises of the other. Ordinarily management's facilities are adequate, and it will be the union that raises the objection. This action may be taken because the collective bargaining relationship is new and neither party trusts the motives of the other—both prefer to meet on neutral grounds. Or, the meeting room offered by management may be one where disciplinary action is usually meted out, placing the union at a psychological disadvantage. If these problems can be overcome, a significant savings can be made. Furthermore, if the meeting is held at the workplace, records and witnesses are more accessible and the arbitrator can more readily visit the workplace.

Arbitrator Fees. The fee charged by the arbitrator, which usually represents about 15–20 percent of the total cost of arbitration, falls into three categories: travel time, hotel room, meals, and incidentals; per diem charges for hearing a case or cases; and per diem charges for study time spent in analyzing and writing the award. In general the more experienced the arbitrator, the higher the fee will be. Here, a union can save money without jeopardizing its case by using a lesser-known person, especially with grievances involving routine contract interpretation or minor disciplinary actions.

If a hearing is postponed or cancelled, some arbitrators charge the parties part of their normal fee. This charge can be avoided when both parties make every effort to resolve the grievance internally before selecting an arbitrator. All too often, either one of the parties may decide to hang tough just short of the arbitration date in the hope that the other side will concede the issue. A last minute compromise may be reached by such strategy, and the hearing will then be cancelled. As a result, an arbitrator with a heavy caseload must rearrange his or her schedule. Arbitrators seek to discourage such action by imposing a penalty charge.

The 1981 report of the Federal Mediation and Conciliation Service lists the current charges of arbitrators who appear on its rosters. The report indicated that arbitrators' daily fees and expenses averaged $299.62. Parties were charged a total of 3.21 days per case which was divided as follows:

.33   Travel Days
1.00   Hearing Days
1.88   Study Days

It should be noted that almost two study days are required for each day of hearings. In part this ratio is a result of time spent evaluating lengthy post-hearing briefs.[10]

Post-hearing briefs tend to be very costly, because the parties usually want a transcript of the hearing. Transcripts, although necessary for some cases, substantially add to the cost of arbitration. One study made in 1976 by a staff member of the AFL-CIO cites the average cost for a transcript as about $500 per day.[11] This figure would, no doubt, be substantially higher today.

Table 10 shows the increase in charges that occurred in FMCS cases based on a sample for the fiscal years 1971 and 1981.

Loser-Pay Arbitration. Under most contracts the total charges of arbitrators are split equally between the two parties. However, "loser-pay" arbitration is sometimes offered as a solution for the rising cost. Instead of the contract stating "The expense of the arbitration will be borne equally by both parties," the contract reads "The arbitration fees and expenses will be borne by the losing side of the arbitration." Each side, however, continues to pay for whomever it uses to present its case and the preparation of briefs and exhibits.

The advocates of this proposal believe that if the loser pays the entire cost, both parties will be pressured into screening their griev-

---

[10]34 FMCS Ann. Rep. 37 (1981).

[11]John Zalusky, "Updating a Vital Process," *The AFL-CIO American Federationist* (Nov. 1976), pp. 1–8.

Table 10. Average Per Diem Rates, Fees, and Expenses Charged by Arbitrators Based on Closed Arbitration Award Cases Sampled: Fiscal Years 1971 & 1981

	1971	1981	Percent Change From Fiscal Year 1971	Percent Change Consumer Price Index 1971–1981
Per Diem Rate	$168.88	$ 299.62	77	
Total Charged	566.59	1132.31	100	125.3
Amount of Fee	480.88	988.76	106	
Amount of Expense	85.71	143.55	67	

Source: *Federal Mediation and Conciliation Service: Thirty-Third Annual Report, Fiscal Year 1980* (Washington, D.C.: Government Printing Office, 1981) p. 37.

ances more carefully and the number of cases arbitrated will drop. Furthermore, a management that seeks to bankrupt a union by pushing an excessive number of grievances to arbitration will find this to be a costly practice when it must foot the entire bill. Likewise, the union that, for political reasons, knowingly arbitrates cases which it cannot win will find it a costly practice.

Why then has loser-pay arbitration caught on only in a few small workplaces? On the average unions lose more arbitration cases than they win, though most grievances are filed by the union. The cases arbitrated are those involving an element of doubt, because management usually concedes well before arbitration those cases demonstrating a clear-cut violation of the contract. A union agreeing to loser-pay arbitration may be discouraged from arbitrating a borderline case because of the possibility of increased cost. Yet a major purpose of the grievance procedure is to resolve complaints where the contract is silent or unclear. Likewise loser-pay arbitration is detrimental to the cathartic effect of arbitration. Even a worker losing an arbitration case many times feels that the workplace system of justice functions because he or she received a hearing. The loser-pay system, however, may discourage unions from taking cases for such purely political reasons.

Critics of loser-pay arbitration also charge that the arbitrator may be more inclined to split decisions in a multigrievance hearing in order that one side not be overburdened financially. A more important criticism of loser-pay arbitration is the difficulty in determining who is the loser. Usually the arbitrator has this responsibility, and it is not always easy. For example, who is the loser if (1) an arbitrator reinstates a discharged worker but does not award back-pay, or (2) a worker grieving a denial of promotion is not awarded the job, but the arbitrator rules that the worker must be promoted to the next open position?

Streamlining the Arbitration Process. Today, delay is a major problem with arbitration. Speedy action was an original reason for advocating arbitration rather than using the courts for settling grievances, for "justice delayed is justice denied." Except for some contracts negotiated by the Steelworkers union which allow workers to stay on the job and on the payroll until the award is made, a management decision remains in effect unless overturned by the grievance procedure. For example, a discharged worker remains off the job until the dismissal is overturned, or in the case of an improper work assignment, the worker must continue to perform until the order is changed. When an award calls for retroactive pay, the cost to the employer is no greater than if it had not violated the agreement and sometimes it is less, because any income earned elsewhere by the worker before reinstatement is deducted from the award. This practice is justified on the grounds that the grievant should not receive benefits over and above the actual loss. Finally, the speed with which a union settles grievances determines whether it is regarded as an effective organization by its members.

Table 11 compares, in days, the time between filing a grievance and the date the arbitrator rendered the award. It shows the level at which delay occurs.

This table shows that over the past 10 years the *total* number of days spent in processing a grievance from its original date of filing through arbitration has fallen almost 10 percent. Increased FMCS efficiency during the prehearing phase, resulting from the use of computers, enables the agency to respond faster to requests for a panel of names.

On the other hand, increased delay occurs between the date of appointment and date of hearing. This delay is caused by the number of other cases an arbitrator has taken on and the insistence by both parties on using the most experienced, and busiest, personnel.

Expedited Grievance Procedures. There are a number of actions the union can take to eliminate delay,[12] though unions may not want to employ some of them if they create as many problems as they correct. Depending on the number of workers covered by the contract, one of these actions is to reduce the number of steps in the

---

[12]Some of these proposals are excerpted from the Zalusky article cited above.

Table 11. Days Elapsed From Grievance Filing Date to Arbitrator's Award, 1971–1981

	1971	1981	Percent Change From 1971
Total Days	250.9	230.3	− 8.2
Pre-Hearing Phase	203.8	196.7	− 3.5
Between grievance filing and request for panel	83.3	79.2	− 4.9
Between panel request date and panel sent	11.1	5.1	− 54.1
Between date panel sent and appointment of arbitrator	46.0	41.7	− 10.4
Between date of appointment and date of hearing	63.4	70.6	+ 11.4
Post-Hearing Phase Between hearing date and date award rendered by arbitrator	47.1	33.6	− 28.7

Source: Federal Mediation and Conciliation Service: Thirty-Fourth Annual Report, Fiscal Year 1981 (Washington, D.C.: Government Printing Office, 1982) p. 39.

grievance procedure. Most establishments do not need a five-step nor, in some cases, even a four-step procedure.

In addition, after studying the decision-making structure of management, the union may conclude that some types of grievances should bypass one or more of the steps in the grievance procedure. For example, there is not much point in filing a discharge grievance with the immediate supervisor when only the industrial relations department has the authority to rehire. Likewise grievances about pension eligibility or disputes over an incentive system may require a decision by higher level supervisors. Time can be saved if the grievance is filed initially with the management representative who has the authority to deal with it.

Some unions negotiate an agreement with management that provides that no precedent is set when a complaint is settled at the first or sometimes second step in the procedure. Management is usually willing to grant the immediate supervisor more authority to make decisions when it knows that it will not be haunted later by the settlement. As a result of increased authority, the immediate supervisor can make an agreement with the steward without first getting the approval of someone higher in the management. Therefore, more emphasis is placed on oral settlement rather than written grievances, since there is less need for careful record keeping when the emphasis on precedent is reduced.

This method also presents certain dangers. Different standards may develop in different departments. Workers in a department having what they perceive as inferior conditions may demand equal treatment and may not be persuaded when the union tries to explain that the lack of standardization is the trade-off for faster handling of grievances.

An agreement that permits no grievance settlement to serve as a precedent allows a union to engage in wholesale wheeling and dealing. Some Teamsters contracts contain such provisions. Under them one worker may win a grievance but a month later another may lose a similar grievance. Why have two different settlements for the same problem? Sometimes the union trades off the grievance of a second worker in return for winning one considered to be more important to the organization. At times, a union may concede the grievance because the member is in the bad graces of the organization or because management has paid off the union representative. The lack of precedent makes such actions possible.

Time and money are saved when the union and management agree to submit to the arbitrator an agreed-upon statement of the nature of the grievance, known as a submission. As a result fewer witnesses are required. Sometimes, however, the hearing itself is postponed in the hope that an agreement on the facts can be reached. If no agreement results, however, additional time is wasted that might be better spent preparing for the hearing.

The decision-making mechanism used by the union to determine which cases to submit to arbitration may also involve delay. Bylaws of a number of local unions authorize the membership to make this decision. Many local unions, however, do not hold meetings during one or more of the summer months. The requirement of membership approval may postpone a request for a panel of names for as long as four months.

Expedited Arbitration. Expedited arbitration is a method for dealing with the dual problems of cost and delay. It seeks to streamline arbitration by discarding some conventional arbitration procedures and speeding up others. Effort by both parties is directed at agreement on a submission to be presented to the arbitrator. Usually the opening statements of both sides are shortened as well. Major savings in both cost and time are achieved by the elimination in expedited arbitration of post-hearing briefs and transcripts.

Expedited arbitration relies on the early issuance of the award to reduce delay. This may be done through a bench decision, where the arbitrator issues an award upon the completion of the hearing without any additional time spent in study or in writing the award. Or, the arbitrator may issue a decision soon after the hearing and follow with a full written opinion at a later date.

In order to work effectively, expedited arbitration requires specific guidelines in several areas:[13]

(1) Clear identification of the type of cases eligible for expedited arbitration;

(2) An adequate supply of trained arbitrators;

(3) The prompt appointment of arbitrators;

(4) The prompt scheduling of cases;

(5) The prompt rendering of awards; and

(6) The cooperation of all parties to make the system work.

The best-known examples of expedited arbitration exist in the U.S. Postal Service and in the basic Steelworkers contract covering 10 major steel companies. Expedited arbitration has also been used for several years by the United Paperworkers International Union and the International Paper Company and by the International Union of Electrical Workers with the General Electric Company.

Expedited arbitration is expanding into the public sector. It is contained in contracts between the American Federation of Government Employees and the San Francisco regional office of the Social Security Administration, the United Transportation Union and the Long Island Railroad, and the city of New York and its unions.

Postal Expedited Arbitration. The single largest group covered by expedited arbitration are the 600,000 workers employed by the U.S. Postal Service. This procedure was first written into the 1973 contract in an effort to reduce the 10,000 grievances involving minor disciplinary action that were awaiting conventional arbitration.[14]

All Postal Service expedited hearings are conducted informally. No transcripts or briefs are used and the awards are not precedents. If the case turns out to be more complex than anticipated, it

---

[13]Michael F. Hoellering, "Expedited Grievance Arbitration: First Steps," *Proceedings of the 27th Annual Winter Meeting of the National Academy of Arbitrators*, ed. James L. Stern and Barbara Dennis (Madison, Wisconsin: Industrial Relations Research Association, 1974), p. 325.

[14]Frederic W. Frost, "New Developments in Labor Arbitration," 29 LAB. L.J. 466 (1978).

is referred to the regular arbitration procedure. The arbitrator's decision usually consists of a single-page award and is made available within 48 hours. The arbitrators are paid their normal hearing-day fee, which averages about $200.00, plus expenses. They are not, however, paid for study or writing time, and they are required to hear up to three cases per day.

The expedited arbitrators are appointed on a rotating basis from the members of 30 area panels throughout the country.[15] Most are experienced arbitrators on the AAA and the FMCS lists.

Two problems have been associated with postal expedited arbitration. It has been difficult to find enough arbitrators willing to serve, and initially, both the union and management found they lacked trained personnel to present their case at a hearing. The U.S. Postal Service used the AAA to train its regional staff, while postal unions used university labor education programs and the George Meany Center for Labor Studies.

Steelworker Expedited Arbitration. The Steelworkers' program of expedited arbitration in the basic steel contract began a few years earlier, in 1971.[16] It was instituted because a large backlog of cases developed as local unions, unable to settle grievances at the plant level, sent them to the fourth step, where the international union representative and company headquarters tried to reach settlements. Many were routine factual disputes. By utilizing expedited arbitration for easier cases, it was hoped that conventional arbitration could be devoted to the more complex issues. As a result, panels of arbitrators were set up in 12 steel centers. In contrast to the U.S. Postal Service system of expedited arbitration where experienced arbitrators are used, the steel panels are staffed primarily by 200 young attorneys. Cases are assigned on an alphabetical rotation of the panel members. If a case proves to be more complicated than anticipated, the arbitrator or both parties by mutual agreement may refer the grievance to conventional arbitration. Although attorneys hear the case, neither party uses an attorney to present its position.

Steelworker hearings and decisions are completed from within 10 days to three weeks from the time the decision to arbitrate is made. Awards are usually issued within 48 hours. There is agree-

---

[15]Bernard Cushman, "Some Reflections Upon the Postal Experience With Expedited Arbitration," *Proceedings of the 27th Annual Winter Meeting*, ed. James L. Stern and Barbara Dennis (Madison, Wisconsin: Industrial Relations Research Association, 1974), p. 332.

[16]Zalusky, "Updating a Vital Process," p. 5.

ment that the written award should be understandable to the parties rather than only to attorneys, that it should state the factual situation in dispute, the decision itself, and the rationale for the conclusion arrived at by the arbitrator. An analysis of the awards indicates that the decisions made by the relatively inexperienced arbitrators are equal in quality to those found under conventional arbitration. This is due in part to the fact that these arbitrators handle less complex cases dealing with minor discipline disputes, allocation of overtime, or supervisors who are doing bargaining unit work.

Some conclusions can be drawn from these two plans. In the steel industry the local parties who handle the expedited arbitration cases acquire a greater understanding of the contract, and employee complaints about the inadequacy of the grievance procedure have been reduced.

The backlog of grievances both in the steel industry and the Postal Service has decreased, but not at the rate anticipated. Under both systems the local unions still do not screen grievances as closely as they should. Because the Postal Service insists on the use of experienced arbitrators who are in short supply, delays result from the unavailability of persons to hear the case.

The use of expedited arbitration by Steelworkers' locals other than in basic steel has not spread as rapidly as expected, perhaps because members feel that if their case merits an arbitration hearing, they are entitled to the conventional one.

Management has its own objections to expedited arbitration. For example, it has no control over the selection of the arbitrator assigned from a panel on a rotating basis. Because post-hearing briefs are prohibited to reduce delay and cost, management argues that arbitration becomes too cheap.

New arbitrators have a complaint of their own. They charge that arbitrators, whether desiring to enter the conventional or expedited field, become acceptable by experience and that they can obtain experience only when acceptable. The shortage of arbitrators in general, therefore, continues.

In theory, at least, expedited arbitration appears to be an ideal answer for discharge cases, most of which require no contract interpretation but simply a determination as to which set of conflicting testimony is the most credible. In practice, however, it is over discharges that unions might face suits charging a breach of their duty of fair representation. A court's determination as to whether there has been a breach of duty may well be decided by examining the transcript of the arbitration hearing. If expedited arbitration is used and no transcript exists, the union may find it difficult to present an adequate defense of its actions. Therefore, it may not be advisable to refer discharge cases to expedited arbitration.

The Legal Status of Arbitration

In many respects the legal status of arbitration is firmly established as a result of decisions by the U.S. Supreme Court.[17] The Court in *Textile Workers v. Lincoln Mills* ruled that a union may sue an employer in either federal or state court to enforce a contract, including a clause to arbitrate. Usually the union will use the federal courts, citing Section 301 of the Taft-Hartley Act, because historically state courts have been more antilabor.[18]

Furthermore, the Supreme Court stated in its *Steelworkers Trilogy* decisions that if the employer argues that an issue is not eligible for arbitration under the contract, the arbitrator, not the courts, should determine arbitrability and that any doubt should be resolved in favor of arbitration. Arbitration has been upheld because it is considered a trade-off for a no-strike pledge by the union for the duration of the contract. The Court stated in one of the *Trilogy* cases that it would not substitute its judgment for that of the arbitrator's because:

> The labor arbitrator is usually chosen because of the parties' confidence in his knowledge of the common law of the shop. . . .
> The ablest judge cannot be expected to bring the same experience and competence to bear upon the determination of a grievance, because he cannot be similarly informed.[19]

Not all judges agree with this idealized version of arbitrators as we shall see later.

In general, it can be said that, on the merits of the case, an arbitrator's decision is final and binding. On procedural questions an award may be overturned where there is evidence that: it was based on fraud; the rights of either party were prejudiced by the misconduct

---

[17]*Textile Workers v. Lincoln Mills*, 353 US 448, 40 LRRM 2113 (1957); *Steelworkers v. Enterprise Wheel and Car Corporation*, 363 US 593, 46 LRRM 2423 (1960); *Steelworkers v. Warrior and Gulf Navigation Co.*, 363 US 574, 46 LRRM 2416 (1960); *Steelworkers v. American Mfg. Co.*, 363 US 564, 46 LRRM 2414 (1960).

[18]"Sec. 301. (a) Suits for violations of contract between an employer and a labor organization . . . may be brought in any district court of the United States. . . ."

[19]*Steelworkers v. Warrior and Gulf Navigation Co.*, above, note 17.

of the arbitrator; the arbitrator exceeded his or her authority under the contract; the hearings were concluded before the losing party could present its case; or the union breached its duty of fair representation. (See Chapter 7 for a discussion of fair representation.)

The Supreme Court has found two important exceptions to the final and binding nature on the merit of an arbitrator's decision. In *Alexander v. Gardner-Denver* it ruled that complaints charging discrimination based on race, color, religion, sex, national origin, or ancestry are reviewable by the courts.[20] This decision stated that, although arbitration is informal and proceeds more quickly than the court and is ideal for contract interpretation, it is less useful for judicial fact-finding, because the competency of the arbitrator is restricted to the law of the shop and not the law of the land. The opinion concluded that an arbitrator's decision may be submitted as evidence in court and will be given appropriate weight. Therefore, a worker who feels he or she has been a victim of discrimination has two options available, and the union should see that the worker is protected under both rights.

This Court decision created a dilemma for the union. On the one hand, if the union appeals a discrimination grievance all the way through arbitration, it may have wasted its money, because the issue can be raised all over again through the federal court system. On the other hand, if it chooses not to proceed with the grievance, it runs the risk of losing the support of its members who have the right to have their complaints processed.

The second exception occurred in *Hines v. Anchor Motor Freight* when the court ruled that an arbitrator's decision is not final and binding if the union breaches its duty of fair representation.[21] In this case several Teamsters were discharged for allegedly falsifying motel receipts. They protested their innocence and asked their union representative to investigate the motel and were assured appropriate action would be taken. In fact no investigation was conducted and the discharge was upheld in arbitration. (Under this contract a joint labor-management committee was empowered to issue a final and binding decision.) Later it was learned that a motel clerk had falsified the books and pocketed the difference. The court then ordered the Teamster members reinstated because the arbitra-

---

[20]*Alexander v. Gardner-Denver*, 415 US 36, 7 FEP CASES 81 (1974).
[21]*Hines v. Anchor Motor Freight, Inc.*, 424 US 554, 91 LRRM 2481 (1976).

tor issued an erroneous decision as a result of the union breaching its duty of fair representation by failing to investigate the motel.

Deferral to Arbitration. Over the years the NLRB has had difficulty in deciding how to handle complaints that charge both a violation of a contract and an unfair labor practice. For example, a steward allegedly discharged for causing trouble and filing frivolous grievances could file an unfair labor practice under Section 8(a)(3) of the Taft-Hartley Act which makes it illegal for an employer "by discrimination with regard to hire or tenure of employment or any term of condition of employment to encourage or discourage membership in any labor organization." The same complaint may also be a contract violation and therefore subject to the grievance procedure and ultimately arbitration if the contract contains a clause prohibiting discriminatory treatment based on union activity. The union must then decide if it wishes to utilize the NLRB, the grievance procedure, or both. If the union files its complaint with both, then the NLRB must make a decision. Should it process the union's complaint as an unfair labor practice, or should it defer to arbitration?

NLRB policies on deferral have swung back and forth over the years depending in part on the labor philosophy of the President who appoints the Board members.[22] The proponents of deferral have several arguments:

(1) The parties to the dispute should be encouraged to use their own procedure, because the use of arbitration will have a positive effect on labor relations. Equally important, the arbitrator better understands the common law of the shop, while the decisions of the administrative agency may disrupt the collective bargaining process.

(2) Because neither party is faced with any direct cost when processing an unfair labor practice complaint, deferral to arbitration may put pressure on labor and management to voluntarily settle the dispute in order to save the expense of arbitration.

(3) Arbitration can produce the most acceptable solution in the shortest period of time.

(4) Arbitrator's decisions have a higher degree of finality than do those of the NLRB which can be appealed through the federal court system.

---

[22]*Speilberg Mfg. Co.*, 112 NLRB 1080, 36 LRRM 1152 (1955); *Collyer Insulated Wire*, 192 NLRB 837, 77 LRRM 1931 (1971). These are the two major cases dealing with deferral.

(5) A deferral policy discourages the union from forum shopping—first trying one approach and then the other when not satisfied with the initial decision.

(6) Deferral reduces the NLRB's heavy case load.[23]

The opponents of deferral have their arguments as well. They reason that: deferral ignores the intent of Congress which granted the NLRB exclusive jurisdiction over unfair labor practices; the cost of arbitration may result in unions allowing valid complaints to die; the scope of review in arbitration is too limited for the full treatment of statutory matters; the remedies available to the arbitrator are more limited than those of the NLRB; a number of arbitrators lack the appropriate training to make legal interpretations.[24]

The NLRB will defer to arbitration if the following conditions are met:

(1) The parties contractually agreed to be bound by the arbitrator's decision;

(2) The proceedings were fair and regular;

(3) The arbitration decision covers the alleged unfair labor practice; and

(4) The decision of the arbitrator is "not repugnant" to purposes and policies of the National Labor Relations Act.

If the case fails to meet any of these criteria, the NLRB General Counsel may issue a complaint and prosecute the case under the Taft-Hartley Act. Most public employment relations boards at the state and local government level also have procedures governing deferral to arbitration which closely follow NLRB criteria.[25]

As a matter of policy, unions should continue to file unfair labor practice charges even though the NLRB may defer to the grievance procedure and arbitration. Filing the charge guarantees the union's claim to NLRB action if problems occur when the complaint is processed through the grievance procedure. It also ensures that the Board will examine as part of its tracking process the arbitrator's handling of the case to see that it meets NLRB standards. It is important for the union to remember that it has only a six-month period in which to file an unfair labor practice charge.

---

[23]Stephen L. Hayford and Lynelle M. Wood, "Deferral to Grievance Arbitration in Unfair Labor Practice Matters: The Public Sector Treatment," 32 Lab. L.J. 680 (1981).

[24]*Ibid.*, p. 681.

[25]*Ibid.*, p. 682–83.

Standards Evolving Out of Arbitration

Standards of Contract Interpretation. In theory arbitrators are not bound by precedent to the degree that judges are. In practice, however, common guidelines have evolved that are followed by most arbitrators. They relate to standards governing the interpretation of the contract and the procedures to be followed in evaluating the factual situation surrounding different types of grievances.

The guidelines dealing with contract interpretation are summarized here.[26]

(1) An arbitrator will not give clear and unambiguous contract language a meaning other than that expressed. If, however, the arbitrator finds that, as a result of a mutual mistake or a typographical error, the parties used language or punctuation which does not express their true intent, an interpretation may be made which does express the true intent of labor and management.

(2) Contract language that is specific will usually be held to supersede more general clauses.

(3) To mention one item of a group or a class of items and not to mention another is interpreted to mean that the excluded items were not meant to be covered, unless a list of items is followed by a statement explaining that the clause is meant to be illustrative, but not necessarily inclusive.

(4) The meaning of words and phrases will be judged by the context in which they appear.

(5) An arbitrator will examine the contract as a whole under the assumption that all parts of the agreement have some meaning, or the parties would not have included them. If an arbitrator finds that alternative interpretations of a clause are possible, one of which would give meaning and effect to another provision of the contract while the other would render that provision meaningless or ineffective, the arbitrator will be inclined to use the interpretation which gives effect to all provisions.

(6) Arbitrators give words their ordinary and popular meaning unless there is evidence that the parties meant other-

---

[26]Harrison, *Preparing and Presenting Your Arbitration Case*, pp. 23–45; Elkouri and Elkouri, *How Arbitration Works*, pp. 296–320.

wise. Technical terms will be interpreted in a technical sense unless clearly used otherwise. A word used by the parties in one sense is to be interpreted the same way throughout the contract unless there is a specific definition to the contrary.

(7) Where the contract is silent or unclear, the arbitrator will attempt to determine what the parties meant when the agreement was written. This meaning will govern the arbitrator's interpretation rather than any intent of the parties that can be read into the language.

(8) The arbitrator may study the history of negotiations as an aid in interpreting the contract, by examining minutes and records or by accepting oral testimony.

(9) The arbitrator will not consider compromise offers made by either party during negotiations prior to arbitration because they are aimed at reaching a settlement that might be less than that to which they are entitled under the contract.

(10) Most arbitrators will not support a past-practice grievance if it challenges contract language that is clear and unambiguous. The union must show that the practice was of a recurring nature over a substantial period of time and that both parties indicated acceptance by implicit or explicit agreement.

(11) When two interpretations of the contract are possible, one making the agreement lawful and the other making it unlawful, the former is adopted on the grounds that the parties intended to have a valid contract.

(12) If the contract language is ambiguous, arbitrators will usually strive to apply it so that it is reasonable and equitable to both parties.

(13) When one interpretation of a contract will bring just and reasonable results and another would lead to harsh or nonsensical results, the former will be used.

(14) Both arbitrators and the courts are reluctant to assess a penalty if another interpretation is reasonably possible. A discharged worker who is reinstated will usually have earnings received elsewhere deducted from any backpay award.

(15) Arbitrators are less inclined to apply a strict interpretation of contract language when the negotiators are inexperienced.

(16) Arbitrators require a heavy burden of proof from the party who urges that a prior arbitrator's decision should be reversed.

Just Cause in Disciplinary Proceedings. In most workplaces disciplinary actions are the major source of arbitrated grievances. It is in this area that arbitrators have developed the most comprehensive form of workplace common law. Most contracts give management the right to discipline for "just" or "proper" cause but provide no definition of the term. Principles extracted from arbitrators' decisions are used to fill the void. Seven general principles follow that are used to determine whether disciplinary action was taken for "just cause."[27] If one or more of them are violated, it is assumed that management's actions were arbitrary, capricious, or discriminatory.

(1) Management must inform the worker what conduct could result in possible or probable disciplinary action. The method of communication it uses may vary. In some workplaces information customarily is transmitted orally by the supervisor to the worker. In others, written statements may be distributed or work rules posted. Certain offenses, however, are considered so serious that official notice prohibiting them is not required before disciplinary action be taken. They include intoxication on the job, theft of property, insubordination, and fighting.

(2) The work rule must be reasonably related to the orderly, efficient, and safe operation of the employer's activity. Although a work rule can be challenged on the basis of unreasonableness, the worker must observe it until it is overturned through the grievance procedure. The only exceptions are rules that require illegal action or pose an immediate threat to the health or safety of the worker.

(3) Management must investigate whether a violation occurred before it takes disciplinary action. This requirement is an attempt to assure that the employee will know the details of the offense that is charged. Sometimes an employee's behavior requires immediate action by management before an investigation is completed if it appears that either the worker's safety of that of others may be

---

[27]*Grief Brothers Cooperage Corp.*, 42 LA 555 (Daugherty).

jeopardized. In such a case an employee who is later found innocent will be made whole again.

(4) Management's investigation must be conducted fairly and objectively. Its representative may act as both the prosecutor and judge, compiling the information and then issuing a decision, but may not also act as a witness against the worker.

(5) The evidence obtained by the investigation showing that the worker was guilty as charged must be substantial. This "preponderance of evidence" test must show that facts presented by management outweigh those offered by the union. When long-service employees are fired, a higher standard of proof, "beyond reasonable doubt," may be required by the arbitrator to sustain the discharges.

(6) Management must apply its rules, orders, and penalties on a nondiscriminatory basis. If it has been lax in enforcing them in the past, it must inform its work force of its intention to enforce them in the future. Otherwise, disciplinary action may be overturned on the grounds that it was discriminatory because others guilty of the same offense were not penalized.

(7) The degree of discipline administered must be reasonably related to both the seriousness of the proven offense and the service record of the employee. A trivial proven offense such as tardiness does not merit harsh discipline unless the worker was found guilty of the same offense a number of times in the past. A worker's past record may not be used to determine guilt on the present charge. It may be used, however, to determine the severity of the punishment if found guilty for the current offense. Therefore, based on past work records, management may assess some workers a lesser penalty than others who are guilty of the same offense.

Due Process. Disciplinary cases do not involve the interpretation of complex contract language.[28] Yet they often present difficult prob-

---

[28]Information summarizing the various reasons for disciplinary actions are found in Joel Seidman, *A Guide to Discipline in the Public Sector* (Honolulu: University of Hawaii Industrial Relations Center, 1977); *Grievance Guide* (Washington, D.C.: The Bureau of National Affairs, Inc., 1972); *Administration of the Labor Contract*, vol. 1 (Mundelein, Illinois: Callaghan & Co., 1963), pp. 369–430; Beeler, *Arbitration for the Local Union*, pp. 61–73; Elkouri and Elkouri, *How Arbitration Works*, pp. 610–66.

lems for arbitrators because both the facts and the testimony are usually in dispute, with no impartial witnesses available. Therefore, the arbitrator has the heavy burden of determining which testimony is most credible and the severity of the penalty to be applied. As a result, emphasis is placed on due process.

Due process implies that procedural requirements must be followed for the protection of the individual. The formal charges must be filed in a timely manner. Where the contract contains no time limit, the rule of reasonableness applies. The worker must be informed of all charges and additional ones may not be introduced after suspension or discharge. The union must be given a chance to protest management's action and the union must receive an opportunity to prepare a defense. Management has the burden of proof to show the misconduct occurred, but after doing so, the burden shifts to the union when its defense is that the penalty is excessive.

Disciplinary Action

Before upholding severe disciplinary penalties, arbitrators will often require evidence that corrective discipline was used on the grounds that the worker should be given an opportunity for improvement. As in the case of notification, corrective discipline is not required for serious offenses, such as fighting or stealing, on the grounds that everyone is well aware of the consequences of such acts.

There are recognized limits to the penalties that may be applied for disciplinary reasons. Negotiated benefits automatically due to workers, such as vacation time, may not be withheld. Demotions or transfers should not be used for disciplinary purposes, because such measures are suitable only when the worker is unable to perform the present job competently rather than used as forms of misconduct penalties.

Frequent reasons for disciplinary action include:

- Insubordination
- Abusive language
- Theft
- Damaging the employer's property
- Incompetency
- Violation of dress codes
- Absenteeism
- Fighting
- Drug Abuse

These reasons will be examined in an effort to provide clues to unions as to the kinds of arguments they must make before an arbitrator. The same degree of widespread agreement does not exist on these issues among arbitrators as it does on the procedural guidelines discussed earlier.

Insubordination. Insubordination is best defined as a refusal to obey a direct order of an authorized supervisory official during working hours on management's property. It occurs most commonly when a worker is told to perform an assignment which the worker feels is not within his or her classification, when it presents a health or safety hazard, or when production methods have changed. Merely questioning the legitimacy of an order is not insubordination. In order for behavior to be classified as such, management must clearly give an order, the worker must refuse to carry it out, management must repeat the order, and then management must clearly state the penalty for failing to comply.

A union representative, acting in an official capacity, is not usually subject to discipline for insubordination except for holding supervision up to ridicule in the presence of employees. The representative is entitled to present the union's position with vigor. Professional employees have more leeway in debating assignments with management on the grounds that they have the same background and training as their supervisors and therefore are in a good position to question their judgment.

The justification for "work now and grieve later" is found in a decision rendered by Harry Shulman when he was the umpire under the Ford Motor Company contract.

> But an industrial plant is not a debating society. Its object is production. When a controversy arises, production cannot wait for exhaustion of the grievance procedure. While the procedure is being pursued, production must go on. And someone must have the authority to direct the manner in which it is to go on until the controversy is settled. That authority is vested in supervision.[29]

Insubordination charges arising out of the refusal to perform work assignments reflect the frustration of workers with a system that requires compliance with an order of management but which provides no effective remedy when overturned. The best the worker can hope for in this type of case is that management will be told its

---

[29]*Ford Motor Co.*, 3 LA 779 (Shulman).

order was improper and admonished not to do it again. Any disciplinary penalty applied to the worker is usually upheld. Below are the type of questions to which the union should have answers when grievances related to insubordination are arbitrated.[30] The union should be prepared to answer similar questions relating to other reasons for disciplinary action.

(1) What job did the employee allegedly refuse to perform?
(2) Did the supervisor clearly assign the job by giving a direct order?
    (a) What were the instructions?
    (b) What was the conversation between parties?
    (c) Was abusive language involved?
    (d) Who are the witnesses and what are their versions of the incident?
(3) In what manner did the employee allegedly avoid the order?
(4) Was the employee involved in previous arguments of a similar nature?
(5) Were other workers prevented from doing their own work due to the alleged refusal?
(6) Was the steward called?
    (a) What role did the steward play?
(7) Was there a claim of physical inability to perform the job?
(8) Did the worker eventually do the job assigned?
(9) Did the worker give a reason for refusal to perform the assignment?
(10) Was management's request reasonable?

Abusive Language. Abusive and profane language is often associated with a refusal to obey a work order and is usually subject to severe discipline. The language used must be over and above that considered acceptable in the shop, which may vary considerably from that used with the general public. There are several common situations in which abusive language is often used: a worker is told to perform a work assignment, refuses, and calls the supervisor a foul name; a worker may call the supervisor foul names in front of other workers; a worker may call the supervisor a foul name privately and

---

[30]*The Grievance Handler's Handbook* (Detroit: United Auto Workers, 1979), pp. 25, 31.

then brag about it publicly; or the worker calls the supervisor names, is ordered to stop, but continues the name calling. In all of these situations the worker may be subject to disciplinary action.

Theft. Workplace theft is a major reason for disciplinary action. Management takes a hard line both against the theft of its own property and that of its employees. Arbitrators are reluctant to rely on the traditional "preponderance of evidence" proof in theft cases and instead apply the higher standard of "proof beyond a reasonable doubt" because workers discharged for this reason often find it difficult to obtain employment elsewhere. On the other hand, they agree that the employer is not required to inform the workers that theft may result in discharge nor comply with a corrective punishment procedure even when the stolen item is of limited value.

Some arbitrators may overturn disciplinary action when the methods employed to detect theft invade the worker's right to privacy. The requirement of a submission to lie detector tests or the search of personal property such as lockers, purses, lunch boxes, or cars may fall into this category. Many arbitrators, like the courts, will refuse to accept the results of lie detector tests because of their proven unreliability. Some states have outlawed them either as a condition of obtaining or retaining a job, or both.

The search of the private belongings of workers raises a constitutional issue: Should a private employer have the right to conduct random searches as it sees fit, when a law enforcement agency is required to obtain a search warrant based on reasonable cause before it can invade the privacy of citizens? Unfortunately, most arbitrators will not grant a worker in private employment the same protection enjoyed in this area by a counterpart in the public sector who is not subject to random searches by an agent of the state.

Damaging the Employer's Property and Incompetency. Management's property may be damaged as a result of carelessness, incompetency, or malice. Arbitrators apply different penalties for each. Carelessness is regarded as a form of misconduct because it is based on the assumption that the employee knows the job assignment, but has failed to carry it out. In reaching a decision an arbitrator will examine several factors: What is the probability of the same act of carelessness occurring again? Does the attitude of the employee demonstrate a desire to learn from past mistakes? What is the extent of the actual or potential injury resulting from the act of carelessness? What is the effect of the act of carelessness on management's customers? What effect will disciplining this employee have on the work habits of other workers? What is this worker's length of service? Management may discharge for carelessness, but it must show that discharge is an established penalty for the type of neglect involved in the case.

A charge of incompetence implies that the worker, for reasons beyond his or her control, is unable to perform an assignment adequately, even though the worker wishes to do so. Failure to perform properly may be due to a misunderstanding about what to do or a lack of knowledge of how to do the job. This situation calls for corrective rather than punitive action. Although arbitrators uphold discharges based on incompetency, they prefer to see management deal with the problem by retraining, demoting, or transferring the worker rather than by discharging him or her.

Malicious or deliberate destruction of management's property is dealt with severely. If the action is malicious, the dollar amount of damage is unimportant and management need only prove that it was done deliberately.

Dress Code Violations. During the last two decades a number of grievances relating to personal appearance have been arbitrated when the employer disciplined workers for violation of its dress code.

Arbitrators will uphold dress codes if there is a reasonable relationship between the grooming standard and health and safety considerations or if it can be shown that the code is necessary to protect the employer's image with the public. Sometimes its announced purpose is to prevent employees from being distracted while working. In addition the standard must be clear, unambiguous, and consistently enforced.

Arbitrators expect the employer's dress code to conform to contemporary mores. Since there is no clear consensus as to what is appropriate here, the question becomes one of whose standards should be adopted.

The employer may seek to relate the dress code to safety. For example, the fire fighter may be instructed to shave his beard because management says the required gas mask will not seal properly. Here, arbitrators have ruled that the employer must test to see if, in fact, the gas mask will not fit.

Again public employees, with the exception of the uniformed protective services, have more freedom in personal grooming than their counterparts in private employment, because the constitution prohibits government from invading an individual's privacy.

Absenteeism. There are many reasons for absenteeism: excessive overtime; inadequate transportation; poor health of the worker, or a member of the worker's family; bad work habits; alcoholism and/or drug abuse; and hard or dangerous work. Management views absenteeism as a cost because it interferes with the production process. Even if provision is made for paid sick leave, there may be an additional cost in paying for a replacement for the absent person.

The worker, on the other hand, feels there should be some leeway in this matter. If paid sick leave exists, the worker regards its use as a right rather than a privilege. Therefore, if the individual's accumulated sick leave is not exhausted for health reasons, the worker may feel entitled to use it as additional vacation time, particularly when others have exhausted their leave. Because the employer and the worker look at the use of sick leave from different perspectives, grievances challenging disciplinary action are often arbitrated.

A worker's use of sick leave for other purposes justifies disciplinary action: a worker may be disciplined for taking leave after a request was denied or for leaving work without permission. Absence while in jail may not be regarded as a good excuse. An employee who cannot get to work because of an emergency may still be subject to discipline if he or she fails to notify the employer.

Intoxication and Alcohol. Alcohol, widely used and socially acceptable, is also the source of major substance abuse in this country. Intoxication and drinking on the job are old problems that have always been subject to discipline, including discharge, because they lead to frequent absenteeism, an inability to perform one's job, and sometimes to improper behavior that may result in criminal activity. Drinking may also affect the employer's business, particularly when the worker has contact with the public, or it can lead to lowered morale among employees who need to perform additional work in order to cover up for the individual. This effort to protect an alcoholic backfires if an undetected worker feels no pressure to seek professional help and ultimately is discharged. Furthermore, drinking on the job may pose a health and safety hazard both to that individual and others.

An arbitrator's approach to a drinking grievance will in part be determined by his or her attitude toward alcoholism in general. By reading arbitration awards, a union may be able to learn how individual arbitrators treat this subject. A first offense of drinking on the job will not usually result in discharge, particularly if the employee has several years of seniority. The arbitrator will require proof of intoxication or drinking on the job in which the details of the worker's appearance and conduct and the manner in which the worker was apprehended must be described. A supervisor who is a witness is expected to explain how the worker's appearance and work habits differed from when he or she is sober. If blood tests were obtained, they will be accepted as conclusive proof.

If an employee voluntarily seeks treatment for alcoholism, an arbitrator may give this action favorable consideration, and sometimes reinstatement may be based on the successful completion of such a program.

Off-duty drinking is not the business of the employer unless the worker comes to work under the influence of liquor. Notable exceptions are airline pilots and other airline employees who are prohibited from drinking for a prescribed number of hours before flight time. Surgeons and others should be governed by like restrictions where employment requires unquestioned sobriety.

Drug Abuse. Drug discharges may involve use, possession, or sale of drugs on the job during working hours or off the job during nonworking hours. In the past arbitrators usually upheld management's position that drug involvement could result in immediate discharge. With the trend toward decriminalization of marijuana, a new element has been introduced, and arbitrators are split, at least in respect to this drug, as to whether immediate discharge is justified.

There is no consistency in the standards of proof required by arbitrators in drug cases.[31] Some rely on the "preponderance of evidence" standard which is the least rigorous in its requirement of proof. Others demand "proof beyond a reasonable doubt," a tougher test to meet. A third category of "clear and convincing proof" is sometimes used. It falls midway between the other two in the degree of verification required.

A discharge is not automatically upheld when a worker is arrested or convicted for the off-premise use of drugs, on the grounds that what the worker does away from the workplace is his or her own business. The validity of the discharge is examined in respect to several factors: the impact the arrest or conviction may have upon the worker's personal relationship with other employees; the impact it may have on the business operations of the employer; and whether the retention of the worker poses a health and safety hazard for others in the workplace.

---

[31]Pat Wynns, "Arbitration in Drug Discharge Cases," *The Arbitration Journal* 34, no. 2 (June 1979), pp. 19–27.

One might expect that these limitations on the right of the employer to discharge for off-premise drug use would result in the reinstatement of a number of workers by arbitrators. In practice, however, this has not proven true because more often than not the employer has issued a work rule which authorizes discharge for the conviction of a crime or for engaging in unlawful behavior. In general, arbitrators feel that such rules should be upheld.

The type of drugs and the worker's involvement with them are taken into consideration in discharges. A relationship with hard drugs such as cocaine and heroin is dealt with more harshly than involvement with other drugs like marijuana and amphetamines, even though no more than personal use is involved. Discharge upon conviction for the sale of drugs *off* the premises is usually upheld on the grounds that the employer has reason to believe that a pusher will logically seek to sell to those with whom he or she is in contact, i.e., fellow employees, thereby creating the possibility of a drug problem within the workplace.

Discharges involving the use of drugs *on* the employer's premises are upheld, particularly when clearly prescribed work rules forbid such conduct. Disciplinary penalties for the use and possession of hard drugs on the employer's property are more harsh than for the same involvement with "soft drugs" and usually bring immediate discharge on the grounds that strict and speedy discipline is necessary. Sometimes an employee's prior work record is considered by the arbitrator when soft drugs are involved.

The use of drugs at the workplace has increased significantly during the past two decades, yet it is not as widespread as that of alcohol.[32] Unions preparing to arbitrate discharge cases involving drugs must be prepared to answer the same type of questions that relate to grievances dealing with the use of alcohol. In general, it can be said that the union will have greater difficulty in winning drug cases than alcohol cases since alcoholism is increasingly regarded as an illness.

Summary

Arbitration has been viewed for some years in the private sector as the appropriate method for settling grievances involving violations, interpretation, or application of the contract. Today, it has

---

[32]United States Department of Health, Education and Welfare, *Let's Talk Drug Abuse* (Rockville, Md.: National Institute on Drug Abuse, 1979), pp. 1, 30.

attained the same stature in all levels of public employment. A dramatic illustration is found in the federal sector—initially only advisory arbitration was permitted, but now all agreements are required to have provisions for binding arbitration.

Although at one time tripartite arbitration panels were commonly used, today the single arbitrator mutually selected by the union and management predominates, except in the railway and airline industries. If the union and management cannot agree on an arbitrator, most contracts provide for either the American Arbitration Association or the Federal Mediation and Conciliation Service to present a panel of names from which an arbitrator is selected.

There is no foolproof method to assure that a union will obtain the best qualified arbitrator for a particular grievance. The awards of a prospective arbitrator should be examined, but it must be remembered that only a small percentage of all decisions are published. Furthermore, the reasoning an arbitrator uses in reaching a decision may be a more important clue on rulings in future cases than the actual decision itself, because each case is judged on its own facts. In general both unions and management try to select as an arbitrator someone with whom they have had a previously favorable experience. If such a person is not available then, all other things being equal, the parties will select the available person with the most arbitration experience.

Disciplinary actions are by far the major reason for the arbitration of grievances. Cases of this kind increase during periods of unemployment when management seeks to reclaim so-called lost rights. Other major reasons for arbitration are work assignments, procedural challenges, seniority questions, overtime assignments and pay, fringe benefits, and disputes over management rights.

The union must exhaust the prior steps in the grievance procedure before invoking arbitration. At the hearing the union must be prepared to prove its case either through the use of written documents or oral testimony. It must decide who is to present its case, a decision that has financial implications. If an attorney rather than a union representative is used, the lawyer's fee may be the single largest cost to the union.

Both time and money are saved if union and management can agree on a submission that states the precise issue which both parties want decided. Otherwise, considerable effort may be spent in determining this fact.

Unions, critical of the rising cost of arbitration, can cut these costs by having a union representative present the case, rather than a lawyer, and by dispensing with transcripts and briefs.

Some unions use expedited arbitration to reduce the time required to complete the arbitration process, to cut costs, and to reduce the backlog of cases. Under these procedures, no lawyers are involved, no briefs or transcripts are used, and the arbitrator is required to issue a speedy award without a detailed explanation of the decision. Although expedited arbitration has proven useful to some unions, this process has not spread as widely as anticipated.

As a result of the decisions of the U.S. Supreme Court in the *Steelworkers Trilogy* cases, the arbitrator's decision, with limited exceptions, is enforceable in the courts. The major exceptions are in decisions dealing with discrimination based on race, color, religion, sex, national origin, ancestry, or when a union breaches its duty of fair representation. Here the court has ruled that the grievant is entitled to process the complaint through the federal court system even though the arbitrator may have given an adverse ruling.

Both the NLRB and the courts have wrestled with the problem of what to do when a complaint is both the subject of a grievance and also the basis for an unfair labor practice complaint. The issue that arises is under what circumstances, if any, the NLRB should defer to arbitration. As a result of a number of policy shifts, it is unclear where the NLRB and the courts will finally wind up.

Although arbitrators are not as bound by precedent as the courts, standards do exist that most arbitrators follow. For example, charges of insubordination are handled in the same manner in regard to the amount of proof required and the kinds of penalties applied. On the other hand, arbitrators differ widely as to how disciplinary actions involving the use, possession, and sale of drugs both on and off the employer's premises should be treated.

Although no legal code exists establishing criteria as to how arbitrators are to function, a common law of the workplace has developed in many areas through the process of trial and error. Well-defined standards exist governing the interpretation of contract language as do criteria governing most forms of disciplinary action.

Key Words and Phrases

ad hoc arbitration
American Arbitration
  Association
bench decision
common law of the workplace
cross-examination
disciplinary action
due process
expedited arbitration
Federal Mediation and
  Conciliation Service
interest arbitration
just cause

loser-pay arbitration
National Railroad Adjust-
  ment Board
oral testimony
prehearing briefs
post-hearing briefs
rights arbitration
Steelworkers Trilogy
submission
tripartite board
umpire system
War Labor Board
written records

Review and Discussion Questions

1. Explain the role the War Labor Board played in World War II in the development of arbitration.

2. From what sources can a union obtain information about an arbitrator's background?

3. What are some of the major issues arbitrated today? Why are these so common?

4. What methods are available to cut the costs of arbitration?

5. Explain how the law impinges on the arbitration process.

6. Explain the seven general principles governing disciplinary action.

7. Discuss the pros and cons of using a union representative rather than an attorney to present the organization's case in arbitration.

9

Problems in Contract Administration

The administration of the collective bargaining agreement is carried out in large part through the grievance procedure. The process by which representatives of labor and management determine whether the contract is violated has introduced a form of industrial democracy into the workplace, because the worker now has a mechanism for protest.

The grievance procedure is also important for other reasons: it serves as a substitute for the courts by providing a systematic method of handling disputes; it specifies where a grievance starts and then enumerates the appeal steps to be followed; it is a channel for the bargaining agent to protect the interests of its members by placing the power of the organization behind the individual; it serves as a method for interpreting the contract and thereby contributes to the formation of workshop common law; it serves as an informational source for management by informing it of the problems which the work force finds objectionable; and it serves as a substitute for the strike.

The Supreme Court in its *Steelworkers Trilogy* decisions institutionalized arbitration as an integral part of the grievance procedure when it spoke in glowing terms of the value and virtues of relying on an impartial third party for a final and binding decision. The Supreme Court enunciated these concepts about arbitration:

(1) It is a relatively *speedy* system of justice.
(2) It is mostly *informal*.
(3) It is *therapeutic* in the sense that it allows workers to have their say.
(4) It is *voluntarily binding*.
(5) It usually involves judgment from someone known and respected by the parties.

    (6)   It is relatively *cheap*.

    (7)   It is a *flexible* process that can easily be changed to suit the needs of the parties.

    (8)   Most importantly, arbitration is an extension of *collective bargaining*, i.e., a system of jurisprudence, created by and for the benefit of the parties.[1]

Alternatives to Arbitration

There are, of course, possible alternatives to arbitration. They include the right to strike, the use of federal or state courts for enforcing the agreement, or the creation of separate labor courts whose jurisdiction would be restricted to disputes arising out of the collective bargaining relationship.

From time to time demands for the right to strike on grievances are heard particularly from younger members, but no union in recent years has shown a desire to move in that direction. In fact, the opposite appears to be true. A union that is unable to negotiate binding arbitration is viewed as weak. Although the right to strike is sometimes advocated as a speedier and cheaper method for settling disputes, no evidence supports this view.

Nor is a move to use the court system any more likely to develop. The American labor movement has never suffered from the illusion that either the federal or state courts are friendly to unions. As a result there is no interest in scrapping arbitration in favor of utilizing the federal or state courts, even if time and cost were comparable.

Labor courts have been utilized successfully in a number of European countries. In part this is due to the unions' exercise of direct political influence, because they are closely associated with a socialist or labor party that is either in power or has reasonable expectations of attaining it in the near future. Therefore, these unions are in a position to exert considerable pressure on behalf of legislation that will produce an acceptable labor court system. In this country, however, labor is much more reluctant to see government participate directly in the collective bargaining process because of labor's limited ability to influence the election of candidates sympathetic to its views.

In addition to proposals to substitute a new system for arbitration, others have urged that emphasis be placed on modifying it.

---

[1]Harry T. Edwards, *Contributions of Grievance Arbitration to Industrial Relations and Industrial Peace* (Amherst: University of Massachusetts, 1977), p. 5.

These suggestions include proposals for free arbitration and greater emphasis on expedited arbitration or loser-pay arbitration.

Because mediation is currently provided free by the Federal Mediation and Conciliation Service (FMCS), it has been suggested that arbitration services should be offered on the same basis. It is unlikely, however, that this proposal will be adopted. (In fact just the opposite is more likely—in 1982 the FMCS proposed a new policy calling for a fee of $25 from each party requesting a panel of names and a $30 fee for direct appointment of an arbitrator in lieu of furnishing a panel of names. Opposition from users of the service was so great that the proposal was dropped. But, the incident illustrates the problem of obtaining additional services from the FMCS.) An enormous increase in the size of the FMCS staff would be required at the very time its budget is being slashed. Even more serious, however, is the argument that if arbitration were provided free of charge, there would be little or no incentive for the union to drop cases that lacked merit. On the other hand, there is no question that a small union may not be able to afford the luxury of arbitration, since one case could empty its treasury. As a result its members may be denied justice.

Although expedited arbitration is now utilized by some unions, it has not become widespread. The shortage of experienced arbitrators who would be available at a moment's notice makes it difficult to implement this system on a wide scale. Even if the arbitrators were available, reluctance both on the part of the union and of management to settle for less than a full-scale hearing makes it unlikely that expedited arbitration will replace the conventional form. An additional factor hindering its spread is the increased emphasis by the courts on examining arbitrators' decisions, particularly in matters involving a breach of the duty of fair representation. As a result, both the union and management may request transcripts and briefs, items expedited arbitration is designed to eliminate.

Loser-pay arbitration has little future, at least in respect to unions actively proposing or voluntarily agreeing to such a formula. Despite rhetoric to the contrary, in most cases both labor and management look upon the grievance procedure as a method of settling disputes arising at the workplace rather than a form of score keeping to determine who is right and who is wrong. Unions on average lose more arbitrations than they win, because many of the cases involve complaints where the contract is silent or unclear. Since clear-cut contract violations usually are settled earlier, it is the tough cases, over which a legitimate difference of opinion exists, that are arbitrated.

It is unlikely, therefore, that labor and management them-selves will agree to modify or in other ways restrict the types of com-plaints eligible for the grievance procedure, including the right to seek review by the courts.

Deferral to Arbitration

The question of whether the NLRB and the courts should defer to arbitration appears to be in a state of flux. Only time will tell in what circumstances deferral will be permitted, if at all. If statutory rights, in this case unfair labor practices, are included in the con-tract, does this waive the statutory procedures if the arbitration case is lost? The NLRB has ruled that it will defer to arbitration if the hearing is fair and just, if the parties agree to be bound by the arbi-tration, and the award is not repugnant to the policies of the Taft-Hartley Act.

Separate treatment is accorded to arbitration awards dealing with charges of sex discrimination. These awards may be appealed to the courts. There are two reasons for handling these awards dif-ferently: Arbitrators may not be familiar with the law, and there is a danger that the employer and union may obtain a rigged award by conspiring against the employee in their presentation of the case. There is little danger, however, of collusion between the two parties in an arbitration case charging antiunion activity on the part of the employer.

The debate over deferral involves two conflicting philosophies. Its proponents argue that the parties to a dispute should be encour-aged to use their own procedures because the use of arbitration has a positive effect on labor relations when a mutually agreed-upon method is used to reach a solution. Opponents argue that deferral ignores the intent of Congress which grants the NLRB exclusive ju-risdiction over unfair labor practices.

Unions may also differ regarding deferral. A large, adequately funded union that can afford the cost of arbitration may prefer de-ferral, because the union will usually obtain a faster decision by that route. A small union may prefer to process a complaint through the NLRB, because no direct cost is involved and broader remedies are available. Public policy developed in this area will have significance not only for the private sector, but for the public sector as well, be-cause all states with public employment collective bargaining laws, with the exception of Michigan, have modeled their deferral policy after that of the NLRB.

Grievance Problems in Different Workplaces

Building Trades. Different unions have different problems with the processing of grievances. Historically, disputes in the building trades were settled between the business agent and the contractor. If no agreement was reached, the workplace was struck until the issue was resolved. As a result of law, implemented by court decisions and the possibility of the employer going nonunion in order to avoid work stoppages, construction unions have negotiated grievance procedures paralleling the industrial model and ending in binding arbitration. Because at this time these procedures have not yet been used to a great degree, it is difficult to predict the usefulness of this development. For example, where workers typically remain with the same employer only for a few weeks or a few months, can an arbitration procedure which often takes several months provide speedy handling for workplace complaints? In large communities where it may be possible to have a rotating panel of arbitrators available at short notice, a workable grievance procedure may evolve.

In order to meet nonunion competition, national construction unions sign national or project agreements with large contractors who operate over a wide geographic area. These contracts have priority over local union agreements and guarantee the employer standard conditions that may cut back benefits negotiated locally. For example, the local agreement may provide for the payment of double time for Saturday work while the national agreement may provide overtime for Saturday work only if 40 hours have been worked previously during the week. These reductions may result in members raising objections to what in essence are concessions on local standards. The complaints will be directed at the union officers rather than at the employers.

Public Sector. Public employees at all levels face some common problems relating to the grievance procedure. Some public employers are unwilling to negotiate an arbitration clause, arguing that it is unlawful for them to be bound by a decision of a third party who is not responsible to the taxpayer. More serious is the narrow scope of many public employment grievance procedures. Sometimes this is due to hard-nosed bargaining by the public employer who wishes to retain unilateral control over as many issues as possible. More often a narrow scope is the result of the state public employment collective bargaining law or court interpretations of it. The Michigan public employment law permits public employee unions to negotiate and grieve virtually the same items that private employees do. On the other hand, states like Delaware and New York have limitations in many areas. If one believes that all complaints arising out of the employment relationship should be grievable, then it is imperative that the scope of grievance procedures, particularly in the federal sector, be broadened.

Not to be underestimated is the all too prevalent feeling that it is a privilege to work for the government and that such employees owe extra loyalty to the public employer and should not tarnish this loyalty by complaining about conditions of employment.

Education. In its *Yeshiva* decision[2] the Supreme Court overruled the NLRB and effectively limited union organizing in private universities and colleges. The Court decided that faculty who performed traditional management functions, such as evaluating for hiring, promotions, and salary increases, are members of management and are therefore ineligible for inclusion in a bargaining unit. As a result collective bargaining in higher education will be restricted largely to publicly supported institutions that are not covered by the Taft-Hartley Act. Grievance procedures in public institutions of higher learning are subject to some of the same problems that affect grievance procedures in public employment in general. In addition, the special problem of peer review hampers the process of grievance handling in higher education. Arbitration is also often opposed on the claim that an outsider cannot possibly understand the unique operations of an institution of higher education.

QWL Programs and Contract Administration

The development of worker participation in the management decision-making process, commonly referred to as quality-of-work-life (QWL) programs, may have an impact on the grievance procedure in the future. The current grievance procedures are an outgrowth of an adversary system where representatives of labor negotiate with representatives of management.

QWL programs seek to end the distinction between the two parties and emphasize the need for cooperation. They seek to involve workers in what historically were considered to be management decisions relating to the way in which the production process operates. QWL programs center around small groups of workers

---

[2]*Yeshiva Faculty Association v. Yeshiva University*, 444 US 672, 103 LRRM 2526 (1980).

meeting regularly to discuss mutual problems within a framework jointly determined by union and management. The emphasis in the United States is placed on problems of quality and productivity rather than humanizing the workplace. Originally, this concept was promoted by Karl Marx and his disciples who envisioned the overthrow of the capitalist system by the workers and their subsequent ownership of industry. Inherent in this belief is the idea that those who produce the product or service should make the decisions that traditionally belong to management.

For some years, however, management used programs promoting worker participation to keep unions out of the workplace on the grounds that workers and employers had common problems that could be solved without the interference of an outside organization. It is only recently that some of the major unions, such as the United Auto Workers, the Steelworkers, and the Communications Workers, have become involved in QWL programs.

The Communications Workers program is based on the following principles:[3]

(1) The effort is *joint*—the union is involved as an equal partner from planning through implementation and evaluation.
(2) It is voluntary for the union, the company, and each individual worker.
(3) Collective bargaining and grievance issues are not a part of the quality-of-work-life program; workers' participation in the grievance procedure is a separate process.
(4) No one can be laid off or downgraded as a result of ideas which came from the participation process.
(5) The goals of the process include both human satisfaction and economic efficiency.

An important issue posed by a QWL program is its effect on the contract and the grievance procedure. All of the unions participating in these programs are quick to point out that collective bargaining and grievance issues are off limits. If workplace problems are discussed, however, will it be possible to prevent subjects eligible for the grievance procedure from being handled? Is a national union or even a local union capable of policing a QWL program? If

---

[3]81 Gov't Empl. Rel. Rep. (BNA) 71 (April 27, 1982). Speech delivered by CWA President Glenn Watts before the Association for Workplace Democracy, March 18, 1982. The CWA principles are quite similar to those governing comparable programs of the UAW with Ford and General Motors.

a union is unable to do so, what are the implications for the traditional manner of handling workplace complaints through the grievance procedure?

Glenn Watts, CWA president, has stated that such grievable issues are to be excluded from QWL programs and that "problems of over-supervision or monitoring, of lack of freedom in the workplace, . . . [such as] permission to go the bathroom," have been discussed under CWA's program with the Bell Telephone Company.[4] One would assume that these matters are already subject to the grievance procedure, since they deal with working conditions rather than the traditional management prerogatives of method of production, the price of the product, or the materials used. A further problem will arise when a union member files a grievance charging that a QWL decision violates the contract. Will a union process such a grievance with vigor?

If a QWL group resolves a problem normally settled through the grievance procedure, what then becomes the role of the union? Will different policies and practices develop in different departments? Neither European nor Japanese experience in these areas indicates the effect that QWL programs will have on the grievance procedure. Some critics of QWL programs feel that the Japanese QWL programs are an extension of traditional methods by management of retaining control of the work force.

Those unions opposing QWL programs do so because they feel that, in practice, these programs concentrate on the problems of production rather than dealing with the problems of layoffs or of humanizing the workplace. For example, the management of United Airlines is enthusiastic about its QWL program, yet 2,000 workers were laid off over a two-year period.[5] The UAW, in its General Motors agreement in 1982, received limited protection against future layoffs, but its QWL programs have done little to reinstate the 200,000 auto workers who have been laid off.

At the same time one segment of management advocates QWL programs, another group recommends the recapturing of its rights which they charge have been seized by the unions. Since true QWL programs require management to surrender some of its traditional rights, it will be interesting to note which trend will dominate the next decade. The growth of antilabor consultants and attorneys and

---

[4]*Ibid*.
[5]30 Gov't Empl. Rel. Rep. (BNA) A-9 (Feb. 12, 1982).

their subsequent efforts to keep unions from organizing, or to de-certify them where they already exist, are part of this trend.

Fairness in the Grievance Procedure

Justice and Dignity Clauses. Certain questions of fairness relating to the grievance procedure need to be addressed. Should a worker, when entering the workplace, lose some normal civilian rights? For example, a citizen charged with a crime does not have the penalty applied until after a trial has been held. In the workplace, however, a worker who is disciplined or discharged has the penalty applied immediately and then must seek to overturn the action through the grievance procedure—in short, the worker is guilty until proven innocent. The one important exception is the contracts negotiated recently by the United Steelworkers union.[6] In 1981 the union negotiated a so-called "dignity and justice" clause with the major can companies. This clause provides that a worker who receives notice of a suspension or discharge and who files a grievance within five days will continue to be employed and receive the regular rate of pay until the proposed action is settled by expedited arbitration. Workers may be removed immediately, however, if they are suspended or discharged because they pose an immediate threat to fellow employees or plant equipment or if they engage in such activity as fighting, theft, wildcat strikes, or refuse to perform their assigned work.

In 1983 similar provisions were incorporated into the basic Steelworkers contracts on an experimental basis. By 1985 one-third of all steel-producing plants of all companies are to have similar provisions in operation.

Both management and the union agree that the experience under the can industry contracts indicates that:

(1) There has been no significant increase in the number of suspensions and discharges going to arbitration;
(2) Supervisory authority has not been undermined by keeping employees on the payroll until they have had their hearing; and

---

[6]109 DLR (BNA) D-1 (June 6, 1983). This summary of the justice and dignity provisions negotiated by the Steelworkers union is based on remarks made by Dee W. Gilliam, director of the union's arbitration department, and T. S. Hoffman, Jr., vice president, Continental Packaging Company, to the 1983 meeting of the National Academy of Arbitrators.

(3) The justice and dignity clause has not undermined well-established discipline procedures—management has not administered harsher discipline nor has the union displayed an increased reluctance to settle grievances.

The justice and dignity clause provides direct benefits to both the worker and management: the worker is presumed innocent until proven guilty and therefore is not placed in an economically disadvantaged position before the case is heard; management has no backpay liability since the worker remains on the job until a final decision is reached.

It is difficult to forecast whether the dignity and justice concept will be incorporated into other labor-management agreements. Only one other major contract in this country, that covering postal workers, ever embodied a similar provision, and it was given up by the postal unions several years ago.

Delays in Grievance Adjudication. Almost all union contracts give the employer the right to discipline or discharge for "just cause," with the penalty being a grievable issue. Since the largest number of grievances involve discipline and discharge, the way such matters are handled is of key importance.

The longer the time span between the disciplinary action and the arbitration hearing, the less likely the arbitrator is to award backpay in order to avoid placing an undue burden on the employer, particularly if the worker has earned some money during the interim period. Arbitrators do not award punitive damages, so a discharged worker receives compensation only for the loss of actual benefits, with nothing for the stress of the experience.

A union member improperly disciplined may ultimately have a "day in court," even though the arbitration hearing is long delayed. The unorganized worker, with a few exceptions, may be disciplined or discharged at will with no recourse to arbitration or the courts, except when the disciplinary action is based on union activity, discrimination for a variety of reasons, or violations of the Consumer Credit Protection Act which prohibits discharge based on garnishments for one debt. There are also some state laws that prohibit the employer from requiring lie detector tests or deducting from a worker's paycheck without written authorization. In the absence of a union contract, an employer is free to discharge for virtually any or no reason.

The Right to a Job. The United States stands alone among industrialized countries in not having a standardized labor law governing both the private and the public sector. In private employment the right to a job is a contract right, as contrasted with public employment where it is considered a constitutional right. Therefore, in the private sector if no union contract exists, no contract right exists. Under the common law in this country, an employee has the right to quit a job at any time, and the employer, in the absence of a violation of a statute, has the right to discharge at any time. In the public sector, however, where a constitutional right exists, an employee may not be deprived of property, i.e., a job, without procedural due process.

The unorganized public employee working for an agency of government, in theory at least, has some protection against being discharged. In most cases the public employee is entitled to some kind of hearing either as a constitutional right or under the civil service procedures governing many levels of government. How meaningful such procedures are in practice, however, is open to question. When using the civil service procedure, if one exists, the worker is often appealing to the same body which enacted the policy under which the individual was discharged. Therefore, state or federal civil service commissions (essentially the personnel arms of the public employer) judge decisions reached under regulations which they have promulgated. In the absence of a union, there is no guarantee that the unorganized individual can exercise an appeal right because of the cost and delay involved in litigation.

Time Limits. The unequal application of penalties which apply to the violation of time limits on the grievance procedure appear unfair to many union members. Most contracts provide that if the union fails to comply with the limitations, it loses the grievance. On the other hand if management fails to respond in time the union may appeal to the next step. Since time limitations are negotiable, more unions are proposing language that requires management to comply with the time limitations or lose the grievance by default.

Criticisms of Arbitration

A number of sharp criticisms of the arbitration process have been made in recent years, some relating to the rights of individuals and some questioning the omniscience, and even the impartiality and integrity, of the arbitrators themselves.

Arbitrators differ over whether they have an obligation to intervene directly during a hearing. Some argue that they have a duty to question witnesses and to request either party or both to produce additional witnesses or exhibits that will help to determine the truth of the matter, thus assuring the employee due process, particularly in a case presented by an inexperienced or partially prepared advocate. These actions by an arbitrator may be required in promotion cases where two union members are competing for the same position and the union is reluctant to introduce evidence favorable to the employee with less seniority.

Other arbitrators argue that their responsibility is confined to the evidence introduced. Otherwise they feel that the arbitrator is serving as prosecutor as well as judge. Even though the arbitrator is impartial in questioning, it may appear to one of the parties that bias is displayed and thus trust in the arbitration procedure is destroyed.[7]

Criticism of another sort came from the late Paul Hays, a federal judge and former arbitrator. Hays questioned the ability of many arbitrators, because of lack of specific knowledge, to decide the particular case before them. He was especially critical of the fact that arbitrators were paid by the parties and felt that as a result they often wrote their awards so as to be rehired.[8] Hays cited no specific evidence for his sweeping charges, leading one well-known arbitrator to refer to his writings as "that viperous little book."

Obviously legitimate criticisms of arbitration do exist. In 1974 the National Academy of Arbitrators, the Federal Mediation and Conciliation Service, and the American Arbitration Association adopted a new Code of Professional Responsibility for Labor-Management Arbitrators.[9] It is meant to replace the Code of Ethics and Procedural Standards of 1951 which was far more general in nature. The new code is designed to cover both interest arbitration and the more widely used rights arbitration. Here are some of the main provisions covered in the new document:

(1)   An arbitrator, deciding that he or she does not have the technical competence to deal with the issue under consideration, is expected to withdraw from the case. Commonly included in this category are incentive systems, job evaluation plans, and pension and insurance programs.

---

[7]Benjamin A. Aaron, "Contemporary Issues in the Grievance and Arbitration Process: A Current Evaluation," *Collective Bargaining Today*, Proceedings of the Collective Bargaining Forum—1971 (Washington, D.C.: The Bureau of National Affairs, Inc., 1972), pp. 162–177.

[8]Paul R. Hays, *Labor Arbitration, A Dissenting View* (New Haven, Conn.: Yale University Press, 1966), pp. 111, 112.

[9]Gov't Empl. Rel. Rep. (BNA) No. 605, at E-1 (May 12, 1974).

(2) Arbitrators have a responsibility to help train new arbitrators.

(3) An arbitrator has a responsibility to disclose a current or past relationship with either the union or management involved in the proceeding.

(4) When an arbitrator is acting as a representative of another company or union in labor relations, or has done so in recent years, he or she must disclose such activities before accepting an appointment.

(5) Significant aspects of an arbitration hearing must be treated by the arbitrator as confidential unless this requirement is waived by both parties.

(6) An arbitrator is not to make public an award without the consent of the parties.

(7) If an arbitrator, as a condition of appointment, agrees to mediate he or she must do so.

(8) If a request to mediate is first made after the appointment, the arbitrator may refuse to do so.

(9) An arbitrator must not delegate any of the decision-making function to another person without the permission of the parties.

(10) The parties, prior to the issuance of an award, may jointly request the arbitrator to include in the decision agreements reached between them concerning the issues.

(11) Once the proceedings are closed the arbitrator must stick to the time limits.

(12) Prior to an arbitrator's appointment the parties should be aware of the arbitrator's fees for the hearing, study time, travel time, postponement or cancellation fees, office overhead expenses, and any work of paid assistants.

(13) Arbitrators may not have a fixed ratio of study days to hearing days.

(14) An arbitrator must abide by the mutual agreement of the parties in respect to the use (or nonuse) of a transcript.

(15) If either or both parties object, the arbitrator should not insist on the use of a tape recorder.

(16) If either party requests the arbitrator to visit the workplace, the arbitrator should comply.

(17) An arbitrator should not consider a post-hearing brief that has not been given to the other party.

(18) Clarification or interpretation of an award is not permitted without the consent of both parties.

(19) An arbitrator should not voluntarily participate in legal enforcement proceedings.

The Code appears to contain several shortcomings. Despite all of the concern expressed over the twin problems of cost and delay, little of a specific nature on these subjects is included. Arbitrators are exhorted to avoid delay, but no meaningful way to implement this desire is included. In respect to cost, arbitrators are urged to make known their charges to the parties beforehand and are instructed to make an honest accounting of the time spent on a case.

The provision of the Code that it is consistent with arbitrators' professional responsibility to include in the award prior agreements reached between the union and management has caused eyebrows to be raised. The rigged award, in which the union or management lets the arbitrator know what they regard as the proper settlement, was denounced by Hays in the strongest terms because it permits union and management to conspire to do in a grievant regarded as a troublemaker. This provision of the new code, even though unintended, may appear to lend some support to this practice.

No enforcement provisions as such are in the code and each of the three agencies—the AAA, the FMCS, and the NAA—is expected to work out its own procedures. It is doubtful, however, that these bodies will be any more vigilant or successful in policing their code than have been the American Medical Association or the American Bar Association. It is doubtful that any group of professionals can and will effectively police themselves. Although the new code on paper is certainly an improvement over the old, it remains to be seen whether it can deal effectively with the unscrupulous arbitrator. Unless enforcement is implemented the arbitration process may come under increased scrutiny from the public and the courts.

Collective Rights vs. Individual Rights

Probably the most difficult issue in the field of contract administration is the right of the individual to use the grievance procedure, including arbitration.[10] In order to balance the power of those

---

[10]See Clyde W. Summers, "Arbitration of Unjust Dismissal: A Preliminary Proposal," and Benjamin A. Aaron, "The Impact of Public Employment Grievance Settlement on the Labor Arbitration Process," *Future of Labor Arbitration in America* (New York: American Arbitration Association, 1976).

who worked for industry with those who own industry, the Wagner Act in 1935 adopted the concept of exclusive recognition under which an employer was required to bargain in good faith with a union representing a majority of the employees in an appropriate unit. This same concept applied to the administration of the negotiated agreement. As a result, a form of industrial democracy developed whereby the individual union member, through the organization, was able to challenge decisions of management. The difficult issue not originally foreseen is the relationship between individual rights and the collective rights of the organization. We have seen that under the Taft-Hartley Act the individual has the right to process a grievance free from intervention from the union. Management, however, has the right to refuse to deal with the individual and can require that the complaint be processed through the bargaining agent. More often than not, management welcomes the individual, so in practice, there is little conflict between individual and collective rights.

Two more complicated problems are involved here. In one case the union refuses to handle a worker's grievance for arbitrary or discriminatory reasons, based on such factors as religion or race. More often, however, arbitrary or discriminatory treatment may be meted out to an individual who is out of favor with the union's bureaucracy, such as an opposition candidate for office or a critic of union policies. Obviously a refusal to process a grievance for any of these reasons is indefensible.

Another problem occurs when a union turns down a complaint that it, in good faith, feels is not a legitimate grievance but the worker is convinced otherwise. One region of a union has instructed its staff initially to process all complaints if the worker insists and then to withdraw them at a higher step in the grievance procedure. This policy may create problems for two reasons. First, the grievance process may be bogged down with complaints that have no merit and the settlement of good grievances will be delayed because poor or weak complaints clog the system. Second, the union may be required to show a higher standard of proof, if challenged, for withdrawing a grievance than for initially not processing it. A union that agrees to process any and all complaints may ultimately lose the respect of both its members and of management by filing weak grievances and then withdrawing them.

Another source of conflict between individual and collective rights can be the settlement reached. The individual may feel that the union accepted less than that to which he or she is entitled. Under the present system the grievant has little recourse, since the grievance procedure is owned by the bargaining agent, and it can make any settlement that is not arbitrary or discriminatory in nature.

Summary

Over the years administration of the contract—consisting of a grievance procedure ending in binding arbitration—has gradually emerged. Originally developed in the mass production industries of private employment, it spread into the construction field. Now it also is institutionalized in all levels of public employment. Once concerned with protecting the collective rights of the group, contract administration is now grappling with the more complicated issue of ensuring that the worker is guaranteed due process.

Much of this book has dealt with the techniques of handling grievances, as well as the common law of the workplace and the broad legal considerations that apply. It must be remembered, however, that the negotiation and the administration of the contract result only when workers as a group exert pressure upon an employer to share power, for few individuals or organizations give up power or share it voluntarily. These words from an industrial relations expert written 20 years ago speak to this point:

> Managers do not willingly listen to workers even when they try to consider what *they* think workers interests are. Only when forced to, will managers explicitly and regularly consider the workers' demands and allow the workers to help determine their immediate and particular conditions of work.[11]

In order to attain power it is necessary for a union to obtain maximum membership. It must also ensure that its members are not only informed about the aims and goals of the organization but are actively encouraged to participate in policy making at all levels.

---

[11]James W. Kuhn, *Bargaining in Grievance Settlement* (New York: Columbia University Press, 1961), p. 182.

Key Words and Phrases

Code of Professional
  Responsibility
individual rights
justice and dignity clauses
labor courts

quality-of-work-life programs
rigged award
right to a job
Yeshiva decision

Review and Discussion Questions

1. What major points governing arbitration were established by the U.S. Supreme Court in its *Trilogy* decisions?

2. Discuss the alternatives to arbitration for the settling of grievances. What are their advantages and disadvantages?

3. Will recourse to arbitration or to the courts for settling grievances be the wave of the future? Why?

4. Will collective bargaining be able to coexist with quality-of-work-life programs?

5. Will nonunion employees receive legal protection against unfair disciplinary action? Why or why not?

6. Should public and private employees have identical rights at the workplace? Why or why not?

7. Should workers facing discipline have their trial before being punished or should the present practice of first applying the penalty continue?

8. Judge Paul Hays has strongly criticized arbitration. Which of his criticisms have validity?

9. Can individual rights coexist with the collective rights of the union in respect to the grievance procedure?

Appendix

Arbitration Resource Material*

Arbitration Journal. New York, American Arbitration Association, 1946—. Quarterly.

The journal is oriented to the practitioner. Articles treat all aspects of arbitration. It contains sections reviewing significant court decisions and book reviews.

Grievance Guide, 6th ed. Washington, D.C., The Bureau of National Affairs, Inc., 1982. 375 pages.

This book deals with problems that employers, unions, and workers encounter in the day-to-day business of living under a contract, using awards handed down by arbitrators as examples. The cases selected illustrate general principles applicable to many bargaining situations.

How Arbitration Works, 3rd ed. Frank and Edna A. Elkouri. Washington, D.C., The Bureau of National Affairs, Inc., 1973. 819 pages.

This textbook deals with the workings of arbitration and with numerous questions that have confronted the parties and their arbitrators. It summarizes standards used by arbitrators in interpreting contract language and in judging disciplinary actions. The book contains a detailed table of contents.

Labor Arbitration Awards. Chicago, Commerce Clearing House, 1961—. Weekly, looseleaf.

The reported arbitration awards cover a variety of industries and reflect a wide range of grievance topics. The reporter contains a topical index to awards, an index digest, case tables, and biographical informa-

*Martha Jane Soltow and Jo Ann Stehberger Sokkar, *Industrial Relations and Personnel Management: Selected Information Sources* (Metuchen, N.J., Scarecrow Press, 1979). This handy reference handbook covers all aspects of the employer-employee relationship. The arbitration references are excerpted from it with permission.

tion on arbitrators. Access to awards is facilitated by an extensive subject index.

Labor Arbitration Index. Fort Washington, Pa., Labor Relations Press, 1978—. Monthly, looseleaf.

This index is designed to provide citations to more than 4,000 published and unpublished arbitration and fact-finding awards annually. It includes cases reported by BNA, CCH, P-H, and AAA, as well as awards made to the Steelworkers and those granted within state public sectors where available. The unpublished awards are contained in the *Labor Relations Index* Arbitration Bank.

Labor Arbitration Reports. Washington, D.C., The Bureau of National Affairs, Inc., 1946—. Weekly, looseleaf.

Reports contain, in full text, selected decisions and reports of arbitrators, fact-finding boards, and other agencies concerned with the settlement of labor disputes. The contents of *Labor Arbitration Reports* are periodically reprinted and bound without change of page numbers. *Labor Arbitration Cumulative Digest and Index*. Washington, D.C., The Bureau of National Affairs, Inc., 1946—. The *Digest* contains concise descriptions of arbitration decisions as reported in *Labor Arbitration Reports*, brought together under LA classification numbers that have been assigned to specific topics.

Summary of Labor Arbitration Awards. New York, American Arbitration Association, 1959—. Monthly, looseleaf.

Unpublished AAA arbitration decisions, primarily in the private sector, are summarized. Decisions are indexed by arbitrator and subject. Copies may be purchased from AAA.

Arbitration in the Public Sector

Labor Arbitration in Government. New York, American Arbitration Association, 1971—. Monthly, looseleaf.

A summary of labor arbitration awards and fact-finding recommendations involving public employees. Copies of full text of awards may be purchased through the American Arbitration Association.

Public Employee Bargaining. Chicago, Commerce Clearing House, 1971—. Bi-monthly, looseleaf.

This service contains the full text of court decisions, administrative rulings, and arbitration awards relating to public employee bargaining. State laws are reprinted on major bargaining subjects.

Public Sector Labor Arbitration Awards. Fort Washington, Pa., Labor Relations Press, 1974—. Monthly, looseleaf.

A compilation of arbitration awards indexed by state, arbitrator, and subject. Types of arbitration are indicated: grievance, impasse, advisory, and fact-finding.

Arbitration in the Schools. New York, American Arbitration Association, 1970—. Monthly, looseleaf.

A summary of awards and fact-finding recommendations published for the American Federation of Teachers, the National Education Association, and the National School Boards Association. Full text of awards available from the American Arbitration Association.

Glossary

AAA (American Arbitration Association) A private organization that supplies a panel of names to interested parties. It also publishes material and produces films dealing with arbitration.

AAUP (American Association of University Professors) An organization originally engaged in setting professional standards in higher education. It now, along with the American Federation of Teachers and the National Education Association, seeks to unionize faculty members.

ABC (Associated Builders and Contractors) An association of nonunion contractors that will hire union members but will not negotiate a union contract.

ad hoc arbitration The arbitrator hears an individual case rather than all the cases occurring under the contract.

adverse actions In federal employment this term covers discharges, suspensions for more than 14 days, grade and pay reductions, and layoffs of 30 days or more.

advisory arbitration An impartial third party holds a hearing and issues findings which are not binding. In actuality it is fact-finding with recommendations.

agency shop A union security provision requiring employees who are not members of the union to pay a service charge equivalent to union dues minus the portion not spent on negotiating and administering the contract.

ALJ (administrative law judge) Responsible for issuing original findings regarding unfair labor practices under the Taft-Hartley Act and most state public employment laws.

arbitration A process whereby an impartial third party issues a binding decision. Usually used as the last step in a grievance procedure. Sometimes used to settle negotiating impasses.

arbitrator An impartial third party who conducts an arbitration hearing.

boycott Concerted action by strikers to get other union members to refuse to do business with a struck employer.

checkoff A written authorization by the worker permitting the employer to deduct union dues. The duration of the checkoff is one year and is automatically renewed unless the worker contracts out at that time.

Civil Service Reform Act of 1978 This law placed collective bargaining in the federal government under law instead of executive order.

classified employee   A white-collar federal employee whose salary is set as part of a national classification system.

closed shop   A form of union security in which an employer could hire only union members. Illegal since the passage of the Taft-Hartley Act in 1947.

comparable worth   Some women's groups and some unions argue that those jobs employing a high percentage of women are traditionally underpaid, because the comparable worth of those jobs are not compared to male-dominated jobs.

consultation   The union has the right to request a meeting with management to discuss problems of concern to its members. Management has an obligation to discuss proposed changes with the union. In either case management is free to unilaterally take action after it has heard the union's views.

COPE (Committee on Political Education, AFL-CIO)   Responsible for getting union members active in politics.

craft union   Workers are organized on the basis of their skill rather than on their place of employment.

Davis-Bacon Act   Federal law providing that employers in construction work paid for by federal funds pay the prevailing wage rate.

deferral policy   The policy of the NLRB permitting an arbitrator to decide a case involving an unfair labor practice charge.

double-breasted employer   Employer in construction industry who operates both a union and a nonunion division.

duty of fair representation   Both the Railway Act and the Taft-Hartley Act have been interpreted by the courts to hold unions liable if their handling of grievances is "arbitrary, discriminatory, or based on bad faith."

EEOC (Equal Employment Opportunity Commission)   Responsible for enforcing Title VII of the Civil Rights Act of 1964 which prohibits discrimination in employment.

ERISA (Employee Retirement Income Security Act)   Protects workers' pension and welfare benefits in private employment. It requires reporting and disclosure information.

expedited arbitration   An effort to streamline the arbitration hearing by reducing both time and cost. Transcripts and post-hearing briefs are usually eliminated. Often the arbitrator issues a decision upon the completion of the hearing or shortly thereafter.

fact-finding   An impartial third party conducts a hearing and issues recommendations which are not binding.

FLRA (Federal Labor Relations Authority)   Composed of three non-federal persons appointed by the president under the Civil Service Reform Act, it replaces the Federal Labor Relations Council. The FLRA is responsible for interpreting, administering, and enforcing the law. Its decisions are appealable to the federal courts.

FLRC (Federal Labor Relations Council)   Composed of three federal government department heads, it was responsible for administering and interpreting Executive Order 111491, deciding major policy issues, and considering appeals from the Assistant Secretary of Labor for Labor Management Relations.

FLSA (Fair Labor Standards Act)   Sets minimum wage, overtime provisions, and restrictions on the use of child labor.

FMCS (Federal Mediation and Conciliation Service)   Federal agency supplying mediators in private and federal employment to solve negotiating impasses or to settle strikes. Supplies panel of arbitrators to those parties arbitrating grievances.

fractionalized bargaining   Informal method of handling grievances. Part of work force utilizes pressure tactics to obtain gains for itself that the union is unable to obtain for the work force as a whole.

FSIP (Federal Services Impasses Panel)   In federal employment it provides assistance in resolving negotiating impasses. The various techniques it employs are to serve as a substitute for the right to strike.

GAO (General Accounting Office)   The GAO audits the operations of the executive branch of government. It determines if federal funds are properly spent.

garnishment   A court action ordering an employer to turn over to a creditor part of a worker's wages.

General Counsel   The legal officer of the NLRB who has the responsibility to issue complaints involving unfair labor practices.

gratuity   In contrast to benefits gratuities *may* be terminated unilaterally by the employer. Depending on the circumstances they *may* include: Christmas turkeys and parties, bonuses, picnics, employee discounts, check cashing facilities, etc.

Hatch Act   Federal law limiting rights of federal employees to engage in partisan party politics.

hiring hall .   The employer obtains its labor force through the union hiring hall. Commonly used in the construction, maritime, and longshoring industries.

incentive system   Wage payment system in which a worker's pay increases with increased production.

index   Alphabetical listing of subject matter by page which is found at the end of a contract.

industrial union   Workers are organized on the basis of where they work rather than what they do. Semi-skilled and skilled workers are in the same union.

injunction   A court order requiring a union to stop an action such as picketing or boycotting. If a union does not obey the order, it may be found guilty of contempt of court.

jurisdiction   A claim by an industrial union that it represents workers in a specific industry or by a craft union that it represents a specific type of work.

maintenance of membership   Form of union security requiring anyone who is a member of the union at the time the contract is signed to remain a member. Does not require nonmembers or new hirees to join.

management rights   Those rights reserved to management which are not subject to collective bargaining. They include such things as: hiring of employees, method of production, scheduling of work, pricing the product, etc.

mandatory bargaining   Those items included under "wages, hours and other terms and conditions of employment" over which an employer must bargain.

mediation   The use of a third party to end negotiating impasses. He may make suggestions or seek compromises. He does not issue public recommendations, nor can he require the parties to accept his suggestions.

NLRB (National Labor Relations Board)   Five-man board appointed by the president which administers, interprets, and enforces the Taft-Hartley Act.

nonmandatory bargaining   Those items which are considered the rights of the respective parties. They are not required to bargain over them but may do so if they wish. On the part of the union, nonmandatory bargaining subjects include such items as the method of selecting stewards, the method of taking a strike vote, the composition of its bargaining committee, etc.

Norris-LaGuardia Act   Passed in 1932, it prohibited federal injunctions in labor disputes, rendered yellow dog contracts unenforceable, and exempted unions from prosecution under the antitrust laws.

OSHA (Occupational Safety and Health Act)   Passed in 1970. It establishes health and safety standards covering workers in private employment.

past practice   A reasonably uniform response to a recurring situation over a substantial period of time which has been recognized by the parties implicitly or explicitly as the proper response.

plant rules   They are usually unilaterally issued by management to enforce discipline and to maintain efficient production. A plant rule may be grieved because it is unreasonable, in conflict with the contract, unknown to the workers, or not enforced equitably.

policy grievance   It affects a number of workers and is filed by the union. Often an interpretation of the contract is involved.

post-hearing brief   Filed after the arbitration hearing is completed. It not only summarizes the arguments made at the hearing, but also draws conclusions.

prehearing brief   Presented to the arbitrator before the hearing is held. It contains the theory of the case and the factual arguments proving it.

premium pay   An extra rate paid to the worker for such things as holiday and Sunday work, shift work, overtime, hazardous work, etc.

prohibited bargaining   Items which law says may not be bargained. Under the Taft-Hartley Act, a closed shop and clauses promoting discrimination are barred.

QWL (quality of worklife)   Shorthand for programs involving workers in decision making formerly reserved to management.

Railway Labor Act   Passed in 1926 it governs collective bargaining on the railroads and airlines.

RIF (reduction in force)   Commonly used in public employment as term for layoffs.

right-to-work law   Under Section 14(b) of the Taft-Hartley Act, state legislatures are permitted to pass laws outlawing the union shop, the agency shop, and maintenance of membership clauses.

scab   An employee who continues to work while the rest of the work force is on strike.

Sherman Anti-Trust Act   Passed in 1890 to prevent combinations in restraint of trade which were subject to treble damages. Although not mentioned in the law, unions were prosecuted under it.

sovereignty theory   Government represents all the people and therefore it is superior to any group that represents some of the people. Because collective bargaining implies two parties of equal stature, government cannot engage in such a process.

submission   Joint statement of the union and management as to what is the precise question to be arbitrated. It may also include those facts about which the two parties are in agreement.

super-seniority   Fictional seniority awarded the steward and other union representatives involved in processing grievances. Its purpose is to ensure that the work force will have available trained union representation at all times.

supervisor   A representative of management with the authority to hire, fire, discipline, settle grievances, or effectively recommend in these areas.

Taft-Hartley Act   Passed in 1947 as a series of amendments to the Wagner Act, it governs collective bargaining for workers in private employment.

tenure   A condition of employment common in the teaching profession. After successfully completing a probationary period, a teacher can be discharged only for incompetency, unprofessional conduct, or lack of funds.

umpire   An arbitrator who handles all hearings for the duration of the contract.

unfair labor practice   Actions of unions or management that are prohibited under federal or state labor relations laws.

union security   The contract clause explaining the relationship of the worker in the bargaining unit to the bargaining agent.

union shop   A form of union security under which the employer is free to hire whomever it chooses, but the worker must join the union as a condition of employment. The period within which the worker must join is usually after 30 days.

wage board employee   Blue-collar worker employed by the federal government whose wages are based on a survey of comparable jobs in the same geographic area.

Wagner Act   Passed in 1935. Provided collective bargaining rights for workers in private employment.

War Labor Board   Established during World War II. Responsible for handling labor-management disputes and the wage stabilization program.

yellow dog contract   An agreement between an employer and a worker which, as a condition of employment, states the worker will not join a union or if he is a member that he will quit. The yellow dog contract was rendered unenforceable by the Norris-LaGuardia Act.

zipper clause   Contract clause in which union waives its right to engage in mid-term bargaining. It may also prevent a union from filing a grievance charging a violation of past practice.

Bibliography

Aaron, Benjamin. "Unions and Civil Liberties: Claims vs. Performance." *Northwestern University Law Review* 53, no. 1 (March–April 1958): 1–12.

American Federation of Government Employees. *Steward Training Workbook: Evidence*. Washington, D.C.: American Federation of Government Employees, n.d.

AFL-CIO. *AFL-CIO Manual for Shop Stewards*. Washington, D.C.: AFL-CIO, 1982.

Allen, A. Dale. "Organizing the Eggheads: Professors and Collective Bargaining." *Labor Law Journal* 23, no. 10 (October 1972): 606–17.

Amis, Lewis R. "Due Process in Disciplinary Procedure." *Labor Law Journal* 27, no. 2 (February 1976): 94–98.

"Arbitration and the National War Labor Board." *Harvard Law Review* 58, no. 3 (February 1945): 309–360.

Baer, Walter E. *Practice and Precedent in Labor Relations*. Toronto, London: D. C. Heath and Co., 1972.

———. *The Labor Arbitration Guide*. Homewood, Ill.: Dow Jones-Irwin, Inc., 1976.

Bairstow, Frances. "Management Rights and the Professional Employee." In *Truth, Lie Detectors, and Other Problems in Labor Arbitration, Proceedings of the Thirty-First Annual Meeting of the National Academy of Arbitrators*, edited by James L. Stern and Barbara D. Dennis, pp. 232–39. Washington, D.C.: The Bureau of National Affairs, Inc., 1979.

Beall, Edwin F.; Wickersham, Edward D.; and Kienast, Philip. *The Practice of Collective Bargaining*. 4th ed. Homewood, Ill.: Richard D. Irwin, Inc., 1972.

Berenbeim, Ronald. "Non-Union Complaint Systems: A Corporate Appraisal." Conference Board Report, no. 770. New York: The Conference Board, 1980.

BNA Editorial Staff. *Policies for Unorganized Employees*. Personnel Policies Forum, PPF Survey No. 125. Washington, D.C.: The Bureau of National Affairs, Inc., 1979.

Boyce, Timothy J. *Fair Representation, the NLRB, and the Courts*. Philadelphia: The Wharton School, University of Pennsylvania, 1978.

Chamberlain, Neil W. *Collective Bargaining*. New York: McGraw Hill, 1951.

Chandler, Margaret K., and Julius, Daniel J. "The Impact of Faculty Bargaining on Management's Rights." In *Proceedings of the Thirty-Second Annual Meeting of the Industrial Relations Research Association*, edited by Barbara D. Dennis, pp. 119–27. Ithaca, N.Y.: IRRA, 1980.

Cohen, Sanford, and Eaby, Christian. "The Gardner-Denver Decision and Labor Arbitration." *Labor Law Journal* 27 (January 1976): 18–23.

Davey, Harold W. *Contemporary Collective Bargaining*. Englewood Cliffs, N.J.: Prentice Hall, 1972.

Duncan, E. Townes. "Finality and Fair Representation: Grievance Arbitration Is Not Final If the Union Has Breached Its Duty of Fair Representation." *Washington and Lee Law Review* 34, no. 1 (Winter 1977): 309–28.

Edwards, Harry T. "Advantages of Arbitration Over Litigation: Reflections of a Judge." In *Arbitration 1982: Conduct of the Hearing, Proceedings of the Thirty-Fifth Annual Meeting of the National Academy of Arbitrators*, edited by James L. Stern and Barbara D. Dennis, pp. 16–29. Washington, D.C.: The Bureau of National Affairs, Inc., 1983.

————. "Labor Arbitration at the Crossroads: The Common Law of the Shop vs. External Law." *Arbitration Journal* 32 (June 1977): 65–95.

Erickson, Paul N., Jr., and Smith, Clifford E. "The Right of Union Representative During Investigatory Interviews." *Arbitration Journal* 33, no. 2 (June 1978): 29–35.

Feller, David E. "Arbitration: The Days of Its Glory Are Numbered." *Industrial Relations Law Journal* 2, no. 1 (Spring 1977): 97–130.

————. "The Impact of External Law Upon Labor Arbitration." In *The Future of Labor Arbitration in America*, edited by Joy Correge, Virginia A. Hughes, and Morris Stone, pp. 83–112. New York: American Arbitration Association, 1976.

Ferguson, Tracy H., and Desruisseaux, Ella M. "The Duty of Fair Representation: Exhaustion of Internal Union Remedies." *Employee Relations Journal* 7, no. 4 (Spring 1982): 610–18.

Fields, Cheryl F. "High Court Rejects Case of Professor Jailed for not Revealing Tenure Vote." *The Chronicle of Higher Education* 24, no. 16 (June 1982): 12.

Fischer, Ben. "The Steel Industry's Expedited Arbitration: A Judgment After Two Years," *Arbitration Journal* 28, no. 3 (September 1973): 185–91.

Fossum, John A. *Labor Relations: Development, Structure, Process*. Dallas: Business Publications, Inc., 1979.

Fusfield, Daniel. *Don't Get Garnisheed*. East Lansing, Michigan: School of Labor and Industrial Relations, Michigan State University, 1960.

Garbarino, Joseph W. "Faculty Unionism: From Theory to Practice." *Industrial Relations* 11 (February 1972): 1–17.

Glime, Raymond G. "What to Put Into a Grievance Clause." *Journal of Collective Negotiations* 1, no. 3 (August 1972): 251–58.

Gold, Peter A. "A Note on the Duty of Fair Representation in the Public Sector." *Journal of Collective Negotiations* 9, no. 1 (1980): 33-41.

Goldberg, Arthur J. "Management Reserved Rights: A Labor View." In *Management Rights and the Arbitration Process, Proceedings of the Ninth Annual Meeting of the National Academy of Arbitrators*, edited by Jean T. McKelvey, pp. 118-29. Washington, D.C.: The Bureau of National Affairs, Inc., 1956.

Hayford, Stephen L., and Wood, Lynelle M. "Deferral to Grievance Arbitration in Unfair Labor Practice Matters: The Public Sector Treatment." *Labor Law Journal* 32, no. 10 (October 1981): 679-92.

Hays, Paul R. "The Future of Labor Arbitration." *Yale Law Journal* 74 (1980): 1019-30.

Heave, Nicole. *Workbook for Teaching Grievance Writing*. Berkeley, California: Center for Labor Research and Education, University of California, n.d.

Hogler, Raymond L., and Maloney, Greta. "Developments in the Right of Representation During Investigatory Interviews." *Employee Relations Law Journal* 7, no. 2 (Autumn 1981): 224-34.

Kothe, Charles A. *Individual Freedom in the Nonunion Plant*. New York: National Association of Manufacturers, 1967.

Ladd, Everett Carl, Jr., and Lipset, Seymour Martin. *Professors, Unions, and Higher Education*. Washington, D.C.: American Enterprise Institute for Public Policy Research, 1973.

Levine, Marvin J., and Hollander, Michael P. "The Union's Duty of Fair Representation in Contract Administration." *Employee Relations Law Journal* 7, no. 2 (Autumn 1981): 1983-2009.

Lieberman, Elias. *Unions Before the Bar*. New York: Oxford Book Company, 1960.

Lieberman, Myron. "Professors, Unite." *Harpers* 243, no. 1457 (October 1971): 61-71.

Lieberman, Myron, and Moskow, Michael M. *Collective Negotiations for Teachers*. Chicago: Rand McNally, 1966.

Marceau, Leroy. *Drafting a Union Contract*. Boston: Little, Brown and Co., 1965.

McGuire, J. P. "The Individual Employee in Breach of Contract and Duty of Fair Representation Cases: Exhaustion of Remedies." *Arbitration Journal* 34, no. 4 (December 1979): 31-38.

Mitchell, Broadus, and Mitchell, Louise. *American Economic History*. Boston: Houghton Mifflin Company, 1947.

Northrup, Herbert R., and Bloom, Gordon F. *Government and Labor*. Homewood, Ill.: Richard D. Irwin, Inc., 1963.

Peck, Sidney M. *The Rank and File Leader*. New Haven: College and University Press, 1963.

Phelps, James C. "Management's Reserved Rights: An Industry View." In *Management Rights and the Arbitration Process, Proceedings of the*

Ninth Annual Meeting of the National Academy of Arbitrators, edited by Jean T. McKelvey, pp. 102-17. Washington, D.C.: The Bureau of National Affairs, Inc., 1956.

Pops, Gerald M. *Emergence of the Public Sector Arbitrator*. Toronto: D. C. Heath and Co., 1976.

Schaffner, Margaret Anna. *Labor Contract From Individual to Collective Bargaining*. Madison: University of Wisconsin Press, 1907.

Sayles, Leonard R., and Strauss, George. *The Local Union*. Rev. ed. New York: Harcourt, Brace and World, Inc., 1967.

Skelton, B. R., and Marett, Pamela C. "Loser-Pays Arbitration." *Labor Law Journal* 30, no. 5 (May 1979): 302-09.

Staudohar, Paul D. "Negotiation and Grievance Arbitration of Teacher Tenure Issues." *Labor Law Journal* 29, no. 7 (July 1978): 413-419.

St. Antoine, Theodore. "Judicial Review of Labor Arbitration Awards." 75 *Michigan Law Review* 1137 (1977).

Stickler, Bruce K. "Investigating Employee Misconduct: Must the Union Be There?" *Employee Relations Law Journal* 3, no. 2 (Autumn 1977): 225-65.

Stieber, Jack. *Protection Against Unfair Dismissal: A Comparative View*. Research Report Series, no. 169. East Lansing, Michigan: School of Labor and Industrial Relations, Michigan State University, 1979.

Stone, Morris. *Employee Discipline Arbitration*. New York: American Arbitration Association, 1977.

Swedo, Jeffrey A. "Ruzicka v. General Motors Corporation: Negligence, Exhaustion of Remedies, and Relief in Duty of Fair Representation Cases." *Arbitration Journal* 33, no. 2 (January 1978): 6-15.

Trotta, Maurice S. *Handling Grievances: A Guide for Management and Labor*. Washington, D.C.: The Bureau of National Affairs, Inc., 1976.

Trotta, Maurice S., and Bishop, Walter. *Grievance Handling for Foremen*. Ann Arbor: University of Michigan, 1969.

Ullman, Joseph C., and Begin, James P. "The Structure and Scope of Appeals Procedures for Public Employees." *Industrial and Labor Relations Review* 23, no. 3 (April 1970): 323-34.

United Auto Workers Education Department. *Bargainers Are Trained*. Detroit: UAW Education Department, 1972.

———. *6 Keys to Stewards Training*, by Frank Marquart, Marjorie Bailey, Sara Gamm, Joe Glazer, Mark Starr, Robert L. Kahn, and Arnold S. Tannenbaum. Washington, D.C., 1958.

———. *The Union Steward at Work: Accurate Fact-Finding*, by Lee Daws. Detroit, 1973.

———. *The Union Steward at Work: Grievance Writing*, by Lee Daws. Detroit, 1973.

———. *The Union Steward at Work: Presenting a Grievance*, by Lee Daws. Detroit, 1973.

———. *The Union Steward at Work: The Next Move*, by Lee Daws. Detroit, 1973.

————. *You Must Have Facts*. Rev. ed. Detroit, 1974.

Walker, Malcolm J. "Academic Governance: The End of Shared Authority." Paper delivered at Western Social Science Association, April 1976, Tempe, Arizona.

Werne, Benjamin. *Administration of the Labor Contract*. 3 vols. Mundelein, Ill.: Callaghan and Company, 1963.

Yenncy, Sharon L. "In Defense of the Grievance Procedure in a Non-Union Setting." *Employee Relations Law Journal* 3, no. 4 (Spring 1977): 434–43.

Topical Index